Taxcafe.co.uk Tax Guides

Small Business
Tax Saving Tactics

Tax Planning for
Sole Traders & Partnerships

By Carl Bayley BSc FCA
and
Nick Braun PhD

Important Legal Notices:

Taxcafe®
Tax Guide - "Small Business Tax Saving Tactics - Tax Planning for Sole Traders & Partnerships"

Published by:
Taxcafe UK Limited
67 Milton Road
Kirkcaldy KY1 1TL
Tel: (0044) 01592 560081
Email: team@taxcafe.co.uk

ISBN 978-1-911020-82-0

11th edition, January 2023

Disclaimer
Before reading or relying on the content of this tax guide please read the disclaimer.

Disclaimer

This guide is intended as **general guidance** only and does NOT constitute accountancy, tax, investment or other professional advice.

1. The authors and Taxcafe UK Limited make no representations or warranties with respect to the accuracy or completeness of this publication and cannot accept any responsibility or liability for any loss or risk, personal or otherwise, which may arise, directly or indirectly, from reliance on information contained in this publication.

2. Please note that tax legislation, the law and practices of Government and regulatory authorities (e.g. HM Revenue & Customs) are constantly changing. We therefore recommend that for accountancy, tax, investment or other professional advice, you consult a suitably qualified accountant, tax adviser, financial adviser, or other professional adviser.

3. Please also note that your personal circumstances may vary from the general examples provided in this guide and your professional adviser will be able to provide specific advice based on your personal circumstances.

4. This guide covers UK taxation only and any references to 'tax' or 'taxation', unless the contrary is expressly stated, refer to UK taxation only. Please note that references to the 'UK' do not include the Channel Islands or the Isle of Man. Foreign tax implications are beyond the scope of this guide.

5. All persons described in the examples in this guide are entirely fictional. Any similarities to actual persons, living or dead, or to fictional characters created by any other author, are entirely coincidental.

6. The views expressed in this publication are the authors' own personal views and do not necessarily reflect the views of any organisation which they may represent.

About the Authors & Taxcafe

Carl Bayley is the author of a series of Taxcafe guides designed specifically for the layman and the non-specialist. Carl's particular speciality is his ability to take the weird, complex and inexplicable world of taxation and set it out in the kind of clear, straightforward language taxpayers themselves can understand. As he often says himself, "My job is to translate 'tax' into English."

In addition to being a recognised author, Carl has often spoken on taxation on radio and television, including the BBC's It's Your Money programme and the Jeremy Vine Show on Radio 2.

A chartered accountant by training, Carl is a former Chairman of the Tax Faculty of the Institute of Chartered Accountants in England and Wales and is also a member of the Institute's governing Council.

Nick Braun founded Taxcafe.co.uk in 1999, along with his partner, Aileen Smith. As the driving force behind the company, their aim is to provide affordable plain-English tax information for private individuals and investors, business owners, accountants and other advisers.

Since then Taxcafe has become one of the best-known tax publishers in the UK and has won several business awards.

Nick has been involved in the tax publishing world since 1989 as a writer, editor and publisher. He holds a doctorate in economics from the University of Glasgow, where he was awarded the prestigious William Glen Scholarship and later became a Research Fellow. Prior to that, he graduated with distinction from the University of South Africa, the country's oldest university, earning the highest results in economics in the university's history.

Contents

Chapter 1

Introduction

The main purpose of this guide is to help self-employed business owners (sole traders and partnerships) pay less Income Tax and National Insurance on their profits.

Most of the chapters will show you how to claim more tax deductible expenses or bigger tax deductible expenses.

Expenses are vital in business tax planning because, in simple terms, taxable profit is calculated as follows:

Taxable Profit = Income _less_ Tax-Deductible Expenses

So the bigger your tax deductible expenses, the lower your taxable profit and the smaller your tax bill.

Lesser-known and Big Tax Deductions

Most business expenses are tax deductible, providing they are incurred 'wholly and exclusively' for business purposes.

You probably don't need us to tell you that stationery purchased for a business is a tax deductible expense, as is a salary paid to an employee.

The focus of this guide is not the obvious expenses. Our aim is to help you:

Claim tax deductions you didn't know about
and
Maximise big, important tax deductions

Lesser-known tax deductions may include the cost of travelling abroad on business or entertaining staff. They may also include paying wages to your children or claiming tax relief on your _home's_ mortgage interest.

Maximising big important tax deductions may include paying your employees in more tax-efficient ways, increasing the tax relief on your motoring expenses, and maximising your property tax deductions.

Many of the tax planning ideas contained in this guide are not widely known or covered in other tax publications.

We are quite confident that even those with fairly substantial tax knowledge will uncover many useful nuggets that will help them save tax.

Capital Gains Tax & Inheritance Tax

The main focus of the guide is helping business owners pay less Income Tax and National Insurance. These are the taxes that have to be paid year in, year out and are levied at potentially extortionate rates.

Some of the later chapters of the guide also contain important information on reducing other taxes, including VAT, Capital Gains Tax and Inheritance Tax.

Tax Red Tape

The focus of this guide is tax planning, i.e. helping you pay less tax. We do not spend any time explaining how to complete a tax return, compile accounts or do basic bookkeeping. While this is important, there are plenty of accountants out there who will help you with your tax compliance.

We feel business owners are far better served by a guide that focuses solely on helping them pay less tax.

Companies

This tax planning guide is aimed at self-employed business owners, namely sole traders, and partnerships. It is not for company owners. Many of the tax rules that apply to sole traders and partnerships apply differently to company owners.

When putting this guide together we decided that it would make for easier reading if the target market was focused. Having lots of qualifiers and special rules for company owners would muddy the waters.

Taxcafe has a range of other guides aimed at company owners (go to *www.taxcafe.co.uk* for details).

Limited Liability Partnerships

Limited Liability Partnerships (or 'LLPs') **are** covered within this guide. In most cases, the rules are the same as for any other partnership, but there are a few quirks to be aware of. Where the rules for LLPs differ, we will explain these where appropriate, but there are other legal and accounting implications of using an LLP which are not within the scope of this guide, so we would recommend taking professional advice before using this type of business structure.

Scottish and Welsh Taxpayers

The Scottish Parliament has the power to set its own Income Tax rates and thresholds, although it cannot change the personal allowance or the tax rates on savings income or dividends.

In Chapter 2 we explain the key differences and their impact on self-employed business owners in Scotland. Despite these differences, the vast majority of the information contained in this guide remains equally relevant to Scottish taxpayers. However, unless stated to the contrary, all examples, tables, calculations and illustrations are based on the assumption that the taxpayer concerned is not a Scottish taxpayer.

The Welsh Assembly also has powers to vary the Income Tax rates applying to Welsh taxpayers. These powers are more limited in scope than those applying in Scotland and the vast majority of the information contained in this guide will again remain equally relevant to Welsh taxpayers. See Chapter 2 for further details.

Summary of Contents

The following is a brief chapter by chapter summary of the tax planning information contained in this guide:

Part 1 – Working from Home

Chapter 3 explains how you can maximise your tax deduction for home office expenses, including home mortgage interest, council tax, property repairs, and gas and electricity costs. This tax deduction can be claimed even if you only work from home some of the time.

Many part-time businesses are run from home and in Chapter 4 we take a look at the special tax rules that apply to this type of business, including the one that allows part-timers to offset business losses against their other taxable income, eg income from employment.

Part 2 – How Your Family Can Help You Save Tax

In Chapter 5 we look at how your spouse or partner can be employed in your business or made a partner and paid income that is either tax free or taxed less heavily than your own.

Chapter 6 explains how to save tax by employing your children (including minors) or making them partners in your business.

Part 3 – Employing People

When you take on employees you may have to pay employer's National Insurance. Chapter 7 explains how it's calculated and some of the reliefs.

Chapter 8 looks at some of the tax-free benefits that can be paid to employees. These are useful alternatives to cash salary.

Entertaining is not usually a tax deductible expense but certain staff entertainment costs are fully tax deductible. Chapter 9 explains how you can maximise your claim.

In Chapter 10 we explain "auto-enrolment" – the system of compulsory pensions.

Part 4 – Business Travel, Subsistence and Entertainment

Chapter 11 explains how you can claim a bigger tax deduction for your travel costs by making sure that more of your journeys are treated as business travel.

Chapter 12 explains how you can claim a bigger tax deduction for subsistence costs (including restaurant meals and alcohol) when you travel on business.

Entertainment costs are not tax deductible but, as we show in Chapter 13, it is possible to structure your spending so that these costs are partly tax deductible.

Chapter 14 looks at how you can claim a tax deduction for flights, hotels, meals and other costs when you travel abroad on business... even when you take some time out to relax!

Chapter 15 explains how you can claim the additional cost of travelling abroad with your spouse or partner.

Part 5 – Investing in Your Business: Capital Allowances

When you buy computers, motor vehicles and other equipment for your business you can claim capital allowances. In Chapter 16 we explain how they are calculated and in Chapter 17 how you can claim extra tax relief by timing your capital spending carefully. You can even claim a cashback from the taxman, as we reveal in Chapter 18.

Part 6 – Leasing vs Buying Business Assets

What saves you more tax: leasing assets or buying them using HP? In Chapters 19 and 20 we explain the tax treatment of each method and provide a definitive answer to this question.

Part 7 – Motoring Expenses

This part of the guide contains invaluable information for business owners who want to maximise tax relief on their motoring costs.

In Chapter 21, we explain the capital allowances that can be claimed when you buy motor vehicles, including the 100% tax deduction when you buy cars with zero CO_2 emissions. We also explain how self-employed business owners can claim big catch-up tax deductions when they sell their cars.

Chapter 22 looks at vehicle running costs and explains how much you can claim for fuel, insurance, maintenance etc.

Small business owners can either claim tax relief on their actual motoring costs or use HMRC's fixed mileage rates. In Chapter 23 we use some examples to show which method produces the biggest tax saving.

Chapters 24 and 25 are all about maximising the amount of VAT you can recover on your motoring costs. Chapter 24 lists all the purchases that qualify: vans, motorbikes, accessories, repairs, parking costs, number plates etc.

When it comes to reclaiming VAT on fuel you have two choices: reclaim VAT on your actual business mileage only or reclaim VAT on all your fuel and pay the Fuel Scale Charge. In Chapter 25 we reveal which method produces a bigger VAT refund.

If you drive a van you may be able to recover over half the cost in tax relief, including a VAT refund and a 100% capital allowance. In Chapter 26 we reveal which vehicles qualify for the full monty of tax reliefs.

In Chapter 27 we provide a definitive answer to a very important tax planning question: Should I lease or buy my car?

Part 8 – Maximising Tax Relief on Borrowings

Chapter 28 explains how you can claim a bigger tax deduction for interest on borrowed money and how to avoid various mistakes that will reduce your tax relief. In Chapter 29 we reveal how business owners can even make interest on a personal loan (eg a home mortgage) tax deductible.

Part 9 – Business Property

Chapter 30 will help you decide whether it is best to rent or buy premises for your business.

In Chapter 31 we explain the difference between property repairs and improvements. Repairs will generally save you more tax. We reveal how certain spending that may increase the value of your property can be treated as a repair for tax purposes.

When you buy a commercial property you can claim immediate tax relief for the value of all the central heating, wiring, lighting and other 'integral features'. Chapter 32 tells you everything you need to know about this generous tax deduction.

In Chapter 33 we explain how you can accelerate tax relief on loan arrangement fees.

Part 10 – E-Commerce

Most businesses have an internet presence these days. In Chapter 34 we explain the rules for claiming tax relief on the various costs, including website development costs and online advertising.

Dedicated internet businesses may even be able to take advantage of other tax saving opportunities, including moving to a lower tax jurisdiction. We provide a brief summary in Chapter 35.

Part 11 – Year-End Tax Planning & Pro-active Accounting

In Chapter 36, we list the things you can do before your business year-end to reduce your business's tax bill. Normally, this involves accelerating expenses and pushing income into the next year; sometimes it involves the opposite approach.

In Chapter 37, we look at some of the opportunities that exist for business owners to save thousands of pounds in tax by changing their year-end. We also look at forthcoming changes to how business year-ends work for tax purposes. As a result of these changes, some business owners may benefit even more, and sooner, by changing their year-end now, while others will benefit more by keeping their current year-end and waiting to make a change later.

In Chapter 38, we then combine the planning opportunities we looked at in Chapter 36 with the new rules in Chapter 37 to see just how valuable year-end planning is going to be over the next couple of year.

Chapter 39 explains how businesses that sell goods can maximise their tax deduction for Cost of Sales. Chapter 40 explains how you can claim a bigger tax deduction for bad debts. In Chapter 41 we explain what you must do to ensure your accountant does their job correctly.

Part 12 – VAT

Most business owners hate VAT. In Chapter 42 we explain the basics and in Chapters 43 and 44 we look at various special schemes that could save your business thousands of pounds in VAT every year.

Part 13 – Capital Gains Tax

Business owners who sell up are in a privileged position when it comes to Capital Gains Tax: they can pay just 10% tax. This is thanks to Business Asset Disposal Relief (previously called Entrepreneurs' Relief). In Chapter 45 we explain the rules.

In Chapter 46 we reveal how it may be possible to pay just 10% Capital Gains Tax when you sell an investment property by running a business out of it for a short period.

Part 14 – Inheritance Tax

Business owners are also in a fortunate position when it comes to Inheritance Tax: they can completely avoid the grave robbers thanks to business property relief. In Chapters 47 and 48 we explain how this relief works and what you must do to protect it.

Part 15 – Benefits & Drawbacks of Cash Accounting

It is important that readers are aware of the benefits and drawbacks of the voluntary cash basis for small businesses and its impact on all the tax planning strategies contained in this guide.

In Chapter 49 we look at the basic workings of the cash basis, its scope, and its many restrictions. Then, in Chapter 50, we look at the transitional rules applying when an existing business enters or leaves the cash basis: and see these provide tremendous scope for saving or deferring Income Tax.

In Chapter 51, we look at some of the other tax planning opportunities provided by the cash basis.

Unless expressly stated to the contrary, it is assumed throughout the rest of the guide that the cash basis is not being used.

Part 16 – Other Important Tax Issues

In the last part of this guide we look at some other important tax issues not covered elsewhere. Chapter 52 looks at some of the most useful tax planning techniques available to avoid the Child Benefit Charge on income between £50,000 and £60,000.

Finally, in Chapter 53 we take a look at the tax relief cap which places an annual limit on the total combined amount of Income Tax relief available under a number of different reliefs.

2022/23 versus Future Tax Years

The current 2022/23 tax year is an unusual one because there have been several changes to National Insurance rates and thresholds throughout the year. To keep things simple, in many of the examples and illustrations throughout this guide we use the "normal rates" that will apply from next year (2023/24) onwards.

For example, this year sole traders who are higher-rate taxpayers face a marginal tax rate of 42.73% (40% Income Tax plus 2.73% National Insurance). Next year the rate returns to 42% and we use this rate in many of the examples in the guide.

Similarly, basic-rate taxpayers face a marginal tax rate of 29.73% this year, falling back to 29% next year.

This year employers pay 14.53% employer's National Insurance on many benefits in kind provided to their employees. The rate returns to 13.8% next year and this is the rate we use in some of the examples and illustrations.

Chapter 2

How Much Tax Do Small Business Owners Pay?

Income Tax and National Insurance

Self-employed business owners pay Income Tax and National Insurance on their taxable profits.

For the current 2022/23 tax year, ending on 5th April 2023, most self-employed individuals pay Income Tax as follows:

- 0% on the first £12,570 Personal allowance
- 20% on the next £37,700 Basic-rate band
- 40% above £50,270 Higher-rate threshold

If you earn more than £50,270 you' a higher-rate taxpayer; if you earn less you're a basic-rate taxpayer (see below for Scottish rates).

For the current 2022/23 tax year, self-employed business owners pay Class 4 National Insurance as follows:

- 0% on the first £11,908 Lower profits limit
- 9.73% on the next £38,362
- 2.73% above £50,270

Most self-employed business owners also have to pay Class 2 National Insurance (£3.15 per week this year, £164 for the year). Starting in 2022/23 the rules have changed. Class 2 is now only payable if your profits are above the lower profits limit (£11,908 this year). If your profits are below the small profits threshold (£6,725 this year) you can choose to pay voluntary Class 2. If your profits are between £6,725 and £11,908 you don't have to pay Class 2 but will still be treated as having paid it, allowing you to qualify for benefits such as the state pension.

Certain types of income are not subject to National Insurance, including interest from bank accounts (including business bank accounts), pensions and rental income.

Business Profits over £100,000

When your taxable income exceeds £100,000, your Income Tax personal allowance is gradually withdrawn. For every additional £1 you earn, 50p of your personal allowance is taken away.

What this means is that, when your income for 2022/23 reaches £125,140, your personal allowance will have completely disappeared. It also means that self-employed taxpayers who earn between £100,000 and £125,140 face a marginal tax rate of 62.73%.

Example
Caroline's sole trader business has generated taxable business profits of £100,000 so far during the current tax year. If she makes an extra £100 of profit she will pay an extra £42.73 of Income Tax and National Insurance.

She will also lose £50 of her Income Tax personal allowance, which means £50 of income that was tax free will now be taxed at 40%, resulting in extra tax of £20. All in all she pays £62.73 in tax on her extra £100 of profit, so her marginal tax rate is 62.73%.

Business Profits over £150,000

Once your taxable income exceeds £150,000, you start paying the 45% additional rate of Income Tax. From next year (2023/24) onwards you will start paying 45% tax when your taxable income exceeds £125,140.

Marginal Tax Rates

Putting all of the above Income Tax and National Insurance rates together, we can see most self-employed business owners face the following combined marginal tax rates in 2022/23:

First £11,908	£0
£11,908 to £12,570	£164 + 9.73%
£12,570 to £50,270	29.73%
£50,270 to £100,000	42.73%
£100,000 to £125,140	62.73%
£125,140 to £150,000	42.73%
Over £150,000	47.73%

Planning with Marginal Tax Rates

If you know roughly how much taxable profit your business is likely to make, you can do some constructive tax planning:

Example 1
Alana is a sole trader and expects to make taxable profits of £55,000 this year. If she incurs an extra £1,000 of tax deductible expenditure, this will reduce her tax bill by £427 (£1,000 x 42.73%).

Example 2
Shelly is a sole trader and expects to make taxable profits of £35,000 during the current tax year. If she incurs an additional £1,000 of tax deductible expenditure, this will reduce her tax bill for the year by £297 (£1,000 x 29.73%).

Not all business expenditure is immediately tax deductible. For example, simply buying additional trading stock which you still hold on your accounting date will not usually help (unless you are using 'cash accounting' – see Chapter 49). Many other things will work though, and we look at some of these in Chapter 36.

Where your marginal tax rate is the same from one year to the next, accelerating your deductible expenditure will merely defer some of your tax. But where your marginal tax rate is expected to change, the timing of your expenditure may be more critical.

(See below under 'Future Tax Changes' regarding the marginal tax rates for the next tax year used in the examples that follow.)

Example 1 continued
Alana expects her taxable profits to fall from £55,000 to around £30,000 next tax year. Her marginal tax rate will fall from 42.73% to 29%. If she incurs £1,000 of tax deductible expenditure this year she will save £427 tax; if she spends the money next year, she will save £290. Alana should try to spend the money this tax year.

Example 2 continued
Shelly expects her taxable profits to rise from £35,000 to £55,000 next tax year. This means her marginal tax rate will rise from 29.73% to 42%. If she incurs £1,000 of tax deductible expenditure this year she will save £297 in tax; if she spends the money next year, she will save £420 in tax. Shelly may want to consider postponing the expenditure until next year (assuming this is commercially feasible).

Some business owners with income above the £100,000 threshold may be able to enjoy 62.73% tax relief by *accelerating* their tax deductible expenditure.

Example 3

Basil is a sole trader who would normally expect to have total taxable income of around £150,000. However, he expects his taxable income to fall to around £125,000 this year.

If he incurs an additional £10,000 of tax deductible expenditure **this year** *he will claw back £5,000 of his personal allowance and enjoy 62.73% tax relief on the additional expenditure.*

If he spends the money **next year** *(and assuming his income has risen back to around £150,000) he will not claw back any of his personal allowance and will thus enjoy 47% tax relief. He will enjoy 47% tax relief because next year he will be an additional-rate taxpayer (see* below under 'Future Tax Changes').

Spending more money when your income has fallen will not suit all business owners. Some will prefer to hold onto their cash.

Total Tax Bills

A lot of tax planning uses these marginal tax rates and revolves around reducing the tax on the top slice of your income. You may also be interested to see the total tax paid by self-employed business owners at different profit levels. This is illustrated in the table below.

The final column is the average tax rate which is simply total tax divided by total income.

So, for example, someone who earns £60,000 faces a *marginal tax rate* of 42.73% this year and can save £427 in tax by reducing their taxable income by £1,000. However, they don't pay 42.73% tax on all their income, only the top slice. When you take into account the personal allowance, basic-rate tax band, etc, the overall average tax rate is 26%.

Total Tax 2022/23
Self-Employed Business Owners

Income	Income Tax	Class 2 NI	Class 4 NI	Total Tax	Average Tax Rate
£20,000	£1,486	£164	£787	£2,437	12%
£30,000	£3,486	£164	£1,760	£5,410	18%
£40,000	£5,486	£164	£2,733	£8,383	21%
£50,000	£7,486	£164	£3,706	£11,356	23%
£60,000	£11,432	£164	£3,998	£15,594	26%
£70,000	£15,432	£164	£4,271	£19,867	28%
£80,000	£19,432	£164	£4,544	£24,140	30%
£90,000	£23,432	£164	£4,817	£28,413	32%
£100,000	£27,432	£164	£5,090	£32,686	33%
£150,000	£52,460	£164	£6,455	£59,079	39%
£200,000	£74,960	£164	£7,820	£82,944	41%

Older Self-Employed Taxpayers

Older self-employed taxpayers generally pay Income Tax at the same rates as their younger counterparts, but those over state pension age are exempt from both Class 2 and Class 4 National Insurance. For a higher-rate taxpayer over state pension age, the only significant difference this makes is that their marginal tax rate will be 2.73% less this year.

Throughout this guide, unless expressly stated to the contrary, it is assumed for the purpose of all examples, tables, and other calculations, that the business owner is below state pension age.

Marriage Allowance

It is possible to transfer 10% of your personal allowance to your spouse or civil partner (£1,260 during the 2022/23 tax year). Unmarried couples are excluded.

Only basic-rate taxpayers can benefit from this tax break, so the potential tax saving is £252 (£1,260 x 20%). Married couples can generally only benefit from this tax break if one person earns less than £12,570 and is therefore wasting some of their personal allowance and the other person is a basic-rate taxpayer (i.e. earns less than £50,270; £43,662 in Scotland).

Potential winners are married couples where one person does not work (e.g. full-time parents) or only has a part-time job. You must register to use the allowance: www.gov.uk/marriageallowance

Example
During the current tax year Bill, a sole trader, earns profits of £30,000 and his wife Daphne earns £6,000 working part time. Daphne has £6,570 of unused personal allowance. She can transfer £1,260 of this to Bill which means Bill no longer has to pay tax on £1,260 of his income. This will save him £252 in tax (£1,260 x 20%).

In the chapters that follow, it is assumed in all examples and calculations that the marriage allowance does not apply.

The Child Benefit Charge

An additional Income Tax charge is levied on the highest earner in any household where any member of the household has annual income in excess of £50,000, and Child Benefit is being claimed.

The additional tax charge is equivalent to 1% of the Child Benefit claimed in the same tax year for every £100 by which the highest earner's income exceeds £50,000. Once the highest earner's income reaches £60,000, the whole of the Child Benefit will effectively have been withdrawn and the charge will have reached its maximum.

Self-employed taxpayers below state pension age who are affected by the charge this tax year will have an overall effective marginal tax rate on income between £50,270 and £60,000 as follows:

No. of Qualifying Children	Effective Tax Rate
1 Child	54%
2 Children	62%
3 Children	69%
4 Children	77%
Each additional child	+7.5%

Anyone with more than seven qualifying children will be suffering an overall marginal tax rate in excess of 100%!

As an alternative to the Income Tax charge, the claimant can choose not to claim Child Benefit. This may be a simple choice for employed earners with high salaries but, for self-employed taxpayers, it is difficult to know their overall income for the year in advance. Hence, many self-employed business owners with young children will be suffering the charge.

The highest earner's total annual income for the purpose of the charge is their 'adjusted net income'. This means taxable income less 'grossed up' gift aid and personal pension contributions, making these reliefs extremely valuable to individuals subject to the Child Benefit Charge.

Example
Peter makes a business profit of £60,000 for the year ending 31ˢᵗ March 2023. He has no other taxable income for the year. His wife, Jenna, has taxable income of less than £50,000.

Peter and Jenna have four children aged under 16, so Jenna is entitled to claim a total of £3,388 in Child Benefit for 2022/23. As things stand, this entire sum will be clawed back from Peter by way of the Child Benefit Charge.

In March 2023, however, Peter makes a personal pension contribution of £8,000. The taxman will pay a further £2,000 of basic-rate tax relief into his pension pot resulting in a gross contribution of £10,000.

Peter's gross pension contribution reduces his adjusted net income to £50,000 (£60,000 - £10,000), so he now avoids the Child Benefit Charge for 2022/23.

Peter's higher rate tax relief on the contribution will also save him a further £1,946 in Income Tax (20% on the band between £50,270 and £60,000).

Hence, Peter's cash contribution of £8,000 will save him a total of £5,326 in Income Tax (£3,380 + £1,946). Looked at another way, Peter has managed to put £10,000 into his pension pot at a net cost of just £2,674 (£8,000 - £5,326).

We will look at some other ways of avoiding, or at least mitigating, the Child Benefit Charge in Chapter 52. In all other chapters of this guide, unless expressly stated to the contrary, it is assumed for the purpose of all examples, tables, and other calculations, that the Child Benefit Charge does not apply. However, for those who are affected, any tax planning measures that reduce taxable income falling into the band from £50,000 to £60,000, will be of even greater value.

Interest Income

The personal savings allowance offers a 0% tax rate (the savings nil rate) for up to £1,000 of interest income if you're a basic-rate taxpayer and up to £500 if you're a higher-rate taxpayer. Additional-rate taxpayers do not receive this allowance.

The personal savings allowance is useful for self-employed business owners who hold a significant amount of cash.

Income that falls within your savings allowance will still count towards your basic-rate or higher-rate limit and may therefore affect the level of savings allowance you're entitled to and the rate of tax payable on any savings income you receive in excess of this allowance.

The automatic deduction of 20% Income Tax by banks and building societies on non-ISA savings no longer applies. Any tax which remains due on bank and building society interest is now collected through self-assessment. (HMRC may also attempt to collect some of this tax through the PAYE system in some cases.)

Interest from peer-to-peer loans can also be sheltered from tax thanks to the personal savings allowance.

Of course, most individuals can shelter all their interest income from tax by putting their money in a cash ISA. However, the personal savings allowance may give you the freedom to put your savings into an account that pays the most competitive interest rate, which may not be a cash ISA. It may also free up more of your annual ISA allowance to invest in shares and equity funds, if that's what you prefer to do.

The £5,000 Starting Rate Band
There is also a 0% starting rate for up to £5,000 of interest income, however in most cases only those on low incomes can use it.

You can only benefit from the 0% starting rate if your *non-savings income* does not exceed £17,570 (£12,570 personal allowance plus £5,000 starting rate band). Your non-savings income typically includes your self-employment profits, any salary income, rental income and pensions but does not include dividends.

Most readers probably cannot use the 0% starting rate because they will have more than £17,570 of non-savings income. You may, however, be able to benefit from the personal savings allowance (discussed above).

Example
Denise has a self-employment profit of £20,000 and interest income of £2,000. The first £12,570 of her self-employment profit is tax free and the remaining £7,430 is taxed at 20%. The £7,430 of taxable non-savings income effectively "eats up" her £5,000 starting rate band. She is, however, entitled to a £1,000 savings allowance which shelters £1,000 of her interest income from tax. The remaining £1,000 of interest income will be taxed at 20%.

Note the 0% starting rate band is not given in addition to your basic-rate band (£37,700 this tax year). Instead it is part of the basic-rate band.

Scottish Income Tax

The Scottish Parliament can set Income Tax rates and thresholds for most types of income including salaries, self-employment income, rental income and pensions. It does not have the power to tax interest and dividend income. These types of income continue to be taxed using UK rates and thresholds.

The Scottish Parliament also does not have the power to set the personal allowance. National Insurance and most other taxes, including Corporation Tax, Capital Gains Tax and Inheritance Tax, remain the preserve of the UK Government.

Scottish Income Tax 2022/23
Income tax in Scotland is being levied as follows this tax year:

£0 - £12,570	0%	Personal allowance
£12,570 - £14,732	19%	Starter rate
£14,732 - £25,688	20%	Basic rate
£25,688 - £43,662	21%	Intermediate rate
£43,662 - £100,000	41%	Higher rate
£100,000 - £125,140	61.5%	Personal allowance withdrawal
£125,140 - £150,000	41%	Higher rate
£150,000 +	46%	Top rate

Next year (2023/24) the higher rate will be increased to 42% and the top rate to 47%. The top rate will be payable when taxable income exceeds £125,140.

Income Tax: Scotland vs Rest of UK 2022/23

Income	Scotland	Rest of UK	Difference
£20,000	£1,464	£1,486	-£22
£30,000	£3,508	£3,486	£22
£40,000	£5,608	£5,486	£122
£50,000	£8,975	£7,486	£1,489
£60,000	£13,075	£11,432	£1,643
£70,000	£17,175	£15,432	£1,743
£80,000	£21,275	£19,432	£1,843
£100,000	£29,475	£27,432	£2,043
£125,000	£44,850	£42,432	£2,418
£150,000	£55,129	£52,460	£2,669
£200,000	£78,129	£74,960	£3,169

The table above compares Scottish Income Tax with the rest of the UK. Anyone earning more than £27,850 will pay more tax in Scotland. Someone earning £50,000 in Scotland will pay £1,489 more tax; someone earning £100,000 will pay £2,043 more tax.

The combined Income Tax and National Insurance rates for self-employed individuals in Scotland this tax year are as follows:

First £11,908	£0
£11,908 to £12,570	£164 + 9.73%
£12,570 to £14,732	28.73%
£14,732 to £25,688	29.73%
£25,688 to £43,662	30.73%
£43,662 to £50,270	50.73%
£50,270 to £100,000	43.73%
£100,000 to £125,140	64.23%
£125,140 to £150,000	43.73%
Over £150,000	48.73%

Who is a Scottish Taxpayer?

Someone is a Scottish taxpayer if their sole or main place of residence is in Scotland. For example, someone who rents a flat in London where they work during the week will probably be treated as a Scottish taxpayer if they spend their weekends with their spouse and children in the family home in Edinburgh and most of their friends and other social links are also in Edinburgh.

In some cases, however, it may be difficult to establish where the main place of residence is located.

Where no close connection to Scotland (or any other part of the UK) can be identified (for example, because it is not possible to establish the person's main place of residence), Scottish taxpayer status will be determined through day counting.

You will then be a Scottish taxpayer if you spend at least as many days during the tax year in Scotland as you spend in any of England, Wales, or Northern Ireland (taking each country separately).

Welsh Income Tax

Since April 2019 the National Assembly for Wales has been able to vary the Income Tax rates payable by Welsh taxpayers.

However, for the current 2022/23 tax year, taxpayers in Wales will pay exactly the same Income Tax as taxpayers in England and Northern Ireland.

As in Scotland, the powers are limited with the UK Government retaining responsibility for the Income Tax personal allowance and the taxation of savings and dividend income. The UK Government also retains control of most other taxes such as National Insurance, VAT, Corporation Tax, Capital Gains Tax, and Inheritance Tax.

Loss Relief

Sole traders can make a claim to set any trading losses off against their total income for the same tax year and/or the previous one. Where you have claimed to set your losses off against income in one of these years (or you have no such income), you can also claim to set any further losses against capital gains arising in the same year. Any surplus loss remaining is automatically carried forward for set off against future profits from the same trade.

Note that losses set against trading profits will provide relief for both Income Tax and Class 4 National Insurance purposes.

Where trading losses are set against employment income, there is no relief for Class 1 National Insurance purposes. However, this element of the loss can be carried forward, specifically and only, for Class 4 National Insurance purposes, to provide relief from Class 4 National Insurance in the future. The same applies to any element of loss relieved against other types of income not subject to National Insurance, or against capital gains.

Under a separate provision, losses arising in any of the first four tax years of a new trade may also be carried back against your total income in the three tax years prior to the loss-making year. The loss is relieved against earlier years first.

There is an overall cap on the amount of loss relief that can be claimed in any one tax year: £50,000 or 25% of adjusted total income, if greater. This cap is covered in Chapter 53. The cap does not apply to losses set off against profits from the same trade.

Temporary Extension of the Loss Relief Rules
Trading losses arising in 2020/21 and 2021/22 can be carried back for set off in the *three* previous years. Losses carried back to the two years prior to the previous year may only be set against profits from the same trade and this extended relief may only be claimed where the taxpayer has already made a claim to set trading losses off against total income of the current year, the previous year, or both (or had no such income in either year).

Other Taxes Paid by the Self Employed

The main focus of this guide is helping sole traders and partnerships pay less Income Tax and National Insurance on their business profits.

However, there are other taxes that may have to be paid and are covered in this guide:

- Employer's National Insurance when you take on employees (See Chapter 7)
- VAT if your business is VAT registered (See Part 12, as well as Chapters 24 and 25 covering VAT relief on motoring costs)
- Capital Gains Tax when you sell your business or any business assets (covered in Chapters 45 and 46)
- Inheritance Tax (covered in Chapters 47 and 48)

SEISS Grants & Other Coronavirus Support
SEISS grants, Coronavirus Job Retention Scheme ('CJRS') payments, and other coronavirus support scheme payments received from local authorities or devolved administrations, should generally have been included in your taxable business income for the tax year in which they were received. Hence, very few of these payments should fall into the current 2022/23 tax year. For further details of how these payments should be treated for tax purposes, see the previous edition of this guide.

Future Tax Changes

Income Tax
Many key tax thresholds and allowances have been frozen for seven years, until 5th April 2028, including the Income Tax:

- Personal allowance   £12,570
- Higher rate threshold   £50,270

If your income goes up with inflation you will end up paying tax at a higher rate which means you will be worse off after tax (see example below).

The threshold at which the additional tax rate (currently 45%) kicks in will be reduced from £150,000 to £125,140 from 2023/24.

Income Tax thresholds that have never been increased since they were introduced many years ago include:

- £50,000   Child Benefit Charge
- £100,000   Personal allowance withdrawal

It was way back in 2009 when former Chancellor Alistair Darling announced that people earning more than £100,000 would have their personal allowances gradually withdrawn. £100,000 was a lot more money then than it is today.

Example
*Chavez earned self employment profits of £60,000 in 2021/22 and paid Income Tax of £11,432. This means his overall Income Tax rate was **19%**.*

*His profits simply increase with inflation and are £80,000 by 2027/28. His income does not increase in real terms, so he is no better off than before. Because the Government has decided to freeze Income Tax thresholds, Chavez's Income Tax bill will be £19,432 in 2027/28 and his overall Income Tax rate will be **24%**.*

Thus by 2027/28 his overall Income Tax rate has increased by five percentage points.

The Government is taking a bigger share of his income, even though his income is exactly the same as before in real, inflation-adjusted terms. (Remember the tax system is supposed to tax you more heavily as your income goes up… but only if your income goes up in *real terms*.)

The five percentage point tax increase Chavez suffers will probably be permanent. If the Government adjusts Income Tax bands for inflation in 2028/29 this will simply stop his overall tax rate from increasing further. To reduce it back to 19% they would have to adjust tax bands by much more than inflation.

In other words, it is possible Chavez's overall Income Tax rate will be 5% higher for the rest of his working life.

In this example, I have assumed inflation will average 5% per year over the seven year period. This is not an outlandish assumption given that, at the time of writing, it was running at over 10%.

National Insurance
The threshold where employers start paying National Insurance on salaries paid to employees has also been frozen at its current level of £9,100 until 5th April 2028.

On a more positive note, the Health and Social Care Levy, planned for introduction in April 2023, has now been scrapped.

Next year (2023/24) National Insurance rates will fall back to their previous levels (typically 9% for profits up to £50,270 and 2% for profits over this level). The lower profits limit (where National Insurance kicks in) will be raised from £11,908 to £12,570, in line with the Income Tax personal allowance. It will remain at this level until 5th April 2028.

VAT
The VAT registration threshold will remain frozen at £85,000 for a further two years until 31st March 2026.

Future Marginal Tax Rates

The marginal tax rates for most self-employed business owners in 2023/24 are expected to be as follows:

£0 to £12,570	0%
£12,570 to £50,270	29% (plus £179 Class 2)
£50,270 to £100,000	42%
£100,000 to £125,140	62%
Over £125,140	47%

Similar marginal tax rates can be expected to apply until the end of the 2027/28 tax year. We will be using these marginal tax rates in respect of all future years throughout this guide.

Making Tax Digital (MTD)

The Government is in the process of making painful changes to the way businesses must manage their taxes, including compulsory digital record-keeping and, worst of all, quarterly reporting of results to HMRC.

Making Tax Digital for VAT
VAT-registered businesses with taxable turnover above the VAT threshold (£85,000) have been required to keep their VAT records digitally and submit their VAT returns using MTD compatible software since 2019. This has been extended to VAT-registered businesses with taxable turnover below £85,000 (i.e. businesses that have voluntarily registered for VAT) from their first VAT period starting after 31st March 2022.

Making Tax Digital for Income Tax

Until quite recently MTD for Income Tax was a ticking time bomb, due to be made compulsory from 6th April 2023.

Thankfully, its introduction has been repeatedly postponed, first to 2024 and then, following a further announcement in December 2022, by at least another two years.

Sole traders and landlords will now be expected to keep digital records and provide quarterly updates of their income and expenditure from:

- April 2026   Turnover above £50,000
- April 2027   Turnover £30,000-£50,000
- Under review Turnover below £30,000

Partnerships were previously expected to have to comply with MTD from April 2025. This is no longer the case but no specific timetable has been announced yet: although it will certainly be no sooner than the dates for sole traders outlined above.

Under MTD, the business owner will be required to keep records digitally and submit four new quarterly updates plus a fifth report (the end of period statement, or 'EPOS') containing final figures and adjustments. The quarterly updates will be in a summary format.

If you are a sole trader and also own a few rental properties you have two businesses and may eventually have to submit eight quarterly updates!

Bizarrely, while there will be penalties for submitting quarterly updates late, there will be no penalties for any errors or omissions. So, speed will be vital, accuracy will not. Makes no sense to us!

While it is comforting to know any errors will not be punished, it will still make sense to prepare the quarterly updates to the best of your abilities: but at least you won't need to stress too much about getting them exactly right. Naturally, however, just like the annual tax return under the self-assessment system, the EPOS will need to be correct, and there will be penalties for errors or omissions in that final report.

There's nothing wrong with digital records (broadly, records kept using accounting software or spreadsheets), they make sense for most businesses; but we can't understand why they have to be made compulsory. I recently heard someone say the proposed regime is really more about 'Making Accounting Digital': that would certainly give it more appropriate initials!

MTD is absolutely bonkers and we at Taxcafe have said this from day one. Originally, it was scheduled for introduction in April 2018, and we have welcomed the many delays and setbacks to this ridiculous project. We're pleased to see it has been put back another two years at least, but would much rather it was scrapped altogether (although we don't hold out much hope).

Even worse, there is the prospect that eventually it might also become compulsory to make Income Tax payments on account four times a year (compared with twice at present), linked with the quarterly reports under MTD.

Part 1

Working from Home

Chapter 3

How to Claim a Big Home Office Tax Deduction

Many businesses start in a spare bedroom or on the dining room table. Even when they're well established, most business owners work from home at least part of the time, for example during evenings or weekends. And since the pandemic we've all been working at home more than ever before.

Working from home means you can claim part of your household costs for tax purposes. But who can claim, how much and which costs?

Almost everyone in business can make some claim for 'use of home'. We don't know any business owner who doesn't at least take some paperwork home or make business calls from home.

Imagine you're a sole trader running a small garage. You need to renew your business premises insurance. You take the proposal form home to complete after work. You've just used your home for business and you are entitled to make a claim.

It constantly amazes us how many people think they're not entitled to the 'use of home' deduction: there are so many popular misconceptions about it. Many people think they can't claim because they're already claiming for an office, a shop, or other business premises. Not true!

Although the amount of the claim is likely to be less, a 'use of home' claim is still possible as long as some work is carried out at home.

(It's also worth noting that, if you have two or more homes, you can make claims in respect of any business use of any of them.)

Business partners need to ensure the costs go through their firm's accounts. This will need the other partners to agree the claim, but this doesn't stop a claim from being made.

How Much Can You Claim?

Claims should be based on the proportionate use of the property for business. The main factors to consider are *time* and *space*: how much space is set aside for business use and how much time is spent on business. With many people working from home more than ever before, the time element is likely to be greater than in the past.

There are many possible methods for calculating the business proportion. In practice, the most popular method is to simply take the number of rooms used for business as a proportion of the total number of rooms in the house. Hallways, bathrooms and kitchens are excluded from the calculation.

Example
Billie designs rose gardens and uses a room in his house as his office. The house also has two bedrooms, a living room, a dining room, two bathrooms and a kitchen.

We can ignore the bathrooms and the kitchen, so this leaves five rooms for the purpose of our calculation, meaning that Billie can claim one fifth of his household costs. So if Billie's annual household costs come to £20,000 and he uses the office exclusively for business, he can claim a £4,000 tax deduction.

What Expenses Can Be Claimed?

Most people don't realise how many costs can be claimed if they work from home. A self-employed person working from home is entitled to claim a proportion of most household costs, including:

- Mortgage interest or rent
- Council tax
- Water rates
- Repairs and maintenance
- Building and contents insurance
- Electricity
- Gas, oil or other heating costs
- Cleaning

Telephone and internet costs may also be claimed, where relevant, although this tends to form a separate claim as the business element of these costs is usually a far higher proportion than for other household costs.

A proportion of general repairs and maintenance costs relating to the whole property, such as roof repairs or gas maintenance costs may be claimed.

Costs which are specific to an area used for work may be claimed in full – subject to any reduction required for partial private use of that area.

Redecorating a study used for work would be an allowable cost, for example. The flipside of this is that any costs specific to a wholly non-work area may not be claimed at all.

Capital allowances may also be claimed on any furniture and equipment used for business, with immediate 100% relief usually available thanks to the annual investment allowance, subject to a reduction for any private use. (See Chapter 16 for more information on the annual investment allowance.)

Alternative Methods

In the earlier example with Billie the claim was based on the number of rooms used for business purposes. This method is nice and simple, but it is always worth considering whether another method might yield a better result. What if Billie's design work requires a lot of space and the room he uses is actually the largest in the house?

In this case, it would be better if Billie did his calculation based on floor space, as this would produce a greater deduction for him.

There is an almost infinite range of other factors you might consider. Suppose Billie's office requires specialised lighting that consumes a lot of electricity: he might be able to claim a higher proportion of his electricity bills. Billie might argue that his work equipment is highly valuable and he should therefore claim a higher proportion of his contents insurance. (In fact, such equipment may sometimes need a separate policy. If so, this would be allowed in full, but with no deduction allowed for Billie's 'normal' contents insurance.)

Take care when isolating individual costs in this way though. Moving away from the simple method is like opening Pandora's Box; you will need to be consistent and there may be other elements to your claim that go the other way, leaving you worse off than when you started.

In particular, HMRC takes the view that 'fixed' annual costs such as mortgage interest, council tax and insurance need to be allocated on the basis that a room is available for private use whenever it isn't being used for business.

This method creates a great deal of complexity and is not widely followed in practice when there is extensive business use of the home. It may, however, be appropriate to use this method where the business use is less extensive and we will look at this situation later in this chapter.

Wasted Space
It may be worth thinking about the impact on your claim of a room with little or no use of any kind. Let's suppose that Billie never uses his dining room. The room's mere existence means he is claiming just one fifth of his household costs. Arguably, if the room is never used, he might justifiably claim a quarter instead.

Better still, Billie should start using the dining room for business. Then he could claim up to two fifths of his household costs (depending on how much he uses the room).

Using a room for business can take many forms – completing paperwork, taking business calls, meeting customers, storing files or other business items – even just sitting there thinking about your business.

Reduce Your Claim and Save CGT
When there is some private use of a room used for business, you will need to restrict your home office claim. For example, let's say once a week, Billie has some friends round for a game of poker and they use his office. They play for about four hours each week. Billie works in his office for 46 hours a week on average, so his business use amounts to 46/50ths, or 92%.

With total annual household costs of £20,000 and five rooms to be taken into account, this means that Billie may now claim a deduction of £3,680 (£20,000 x 1/5 x 92%).

"Why don't they play cards in the dining room?" you may ask. One possible reason is that Billie wants to protect his Capital Gains Tax (CGT) exemption.

The CGT exemption that you usually get when you sell your home is restricted if part of the house has been used exclusively for business.

Fortunately, as long as there is some private use of each room in the house, no matter how small, your CGT relief is safe.

In fact, you can counter-balance that small element of private use of your 'work room' with a small element of business use in another room, thus restoring your Income Tax deduction to its previous level with no loss of CGT relief. For example, if Billie used his dining room for business 8% of the time, his total claim would be restored to the original one fifth. In cases like this, it is wise to make a note of the logic behind your claim in case of any later enquiries.

Time-Based Claims
For smaller properties, looking at floor space or number of rooms may be unsuitable and it will often make more sense to make claims on a time basis instead.

Example
Donna is a self-employed web designer. She works at home in her small one bedroom flat. Because her flat is so small, Donna is effectively using the whole flat for business when she is working. Conversely, of course, when she isn't working, she is using the whole flat privately.

In this case, we could use what I call the 'work, rest and play' principle - assuming that Donna spends an equal amount of time on each, she should claim one third of her household costs.

Many self-employed people work more than a third of the time, so a greater claim will sometimes be justified.

Since HMRC staff are not self-employed, it may be wise to retain some evidence of your actual working hours in order to convince them of this!

Part-Timers

Those who work from home only part of the time, such as at evenings and weekends, will need to reduce their claim accordingly. All of the methods for allocating household costs described above remain available, but a further reduction in the claim must be applied to reflect the part-time nature of the business use of part of the home.

Establishing this reduction needs to be considered on a case by case basis. The key watchword to remember is: be reasonable!

Let's say, for example, that you use your dining room for business purposes around 20 hours each week, but the room is also used privately (for meals, the children doing their homework, etc) around 30 hours each week. So, 40% of the room's total usage is business use.

Let's also say that there are five other rooms which we need to take into account (excluding hallways, bathrooms and kitchen, as usual) and your total annual household costs are £18,000.

In this case, it would seem reasonable for you to claim £1,200 (£18,000 x 1/6 x 40%) in respect of business use of your home.

As your dining room is used quite extensively (50 hours per week in total), it does not seem necessary, in this case, to look at 'fixed' costs like council tax and mortgage interest, differently to 'variable' costs like electricity. Let's look at another example, however.

Example

Freema is a self-employed freelance medical consultant and she does some occasional work at home amounting to around three hours per week on average.

Based on the usual test, her flat has three rooms to be taken into account, including the spare bedroom which she only uses for work and for the occasional guest. She has very few guests, so her business use of the spare room amounts to 90% of the room's total usage.

Freema's total annual household costs amount to £12,000. If we used our usual formula, this would produce a claim of £3,600 (£12,000 x 1/3 x 90%). However, taking a reasonable view, we see that this amounts to a rather ridiculous and unsustainable claim of over £23 per hour of business use.

Hence, in this case, it seems reasonable to apply HMRC's approach, whereby 'fixed' costs are allocated on the basis of how much time the room is actually used for business as a proportion of how much time the room is available.

Let's say that Freema has £10,000 of 'fixed' costs and £2,000 of variable costs. There are 168 hours in a week, but it is reasonable to assume that a room is only available for use 16 hours per day, or 112 hours per week. Freema's tax deduction is therefore calculated as follows:

Fixed costs:	*£10,000 x 1/3 x 3/112*	*£89*
Variable costs:	*£2,000 x 1/3 x 90%*	*£600*
Total claim:		*£689*

This is a much more reasonable and sensible claim in Freema's case.

For the purpose of these types of calculations, fixed costs would include:

- Mortgage interest or rent
- Council tax
- Water rates (but not if the supply is metered)
- Building and contents insurance

Minimal Use
For cases where there is only minimal business use of the home, HMRC's instructions suggest claims of up to £2 a week (or £104 a year) will be acceptable, although some actual business use of the home is required, even if only very small.

This is particularly useful for those with only a small amount of work to do at home, such as a landlord with just one rental property. It isn't much, but it saves the effort of doing any more complex calculations.

It is worth noting that the £2 per week rate has been included in HMRC's manuals relating to self-employed business income for some time. Meanwhile, the rate allowed to employees working from home has been increased to £6 per week (or £312 a year) and some commentators believe it is reasonable to assume HMRC will now allow this same rate for self-employed business owners rather than the £2 per week shown in the business income manual. Sadly, the position here is not entirely clear!

Flat Rate Deductions

A system of flat rate deductions for business use of your home is also available for trading businesses. The flat rate deductions are an alternative method which is available instead of the proportionate calculation discussed above.

The amount of the deduction is calculated on a monthly basis according to the number of hours spent wholly and exclusively working on business matters. The rates applying are:

Hours worked in the month	Deduction allowed for the month
25 to 50	£10
51 to 100	£18
101 or more	£26

Chapter 4

Part-time Business, Special Tax Rules

Many people start out with a part-time business for various reasons:

- You may have a full-time job and start a sideline business
- You may see a part-time business as an easier way to make the transition to self-employment
- You may already have another business in a different field, or
- You may even be turning your hobby into a business.

In recent years there has been explosive growth in online businesses, some of which are run from home on a part-time basis. As far as the tax system is concerned, there are very few differences between a part-time business and a full-time one. The major differences come in the areas of loss relief and National Insurance and we will look at these later. As far as calculating profits and tax deductions is concerned, there is really very little difference.

The first step, however, is to determine whether you actually have a business in the first place. Although a hobby or other activity can evolve into a business, it can be difficult to tell exactly when this happens. Some old case law gives us six tests to indicate when a business exists:

i)   The activity is a 'serious undertaking earnestly pursued' or a 'serious occupation'.

ii)   The activity is 'an occupation or function actively pursued with reasonable or recognisable continuity'.

iii)   The activity has 'a certain measure of substance as measured by the value of supplies made'.

iv)   The activity is 'conducted in a regular manner and on sound and recognised business principles'.

v)   The activity is 'predominantly concerned with the making of supplies to consumers'.

vi)   The goods or services supplied 'are of a kind which, subject to differences in detail, are commonly made by those who seek to profit by them'.

Where some or all of these tests are met, you probably have a business. The language of the tests is a bit 'legalese' though, so what do they actually mean?

To me, the tests can be summed up by saying that something which you do on a regular basis, in an organised manner, with the intention of realising a profit, is a business.

If you do have a business, it will usually be a trade, but there are some important exceptions to this. For example, a supply of services may sometimes be a profession rather than a trade. There is very little difference in the tax treatment of professions (or vocations) when compared to trades, except when it comes to losses, so we will examine this distinction a little further below.

Property rental businesses have their own special rules and, while it can be a business, investing on the stock market will almost never be regarded as a trade.

For the rest of this chapter, I will assume your part-time business is a trade. Before I move on though, I should point out that, just because you do not have a business, this does not mean any profits or gains you make are not taxable. Although there are many exemptions (like selling your house or car), any time you make money on something, there is a good chance it is taxable!

Property & Trading Income Allowances
Having said this, two allowances of £1,000 each are available to exempt small amounts of property income or trading income. Individuals with total gross property or trading income below the allowance no longer need to declare or pay tax on that income.

Where the gross income exceeds the £1,000 allowance, the individual can either deduct expenses as normal, or deduct the allowance from their gross income (in which case your other expenses cannot be deducted).

This exemption was introduced to help those who earn small amounts of income from websites like eBay or Airbnb.

The allowances may not be used against income from your own company, or a partnership in which you are a partner.

Why Does Having a Business Matter?

The good thing about having a business, as opposed to some sort of casual, windfall, income, is the fact that you can claim deductions against your business income.

The principles here are the same as for any full-time business and hence, as well as your direct business costs, you will be able to claim all the usual things like premises costs, motor expenses, travel and subsistence, legal and professional fees, etc: as long as the costs are incurred for the purposes of the business.

For the part-time business owner, the only 'business premises' they have will often be their own home. This means that they are entitled to claim a proportion of all their household running costs, including: mortgage interest, council tax, insurance, repairs, gas, electricity and other utilities.

It doesn't matter if it only takes you an hour a week to run your business: as long as you have a business, you are entitled to claim tax deductions under the same rules as everyone else.

One thing you should bear in mind, though, is that it naturally follows that, if your business is only part-time, you will generally only be able to claim a lower level of expenses than a full-time business, particularly when it comes to things like motor expenses and 'use of home'.

For example, a 'use of home' claim equal to 25% of your household running costs might be appropriate for a full-time business, but would be hard to justify if you only spend five hours a week on your business!

Each case has to be decided on its own merits, but the key thing to remember is that you need to restrict your claims to something which is reasonable under the circumstances.

Loss Relief

Where a part-time trading business gives rise to losses, the general rule is that these can be set off against the proprietor's other income or capital gains for the same tax year or the previous one (see Chapter 2 for further details).

This is another advantage of having a business rather than casual income and it means many part-time traders are able to claim repayments of tax paid under PAYE on employment income, or else reduce the tax due under self-assessment on other sources of income. There are, however, two areas of difficulty in claiming loss relief for part-time businesses.

The first problem is that, when it comes to part-time businesses, HMRC tend to want to 'have their cake and eat it'. If the business makes a profit, HMRC will want to tax it, if it makes a loss, they may claim that it is just a hobby and thus deny any loss relief.

When a loss arises, therefore, it is important to be able to point to the six tests looked at earlier and show your business meets at least some of them. Most importantly, you need to be able to show you are in business with the intention of making a profit: you cannot claim relief for a loss unless you were trying to make a profit.

There are many ways to demonstrate your intention to make a profit and the facts of the case will often speak for themselves. One of the best defences is to have a business plan which shows not only that you hope to make a profit, but also how!

The other problem for part-timers is that loss relief is restricted to a maximum of just £25,000 in each tax year where you spend an average of less than ten hours per week working in the business. This covers both part-time sole traders and part-time business partners and the £25,000 limit applies to the total losses from all your part-time businesses.

Part-time business partners working less than ten hours per week are also subject to a further restriction on any losses arising in the first four tax years they are in business. For these 'early years' the total amount of losses which they can set off against any other income or capital gains is limited to the amount of capital they have contributed to the partnership (including undrawn profits).

Both of these rules were brought in as an anti-avoidance measure aimed at investment partnerships but, sadly, they also catch many genuine part-time businesses. The second best way to get around them is to make sure you work at least ten hours per week in the business. If you are close to this threshold, it may be worth keeping time records to demonstrate that you are working more than the required minimum number of hours. The best way to avoid these rules though is to make a profit!

The restrictions for part-timers working less than ten hours per week in the business do not apply to professions (doctors, dentists, accountants, lawyers, surveyors, etc). Furthermore, these restrictions do not affect the set off of losses against profits made from the same trade in a different year.

Further restrictions in this type of loss relief for all businesses are covered in Chapter 53.

National Insurance for Part-Timers

You don't usually have to pay National Insurance if:

- You're over state pension age at the start of the tax year
- You are under 16 at the end of the tax year
- Your business is not a trade or profession

You can also claim exemption from National Insurance if your annual business profits are less than the lower profits limit (£11,908 for 2022/23): see Chapter 2 for further details.

If you have more than one trading business, either as a sole trader or as a partner, you will only pay one Class 2 National Insurance contribution of £3.15 per week and your total profits will simply be added together to calculate your Class 4 liability.

The real complication comes when you have both employment and self-employment income and each of them amount to more than the National Insurance 'primary threshold'. The threshold has changed several times this year but will be £12,570 for 2023/24. In this situation, you will be liable for Class 1 National Insurance on your employment income and both Class 2 and Class 4 on your self-employment profits.

Where your total income from both sources amounts to more than the sum of the upper earnings limit (currently £50,270) and the primary threshold, you may effectively 'overpay' National Insurance – i.e. you may pay more than you are required to by law. You cannot simply reduce the amount that you pay: you will either have to put in a claim for exemption or make a repayment claim later.

Part 2

How Your Family Can Help You Save Tax

Chapter 5

How a Spouse or Partner Can Help You Save Tax

Transferring part of your income to your spouse or partner can save a significant amount of tax if they pay tax at a lower rate. Sadly, not everyone has the freedom to transfer their income easily, but most business owners do have some scope to effectively transfer part of their own income to their spouse or partner.

Furthermore, most of this type of planning works whether you're married or not. For the rest of this chapter, we will therefore just refer to 'partners' to cover husbands, wives, civil partners and unmarried partners alike.

Note, National Insurance rates and thresholds have changed several times this year (2022/23). To make matters simpler we will use the rates and thresholds that apply next year (2023/24) throughout this chapter.

Salaries

If your partner works in your business you can pay them a salary. Many business owners' partners contribute to the business on a part-time basis, even when they have a job of their own. The partner might help with the paperwork, take business telephone calls, clean overalls or other workwear, help with purchasing supplies, organise travel arrangements, or carry out any number of tasks associated with the business.

Any of these tasks will justify paying a salary (except entertaining customers which HMRC doesn't generally accept as 'work').

If your spouse or partner does not have any other taxable income, they can receive a salary of at least £9,100 free from both Income Tax and National Insurance. This would save a higher-rate taxpayer sole trader or business partner £3,822 in tax and National Insurance (£9,100 x 42%).

In fact, if we consider the top marginal tax rate of 62% which we examined in Chapter 2, some business owners could save up to £5,642 by paying this amount of salary to their partner.

Employer's National Insurance is payable on salaries over £9,100 at the rate of 13.8%. However, if the business does not use up its £5,000 National Insurance employment allowance paying other employees, a salary of up to £12,570 can generally be paid completely tax free. A salary of more than £12,570 will usually be subject to 12% employee's National Insurance.

The most important point is that you can only get a deduction from your business profits in respect of your partner's salary if the payment to them is justified by the work that they do.

Furthermore, you must actually pay the salary to your partner. There is no automatic deduction just for having a partner. (Even if some might argue that there should be!)

If a payment of, say, £9,100 isn't justified, a smaller payment should be made instead. Even a salary of just £2,000 could save you up to £1,240.

National Insurance is generally payable on any salary payments in excess of £758 per month (or £175 per week). Any salary should therefore be paid on a regular basis and not in one lump sum.

Reporting Requirements

You may have to report payments to your partner to HMRC under the 'Real Time Information' system (RTI). Payments must be reported 'on or before' the point at which the payment is made.

If your business does not have any other employees it may not be operating a PAYE scheme, so employing any family member could lead to additional accountancy fees.

Employers must register for PAYE and report under RTI where at least one employee earns at or above the LEL (£6,396 in 2022/23 and 2023/24), or has another job.

Even if your partner earns less then the lower earnings limit their salary will still have to be reported to HMRC if the business currently operates a PAYE scheme.

If your partner has any other employment income, you will probably have to deduct basic rate Income Tax from their salary.

When Does a Partner's Salary Save Tax?

The best savings naturally arise when the partner has no other income.

If the partner is a basic-rate taxpayer the saving will be smaller but often worthwhile. It now becomes a case of comparing the business owner's marginal tax rate with their partner's.

Remember that a self-employed business owner will be paying National Insurance on their profits as well as Income Tax, but they can employ their partner and pay them £9,100 free from National Insurance regardless of their income level (and possibly up to £12,570 if the employment allowance is available).

Once you start to pay your partner more than £9,100 you may also start to incur employer's National Insurance at 13.8%, unless your partner's salary is covered by the £5,000 employment allowance (see Chapter 7) or the exemption for under 21s and apprentices under 25.

Once you start to pay your partner more than £12,570, they will start to suffer employee's National Insurance at 12% on the excess.

They will also start paying 20% Income Tax if they don't already have any other taxable income. If they already have other income that uses up their personal allowance, they will generally pay Income Tax on all of the salary you pay them.

Even if Income Tax and National Insurance is payable on your partner's salary it may be possible to still enjoy an overall tax saving.

For higher rate taxpayers any salary payment to a basic rate taxpayer partner will generally continue to save tax.

Take care not to pay too much, however. If your partner's salary takes their total income over the higher rate tax threshold (currently £50,270), or reduces your income below it, the salary will actually start to cost you extra tax.

Example

Colin runs a small bakery as a sole trader and expects to make a profit of £65,000 in 2023/24. His partner Bonnie has a part-time job as a secretary, earning £12,570, but also helps Colin in the bakery.

Colin pays Bonnie a salary of £14,047. She pays Income Tax at 20% on this plus National Insurance at 12% on the amount over £12,570 – a total of £2,986. Colin also has to pay National Insurance at 13.8% on the amount over £9,100. This amounts to £683, bringing the total tax cost of Bonnie's salary to £3,669.

Bonnie's salary and the employer's National Insurance paid by Colin amount to a total of £14,730. This is the amount by which his profits exceed the higher-rate tax threshold. The salary and employer's National Insurance are deductible from Colin's business profits, saving him tax at 42%, or £6,187. Overall, Bonnie's salary saves the couple a net sum of £2,518.

BUT if Colin paid Bonnie another £1,000, it would cost a total of £458 in Income Tax and National Insurance while only saving Colin a further £330 on his own tax bill: an overall net cost of £128, or 12.8% of the additional salary.

As we can see, you can pay too much salary to your partner.

In the above example, we assumed the employment allowance (see Chapter 7) was not available to exempt Colin from employer's National Insurance on Bonnie's salary. Let's see what impact the allowance would have had if it had been available.

Example Part 2

Colin has no other employees apart from Bonnie and realises the employment allowance is available to exempt him from up to £5,000 employer's National Insurance on Bonnie's salary. He therefore increases her salary to £14,730. Bonnie now suffers a total of £3,205 in Income Tax and National Insurance, but Colin is exempt from any employer's National Insurance liability. Colin continues to make the same 42% tax saving of £6,187, which now leaves the couple £2,982 better off overall.

As we can see, the employment allowance leads to a decent increase in the potential saving on a salary payment made by a higher rate taxpayer to their basic rate taxpayer partner.

Where there are no other employees, the employment allowance could exempt the employer from National Insurance on a salary of up to £45,332.

However, it remains important to limit the salary so that neither the employee becomes a higher rate taxpayer nor the employer becomes a basic rate taxpayer.

Partners in Partnership

Under the right circumstances you can save more tax by making your partner at home your partner at work too (i.e. making your life partner your business partner).

This has some very important legal implications which should be considered, some (but not all) of which can be resolved by using a Limited Liability Partnership.

This approach can be more tax efficient because the National Insurance position for a business partner is much better than for an employee. Instead of employee's National Insurance at 12% and employer's at 13.8% (where applicable), your partner will only pay Class 4 at 9% (plus £3.45 a week in Class 2).

Savings for High Earners

For those business owners facing marginal tax rates of 47% or 62% on their business profits, even a salary paid to a higher-rate taxpayer partner could save tax.

Example
Ace anticipates making a profit of £110,000 for her accounting period ending 31ˢᵗ March 2024. Her husband Sylvester, who works as an accountant, estimates this will give her a tax bill of £38,199.

Sylvester has always helped Ace with her business but, as he already has a salary of £60,000 from his main job the couple could never see any point in Ace paying him another salary.

This year, however, Ace pays Sylvester a salary of £9,100. As he is a higher rate taxpayer, he will have to pay £3,640 in Income Tax but, since his main employment is not connected with Ace's business, there will be no National Insurance to pay.

Ace's business profits will be reduced to £100,900 and Sylvester estimates this will now give her a tax bill of £32,557. She saves £5,642 and the couple are £2,002 better off overall.

Even if Ace's profits actually turn out to be just outside the 62% marginal rate band (income from £100,000 to £125,140), Sylvester's salary will still give them a small National Insurance saving, so there's usually no harm in trying this technique even if you're not quite sure where you stand.

On the other hand, if you're more certain about your profit levels, you may want to pay your partner even more. Where your marginal personal tax rate is 62%, any salary payment to your partner will nearly always save tax overall unless and until it takes them into the same marginal tax rate band. (Your partner may need to claim a refund of excess National Insurance paid where they already have another salary, or self-employment income, in excess of £50,270 and you pay them more than £12,570.)

Where your marginal tax rate is 47% (income over £125,140 from 2023/24 onwards), a salary in excess of £9,100 paid to a higher rate taxpayer partner will not be tax efficient where the employment allowance is not available to exempt you from any employer's National Insurance liability.

Older Couples

Throughout this chapter we have assumed that both the business owner and their partner are below state pension age.

Where the business owner is over state pension age, the savings on any payment to their partner will be less because the business owner will not be paying Class 4 National Insurance.

Conversely, where the owner's partner is over state pension age, the savings on any salary payment will be greater because the partner will not suffer any employee's National Insurance. The owner will, however, still be liable for employer's National Insurance on any payments over £9,100 (unless the £5,000 employment allowance is available).

Similarly, where a partner over state pension age becomes a business partner, they will not suffer any Class 2 or Class 4 National Insurance on their profit share.

These factors should be taken into account in planning salary payments or other tax saving strategies when either or both partners are over state pension age.

Compulsory Pension Contributions

Under the auto-enrolment regime, many businesses have to make compulsory pension contributions on behalf of their employees. The tax planning in this chapter takes no account of the cost of compulsory pension contributions, nor the administrative cost of setting up a suitable scheme.

Where the partner to whom any salary is paid receives no more than £10,000, or chooses to opt out of the auto-enrolment regime, there will be no pension contributions required. In other cases, however, some costs are likely to arise. We will look at the auto-enrolment regime in more detail in Chapter 10.

Chapter 6

Employing Children and Going into Business with Them

Children can place an enormous strain on your finances. So how about turning the tables and seeing what tax savings your children can generate for you?

Employing Children

Paying salaries to your children is a good way to reduce your taxable profits but which children can you legally employ?

With some limited exceptions for specific jobs (e.g. acting or modelling), it is generally illegal to employ children under 13. This will rule out most businesses from employing very young children, although there will be exceptions. The position for 13-year olds depends on local by-laws. Some areas allow them to do limited work, some allow them to do the same work as a 14-year-old and some do not allow them to work at all.

Children aged at least 13 or 14 (depending on local by-laws), but under school leaving age may do 'light work' (e.g. office work) provided that it does not interfere with their education or affect their health and safety. Certain types of work (e.g. factory work) are prohibited and any business employing children under school leaving age must obtain a permit from the local authority.

Subject to these points, children still attending school can work up to two hours most days. On Saturdays and weekdays during school holidays this increases to eight hours (five hours if under 15). Working hours must fall between 7 am and 7 pm and are subject to an overall limit of 12 hours per week during term time or 35 hours during holidays (25 hours if under 15). The child must also have at least two weeks uninterrupted holiday each calendar year.

16 and 17 year olds over compulsory school age can generally work up to 40 hours per week and can do most types of work, although some additional health and safety regulations apply. However, it should be noted that in England children must remain

in some form of education or training until they reach 18 years old. This could be through part-time education or training whilst they are working; or through an apprenticeship.

Children aged 18 or more are mostly subject to the same employment rules as anyone else, including the working time directive.

In essence, therefore, you can generally employ any of your children aged 13 or more and pay them a salary which is deductible from your own business income.

How Much Can You Pay?

A salary paid to a child must be justified by the amount of work they actually do in your business. If you employed your 15-year old daughter to answer your office phone one hour each evening, you could not justify paying her a salary of £30,000, but a salary of, say, £1,500 should be acceptable.

What about the national minimum wage? If your children are below the compulsory school leaving age the national minimum wage does not apply. The national minimum wage applies to employees aged 16 to 22 and the living wage applies to those aged 23 and over.

However, there is an exemption for relatives living in the employer's household. Hence, these compulsory wage rates will often not apply to your own children, although they may still be a good yardstick to use when setting the salary level for younger children with no particular business skills.

The hourly rates applying from April 2022 are as follows:

- £9.50   Living wage, 23 and over
- £9.18   21-22
- £6.83   18-20
- £4.81   16-17 if above school leaving age
- £4.81   apprentice rate

Subject to the national minimum wage (where it applies), there is no fixed rate of pay which applies to children. The rate paid must, however, be commercially justified: in other words, no more than you would pay to a non-family member with the same level of experience and ability in the job. For a child with no experience carrying out unskilled work, the national minimum wage for 16 to 17 year olds (currently £4.81 per hour) represents a good guide. Where the child has some experience, or the role requires some skill, a higher rate will often be justified.

Assuming a rate of £5 per hour can be justified, the maximum salaries a child could earn (based on an estimated 13 weeks of school holidays per year) would be approximately as follows:

13/14 year olds:	£3,715
15+ but still school age:	£4,265
Over school age but under 18:	£10,400

Subject to this, in 2023/24 a salary of up to £12,570 could be paid free from Income Tax and National Insurance to a child with no other income.

Any salary in excess of £12,570 will be subject to 20% Income Tax and employee's National Insurance at 12% will also become payable if the child is aged 16 or over.

Employer's National Insurance at 13.8% generally applies to any payment in excess of £9,100 unless covered by the £5,000 employment allowance (see Chapter 7). However, salaries up to £50,270 paid to employees aged under 21 or apprentices under 25 are exempt from employer's National Insurance (where higher salaries are paid, only the excess attracts employer's National Insurance).

Within the limits described above, every £100 of salary paid to a child in 2023/24 by a higher rate tax-paying sole trader will save £42. Savings of up to £62 will be available in some cases.

Looked at another way, a higher rate taxpayer needs before tax income of £172.41 to be able to put £100 into a child's hands as pocket money. Alternatively, you can get them to do some work, pay them £100 and be left with £72.41 to spare (£42 after tax).

Junior Partners

Taking one of your children into partnership may be a good way to reduce the overall tax burden on the family. This has important legal implications but using a Limited Liability Partnership ('LLP') is a good way to safeguard the family's private assets.

For children aged 21 and over, the position is much the same as taking a spouse into partnership and has the advantage of typically reducing the overall National Insurance burden from as much as 25.8% to just 9% on a significant amount of the profits allocated to the child when compared with a salary.

In theory, there is nothing to prevent a minor child from being taken into partnership, even though they do not yet have full legal capacity to contract in their own right. Remember, however, that the National Insurance savings are much smaller for younger children because no employer's National Insurance is payable on salaries paid to under 21s who are basic-rate taxpayers.

The savings will also be much smaller if no employer's National Insurance is payable anyway thanks to the £5,000 employment allowance.

For a partnership to exist there must be an agreement for the partners to carry on in business together with a view to profit. This agreement may be express or implied and need not be written (except for an LLP), although this is generally advisable.

It must, however, be acted upon and it is here that HMRC will concentrate their attention and declare the partnership to be 'artificial' and thus null and void if this is not the case.

In other words, any child you take into partnership must genuinely participate in the business at a sufficient level to justify their status as a partner.

Conclusion

There are several different ways to save tax by effectively passing some of your business income directly to your children. It is vital to remember, however, the income must be the child's to keep. Any arrangements requiring the child to pass the income back over to you will mean the planning is ineffective and the income is taxed on you. You must truly give to truly save.

Part 3

Employing People

Chapter 7

The Hidden Cost: Employer's National Insurance

When you employ somebody in your business, the wage or salary is a tax deductible expense.

Your employees will pay Income Tax and National Insurance but it is your responsibility, as HMRC's unofficial tax collector, to deduct it from their pay correctly and pay it over once a month.

You also have to report all payments to employees to HMRC under the 'Real Time Information' system ('RTI'). Payments must be reported 'on or before' the point at which the payment is made.

These requirements will often lead to additional professional fees. Paying all your employees monthly (rather than weekly) will keep costs down, but they are often still a considerable burden. Such costs are at least tax deductible, as you would expect.

Another much more significant cost is employer's National Insurance which can be much higher than the National Insurance paid by the employees themselves. We call this the 'hidden cost' because many employees and budding entrepreneurs do not realise how much National Insurance is paid by employers!

There is, however, no employer's National Insurance on salaries paid to employees aged under 21, or apprentices under 25: provided, in both cases, salaries do not exceed £50,270. Further reliefs apply to ex-service personnel in their first year back on 'civvy street' and employees working predominantly within designated Freeport sites.

Employees will pay National Insurance at the following rates on their earnings in 2023/24:

- First £12,570   0%
- Next £37,700   12%
- Over £50,270   2%

Subject to the reliefs described above, employers pay 13.8% on every pound each employee earns in excess of £9,100, less the £5,000 employment allowance. There is no cap on the employee's earnings for this purpose: the 13.8% rate continues to apply to any level of salary above £9,100. The £9,100 threshold will remain fixed at this level until 5th April 2028.

From April 2020, the employment allowance is only given to employers whose National Insurance bill was less than £100,000 in the previous tax year. Fortunately, most small businesses are unaffected and continue to enjoy this tax break.

Example
Eric employs five people (all aged 21 and over) and pays each of them £25,000 per year. He has to pay £5,970 in employer's National Insurance:

£25,000 - £9,100 = £15,900 x 13.8% =	*£2,194*
x 5 =	*£10,970*
Less employment allowance	*£5,000*
Equals	*£5,970*

In this example, the employer's National Insurance increases the business owner's employment costs by roughly 5%. However, the good news is that employer's National Insurance is a tax deductible expense. For self-employed business owners this means the employer's National Insurance they pay will reduce their own tax bills.

Example continued
Eric is a higher-rate taxpayer. The £5,970 he pays in employer's National Insurance is a tax deductible expense and will reduce his own tax bill by £2,507 (£5,970 x 42%), so the true cost is only £3,463.

Chapter 8

Pay Your Employees Tax-Free Benefits

A business can give its employees various benefits-in-kind that are either tax free or taxed less heavily than regular salary payments. To understand what sort of tax savings are available you have to remember that an employee's salary suffers three different taxes, two paid by the employee and one paid by the employer:

- Income Tax
- Employee's National Insurance
- Employer's National Insurance

With some benefits-in-kind ALL three taxes can be avoided, so there are significant savings for employees and employers.

Employer's National Insurance is the tax most employees forget about or don't even know about. It's currently levied at 13.8% on most salary income over £9,100.

On a salary of £50,000 the employer will pay £5,644 in National Insurance in 2023/24 – that's a lot of money that could have been kept by the employer or used to pay the employee a better salary.

When you add all three taxes together, the total Income Tax and National Insurance rates paid on salaries in 2023/24 are as follows:

- Income from £9,100 to £12,570   13.8%
- Income from £12,570 to £50,270   45.8%
- Income from £50,270 to £100,000   55.8%
- Income from £100,000 to £125,140   75.8%
- Income over £125,140   60.8%

These combined tax rates are extremely ugly and we've never heard any politician mention them.

Premier League Benefits

Clearly any benefit in kind that avoids all of the three taxes is a much better alternative to cash salary. The following are some of the benefits that are exempt from all three taxes:

- Workplace car parking
- Pension contributions and up to £500 of pensions advice
- One mobile phone
- Staff parties (costing up to £150 per head)
- Certain types of childcare
- Relocation costs (up to £8,000)
- Work-related training
- Provision of bicycles and cycling safety equipment
- Long-service awards
- In-house gyms and sports facilities
- Health screening and medical check-ups (one per year)
- Cheap/free canteen meals
- Personal gifts unconnected with work (e.g. wedding gifts)
- Business mileage payments
- Protective clothing and uniforms
- Overnight expenses if away on business
- Equipment for disabled employees (e.g. hearing aids)
- Trivial benefits up to £50

Each of these tax-free benefits is subject to specific rules.

Salary Sacrifice

Salary sacrifice arrangements (also known as optional remuneration arrangements) have allowed employees to give up salary in return for tax-free benefits.

The Government was concerned about the revenue lost from these schemes so the Income Tax and employer's National Insurance advantages of many salary sacrifice schemes have been removed.

Some benefits are not affected and continue to enjoy Income Tax and National Insurance relief. These include employer pension contributions, employer-provided pensions advice, employer-supported childcare and cycle to work schemes.

The Second Division

With many benefits-in-kind, the employee has to pay Income Tax at the usual rates (20%, 40% or 45%) and the employer usually has to pay National Insurance at 13.8% BUT there is no employee's National Insurance.

So most benefits-in-kind provide at least one tax saving: employee's National Insurance.

(Note, the employer's National Insurance rate in 2022/23 is 14.53%. Throughout this chapter we use the more permanent rates applying for 2023/24 and future tax years.)

The employee's National Insurance saving doesn't amount to much if the employee is a higher-rate taxpayer. Higher-rate taxpayers only pay 2% National Insurance.

However, for basic-rate taxpayer employees, the saving is more substantial because they pay 12% National Insurance.

Example
Gaelene, a basic-rate taxpayer, would have to pay £600 per year for a membership at Jim's Gym. Her employer, Trying to Please, offers to pay for her gym membership and Gaelene accepts.

Trying to Please contracts directly with Jim's Gym and pays the £600 annual cost. Adding 13.8% employer's National Insurance means the total cost to Trying to Please is £683. This amount is fully tax deductible, just like cash salary.

How much better off is Gaelene? She still faces an Income Tax charge of £120 but saves £72 of National Insurance (£600 x 12%).

It is essential that the employer contracts directly with the gym and pays the fees direct. If the employer settles an employee's contractual liability, this will be fully taxable, like additional salary.

The tax saving is not large but it is an annual saving, so the same saving may be reaped in future years.

What is more, this is just one of many benefits-in-kind that could be offered to Gaelene, so the total annual saving could be significant.

For the employer, the cost of providing a benefit is generally allowed as a tax-deductible expense because it is provided for the benefit of employees.

If an employer has a significant number of employees, it may be possible to negotiate discounts with suppliers when contracting to provide employee benefits.

Time Cost and Compliance Costs
Although benefits-in-kind can provide attractive tax savings for the employer and the employee, the time cost should also be factored in. Setting up a gym membership is more time consuming than paying a salary. Note too that your accountant will probably also charge a fee to complete a P11D form to report various taxable benefits to HMRC.

Chapter 9

Staff Entertaining Can Be Tax Free

The general rule is that entertainment expenditure is not tax deductible, e.g. entertaining business clients (see Chapter 13).

It comes as a surprise to many people that most staff entertaining is, however, an allowable business expense. VAT registered businesses can also recover VAT incurred on allowable staff entertaining expenditure.

The allowable costs of a staff function include food, drink, entertainment (e.g. musicians) and any other incidental costs, such as venue hire, transport and overnight accommodation. There is no limit to the amount a business can claim in respect of staff entertaining providing there is no other motive behind the expenditure.

There are some restrictions to the scope of the relief, however, plus one major catch!

The first problem is that sole traders and business partners are proprietors, not staff, so entertaining spend for them *alone* is not allowable. So, you need to take some staff with you before any expenditure can be claimed.

Let's say that two business partners take their 12 office staff out for dinner to celebrate winning a new contract. That's fine: this expenditure would all be allowable and there is no need to restrict the claim for the element which relates to the proprietors themselves.

The motive behind the expenditure is important. Any staff entertaining undertaken to boost staff morale is an allowable cost as it is for the benefit of the business. Once there is any other relationship between proprietors and staff, however, the motive becomes less clear.

The most obvious example of this is where the staff member is also a relative: any entertaining expenditure in these cases is potentially a personal expense.

Nevertheless, where the relative is included in a larger group, the expenditure may remain allowable. A sole trader taking his four office staff to dinner could still claim all of the expenditure, even if his own son were one of them. If, however, he took the son out to dinner alone, the position would be very doubtful.

Even less clear is the position when a personal relationship develops between a proprietor and a member of staff. Again, we must look at the motive behind the expenditure. A close personal relationship would effectively put the staff member into the same category as a relative but what about a simple friendship?

In a small business, the proprietors and staff are all colleagues and friendships will often develop. This does not prevent you from claiming staff entertaining but the amount of expenditure claimed must be kept 'within reason'.

What is 'within reason' will depend on the circumstances of each case. A proprietor might take all the staff out for drinks every Friday evening. This is not unusual and the cost could be an allowable expense if motivating the staff appears to be the main reason for the expenditure. This, however, brings us to the catch!

The Catch
In principle, an employee is liable for Income Tax on the value of any benefit provided by reason of their employment. This includes the cost of staff entertaining.

On top of this, the employer is also liable for Class 1A National Insurance (at 13.8% from 2023/24 onwards) on the cost of the staff entertaining. The 'cost' of entertaining, for both Income Tax and National Insurance purposes, must include VAT, even if the employer can recover it.

None of this affects the business's ability to claim a deduction for the expenditure. It's like a salary – the employee pays Income Tax, you pay employer's National Insurance and the business gets a tax deduction. (The only difference is that the employee does not also pay National Insurance, so there is a small saving.)

Nevertheless, taxing employees on entertaining spending is an absolute disaster when the original motive was improving staff morale. Any good done will be completely undone when the employees receive a tax bill. Can you imagine the countless arguments: "I only drank water"; "I only went to show my face"; "I would never have gone if I knew I had to pay for it!"

Fortunately, there are a couple of ways to get around this problem. The employer could make a voluntary settlement. Better still, there's the annual party exemption.

The Annual Party Exemption
Expenditure of up to £150 per head on an annual staff function can be exempted from both Income Tax charges and employer's National Insurance. In fact, it doesn't have to be a single function and several events can be covered by the exemption, as long as the total aggregate cost per head over the tax year does not exceed £150.

This sounds great but there are a few pitfalls to watch out for:

- The exemption only covers annual events: either a Christmas party or a similar event. It does not cover 'casual hospitality', like taking the staff for a drink on a Friday night.
- The event must be open to all members of staff. It can be restricted to staff working at a particular location, such as a branch or regional office, but it cannot be restricted to staff of a particular grade, such as management only.
- Where the total cost of the event, including incidental costs like transport and overnight accommodation, and VAT (regardless of whether the business can recover it) exceeds £150 per head, none of the expenditure can be covered by the exemption. However, where there are several qualifying events in the year, the exemption can be used on any combination of these whose total aggregate cost adds up to no more than £150 per head.

Example

John, a sole trader, spends £160 per head on a Christmas party. None of this is covered by the exemption.

Jane, also a sole trader, spends £30 per head on a staff barbecue in May, £60 per head on a summer ball in August and £80 per head on a Christmas party. The exemption can be used to cover the summer ball and the Christmas party (total cost £140 per head), but the full cost of the staff barbecue will be taxable.

Quite bizarrely, Jane has spent £10 more per head on staff entertaining but her staff are taxable on a cost of only £30 each compared with £160 for John's staff.

As we can see, careful planning of the timing and scale of your staff functions will enable you to make the most of the exemption.

The good news is that the cost per head is calculated by dividing the total cost of the event by the number of people attending, including staff's partners and other guests. Sometimes this could mean that increasing the size of the event reduces the cost per head to the point where the exemption applies.

One way to keep the cost of an event to no more than £150 per head is to advise staff that they will be required to reimburse any costs in excess of this amount. However, this may not be good for morale and a fixed contribution in advance of the event is usually more acceptable to staff.

Staff Entertaining versus Business Entertaining
Where customers or other external parties are present at an event, it may become business entertaining rather than staff entertaining. The business is unable to claim a tax deduction but there is no tax charge on staff attending the event, nor any Class 1A National Insurance.

Given the cost of a PAYE Settlement Agreement, this may actually work out cheaper.

PAYE Settlement Agreements

For expenditure not covered by the annual party exemption, there is another way to prevent morale-shattering tax charges from falling on the staff, but it comes at a cost. The employer can obtain a PAYE Settlement Agreement and pay all the Income Tax and National Insurance. This payment is usually tax deductible.

Information about arranging a PAYE Settlement Agreement can be obtained at: www.gov.uk/paye-settlement-agreements

PAYE Settlement Agreements no longer have to be renewed annually. Agreements can now be arranged that remain in place for subsequent tax years. Under these agreements entertainment costs are grossed up to allow for the fact that the employer is settling the staff's Income Tax liability. Class 1B National Insurance will also be payable at 13.8%.

Example

Omar, a sole trader, spends a total of £3,000 on a staff party (including VAT) which is not covered by the annual party exemption. He advises HMRC that he wishes to enter a PAYE settlement agreement rather than allow his staff to be taxed on this benefit.

Half of the staff at the party were basic rate taxpayers, so the grossed up cost of their benefit is £1,500 x 100/80 = £1,875. The other half were higher rate taxpayers, producing a grossed up cost of £1,500 x 100/60 = £2,500. The total grossed up cost is thus £4,375, giving rise to a tax charge of £1,375 (£4,375 - £3,000) plus Class 1B National Insurance of £604 (£4,375 x 13.8%).

Omar's PAYE settlement is £1,979 (£1,375 + £604). This is 66% of the cost of the party, but at least Omar can claim it as a tax deduction in his own accounts.

Chapter 10

Auto-Enrolment: The Advent of Compulsory Pensions

A system of compulsory pensions called 'auto enrolment' forces employers to enrol nearly all their staff into a pension. Whether you view this as good or bad probably depends on your political leanings... and whether you're an employer or employee.

When it comes to pensions, many small business owners cannot afford to save for their own retirements, let alone those of their entire workforce... they have a tough enough job already paying PAYE, National Insurance, VAT, Business Rates etc, etc, ... as well as their own tax bill on what little income they have left!

Exemptions

Only employees earning more than £10,000 and aged from 22 to state pension age need to be *automatically* enrolled into a pension. However, some older and younger employees and those who earn less than £10,000 also have workplace pension rights:

- If an employee earns less than £6,240 in 2022/23 they don't need to be automatically enrolled but the employer has to provide access to a pension if they request it and are aged 16 to 74. The employer doesn't have to contribute.
- If an employee earns between £6,240 and £10,000 and their age is between 16 and 74 they don't need to be automatically enrolled but do have the right to opt in. If they do decide to join the pension scheme the employer will have to contribute as well.
- If an employee earns more than £10,000 but is aged 16 to 21 or between state pension age and 74 they don't need to be automatically enrolled but do have the right to opt in. If they do decide to join the pension scheme the employer will have to contribute as well.

How Much Does it Cost?

Employers are forced to make a minimum pension contribution and, in practice, so too are most employees. Generally speaking, contributions are a percentage of 'qualifying earnings'. The total minimum contribution is 8% with at least 3% coming from the employer.

The total minimum contribution can be paid by the employer but in practice many small firms will insist the employee makes up the required balance.

This means many employees have to contribute 5% to a pension if they want to benefit from a 3% contribution from their employer.

Employees' contributions enjoy tax relief as normal, which means 4% will come from them personally and the extra 1% will be added by the taxman in the form of basic-rate tax relief.

Qualifying Earnings

The minimum contributions are generally not based on the employee's total earnings but rather on a band of earnings. The lower and upper thresholds for 2022/23 are £6,240 and £50,270 respectively. What this means is that pension contributions are typically based on earnings of up to £44,030 (£50,270 - £6,240).

For example, someone with employment income of £60,000 will have their pension contributions based on earnings of £44,030. Someone with employment income of £20,000 will have their pension contributions based on earnings of £13,760 (£20,000 - £6,240).

Pension Schemes

A state-sponsored pension scheme called NEST (National Employment Savings Trust) is available for employers who do not have their own pension scheme. You can use another scheme if you prefer but it must be a "qualifying scheme". The pension provider will be able to tell you if the scheme is qualifying or not.

Employees Can Opt Out

Employees must be automatically enrolled but employers can postpone this by up to three months. The three month period is designed to make life easier for businesses that employ lots of temporary and seasonal workers.

It is important to note that employees can opt out of compulsory pensions if they choose. Some employees may choose to opt out because it's not just their employers who are forced to make pension contributions. Employees also have to put money in and their contributions are even higher than their employer's (5%, albeit with 1% coming from the taxman).

Many employees may choose to spend their earnings rather than save for the future, especially those in their twenties, thirties and forties, faced with paying off student loans, climbing the housing ladder and bringing up children.

Employers are prohibited from inducing or encouraging employees to opt out. Any decision to opt out must be taken freely by the staff member without influence from the employer. If the employee does, however, opt out the employer doesn't have to make any contributions.

Employers are required to automatically re-enrol eligible employees back into the workplace pension scheme roughly every three years.

Part 4

Business Travel, Subsistence and Entertainment

Chapter 11

Travel Expenses: How to Claim a Bigger Deduction

Travel takes many forms: trains, taxis, planes, cars; the list is almost endless. In most cases, the cost is obvious, such as a train ticket or taxi fare. Motor expenses are a little harder to calculate and we will look at these in more detail in Part 7. Here, however, we focus on the issue of what constitutes business travel.

Whatever method we travel by, the cost is an allowable expense for tax purposes if the journey is classed as a **business journey**. You would think this would be a simple matter. Straight away though, we run into a problem.

Principle 1: Home to work travel is not allowable
Imagine a self-employed woman called Jo, travelling to her business premises every day. To a reasonable layman, this journey is clearly made for business purposes. Sadly, tax law states otherwise and this journey is classed as personal.

Principle 2: Travel from home to a temporary workplace is allowable
What if Jo needs to carry out some work at her customer's premises and travels there directly from home? Now the journey is classed as a business journey.

In general, travel to a workplace remains allowable unless that workplace is the individual's permanent base. Jo cannot claim the cost of travel from her home to her office but can claim the cost of travel from her home to any other business destination unless, and until, it becomes her main base.

People working from home can therefore generally claim all their business travel costs since there is no 'home to work' element to be disallowed.

For self-employed taxpayers, the question of whether any location is their main business base must be decided on the facts of the case. The rule applying to employees, where travel costs relating to a temporary workplace cease to be allowable if they spend 40% or more of their working time there for a period that lasts, or is likely to last, more than 24 months does not apply: although it could be a useful yardstick to consider in some cases.

Principle 3: Where there is 'Triangular Travel' involving home, work and another business destination, two sides of the triangle will be allowable (but not the 'home to work' side)

If Jo leaves her customer's premises and goes straight home, this journey is again allowable. Alternatively, if Jo travels from the customer to her office, this journey is also allowable.

Let's suppose Jo lives in Bedford and works in Luton. A journey from her home to a customer in Milton Keynes would be fully allowable and the subsequent journey from Milton Keynes either to Luton or back to Bedford would also be fully allowable. But if Jo goes to her office in Luton after visiting the customer, her later journey back home to Bedford will not then be allowable.

Principle 4: Any part of a journey which is part of, or similar to, a person's usual home to work journey is not allowable

HMRC views journeys which are similar to a person's regular commute as still being 'home to work travel'. Where there is a clearly separate additional business element to a journey, however, that element should remain allowable.

Let's say Jo visits another customer based a few miles from her office. She catches the train to Luton as usual but, instead of walking to her office nearby, she takes taxis to her customer and back to her office afterwards. Jo's taxi journeys are allowable since they are clearly not part of her usual journey to work.

Principle 5: There is no restriction on the standard, or class, of travel for the purposes of tax relief

Jo visits London on business and travels first class. Despite the increased cost, the journey remains fully allowable.

In fact, Jo could travel to Istanbul first class by Orient Express if she wished and there would be no restriction on her tax relief as long as the journey was made purely for business purposes. If she stopped off in Venice for some sightseeing, however, the journey would cease to be wholly for business purposes and would not be fully allowable.

Principle 6: Small incidental private elements to a journey will not prevent it from being allowable

In theory, the cost of travel is only allowable when incurred 'wholly and exclusively' for business purposes. Taking this literally would mean any personal element to a journey would prevent the entire cost from being allowed for tax purposes.

Thankfully, HMRC is prepared to ignore any minor, incidental element to a journey. If Jo stopped at a garage to buy some milk on her way home from a customer, for example, the journey would remain fully allowable.

This leaves us with the problem of journeys with a more significant private element to them.

Principle 7: The main reason behind a journey will usually determine whether it is allowable

Grant is another customer whom Jo often visits. However, Grant is also a personal friend and Jo will often stay for dinner afterwards.

Here, we have to ask what the main purpose of the journey was. If Jo's main reason for visiting Grant was for business and staying for dinner was merely incidental, then the journey remains fully allowable. On the other hand, if she mainly went to Grant's for dinner and they just happened to discuss a little business then the journey is a private one and not allowable at all.

Principle 8: Where there is more than one purpose to the journey, an apportionment will usually be accepted

So what about that trip on the Orient Express? Theory says the journey is not 'wholly and exclusively' for business purposes and therefore not allowable.

In practice, however, for self-employed taxpayers, HMRC will usually accept a reasonable apportionment between the business and private elements. Some claim might therefore still be justified, although the exact proportion will depend on the facts of the case and any additional costs relating directly to Jo's stay in Venice would have to be disallowed.

We will return to the subject of international travel in Chapter 14.

Chapter 12

Subsistence:
How to Claim a Bigger Deduction

Almost every business owner incurs subsistence expenditure such as meals, drinks and other refreshments, yet in practice it can often be one of the most difficult areas of tax to deal with.

Business Proprietors
The greatest area of difficulty tends to arise with business proprietors' own subsistence costs – the expenses incurred directly by sole traders, business partners and individuals with property rental businesses.

Claims for proprietors' own subsistence must usually be based on actual expenditure and 'round sum' allowances are not generally available.

The first problem is evidence. Many business owners neglect to obtain receipts for some of their subsistence expenditure. Here, I would make two points:

- Firstly, in an ideal world, you should really try to get a receipt for every last penny of your business subsistence. It doesn't necessarily have to be a printed till receipt: I have even resorted to getting a receipt written on a napkin!
- Second, don't give up and not claim just because you don't have a receipt. Reasonable subsistence claims are seldom refused, especially if you make a note of the expenditure at the time – but do try to get receipts in future.

Business Trips
The basic rule is that business proprietors may claim reasonable subsistence costs incurred during a business trip. In essence, a business trip is any trip away from the proprietor's normal place of business made for business purposes and which does not form part of their normal pattern of travel. Let's look at some examples to see what this means in practice.

Example 1
Mike is based in Scotland and has to spend a day in London on business. He has an early morning flight, so he has breakfast at the airport. He grabs a coffee and a Danish pastry when he arrives in London. Later, he goes out for lunch in a pub near his customer's office. He buys another coffee and a piece of cake in the airport on the way home. All of this expenditure was necessitated by Mike's business trip and can all be claimed for tax purposes. If, however, Mike buys himself a takeaway on the way home from the airport that evening, it would not be allowable. If he had dinner in London before catching his flight home though, this would be allowable.

An interesting planning point emerges here. By and large, any meals, snacks or drinks you have while you're away will be allowable. As soon as you're back on your own 'patch', any further expenditure is purely personal and cannot be claimed.

Example 2
Emma normally works from home but needs to visit one of her customers just a mile away. She buys herself a coffee on the way to her customer's office and goes for lunch in a local cafe. Sadly, this expenditure is not allowable. Emma could have made herself a coffee before leaving home and could have returned home for lunch. Her subsistence expenditure cannot be claimed as a business expense because she had a reasonable alternative.

It would have been exactly the same if Emma had her own office premises and her customer's office was only a mile away. Her subsistence costs would still have been a personal expense because one cannot say that her expenditure was any different to that which she might incur during a normal day at her own office.

Mike, on the other hand, flew all the way to London. It would have been ridiculous to expect him to go home to Scotland for lunch, so his subsistence costs were a reasonable business expense.

There is no set rule on how far you must travel before your subsistence costs become allowable. It is a question of whether it would have been reasonable for you to return home, or to the area in which your own business premises are located, before incurring the expense.

You must also actually incur the expenditure during the business trip. In Mike's case, it would be quite reasonable for him to have dinner in London, which would be allowable, but if he chose to go home first, he could not claim the cost of his dinner in Scotland.

While subsistence expenditure needs to be reasonable, it doesn't need to be frugal. If you're in a town with a nice Italian restaurant and a burger bar, there is no requirement for you to take the cheaper option.

Some people assume all alcohol must be a personal expense and hence not allowable. Not so! Just because something provides an element of personal enjoyment, this does not prevent it from being a business expense. You wouldn't just assume that desserts weren't allowable, would you?

You have to drink, so if you choose to drink one or two glasses of beer or wine with a meal instead of water or lemonade, it's still subsistence. A single glass of beer or wine in an airport or railway station on your way home would also generally be allowable.

But, any expense you claim must be reasonable. There can come a point when the expense is incurred purely for personal enjoyment and is no longer allowable. A half bottle of wine is usually fine, but a magnum of vintage champagne is probably not.

Similarly, while drinks taken with a meal are usually considered reasonable, further alcoholic drinks after an evening meal would generally be regarded as a personal cost that cannot be claimed.

Business Meetings and Entertaining
So far, we've talked about personal subsistence. Once you're with a customer or business contact, the situation changes. For business meetings, we must again consider what is reasonable. A cup of tea or coffee while you discuss some business would usually be acceptable. Beyond that, we're into the realm of business entertaining and that's another story (see Chapter 13).

In the meantime, if you're reading this in an airport or railway station on your way home from a business trip, why not have a drink on the Chancellor of the Exchequer?

Chapter 13

Entertainment Can Be Tax Deductible

Back in the 1980s, the cost of entertaining foreign customers was an allowable expense for tax purposes. Sadly, however, despite being a vital and unavoidable expense for many businesses, there is no longer any tax deduction available for any business entertaining, foreign and domestic alike.

At first glance, therefore, there might seem to be little point in writing a chapter on business entertaining. In my experience, however, a great deal of allowable expenditure is wrongly classed as business entertaining and disallowed when it could legitimately be claimed as something else.

Furthermore, with a few minor changes in business behaviour, even more expenditure might be deductible.

The first area of confusion is the difference between subsistence and entertaining. If you take a customer to lunch, the cost of their meal is business entertaining and not deductible. If you took them to lunch locally, the cost of your own meal must be treated the same way.

If you have travelled some distance to meet the customer, however, your own meal might represent a legitimate subsistence cost which may be claimed (see Chapter 12).

This is why it is generally a mistake to 'play host' to your visitors. A policy of 'visitor pays' could convert half of your entertaining expenditure into allowable subsistence costs.

Example
Every month, Mike travels 100 miles to visit Linda, one of his suppliers. Linda pays for their lunch in a local restaurant. Linda also visits Mike once a month and he then pays for lunch. All of the costs incurred by both Mike and Linda are disallowable business entertaining.

Let us suppose, however, that Mike and Linda reverse their arrangements to a 'visitor pays' policy. Half of the cost of each lunch now becomes allowable subsistence expenditure.

The position changes if a visitor is actually making a direct contribution to your business – i.e. they are personally performing work directly for your business during their visit.

Let us suppose that Linda is an IT consultant and, during her visits, she carries out maintenance work on Mike's computer system. If Mike pays for Linda's lunch under these circumstances, he can claim this as part of his IT support costs.

Furthermore, where there is a contractual obligation to provide visitors with food, drink, etc, this cost is also usually allowable.

Staff Entertaining
Staff entertaining is an exception to the normal rules on entertaining and is generally an allowable expense for tax purposes, although it can lead to additional PAYE costs (see Chapter 9 for details). However, this exception does not apply if the staff entertaining is merely incidental to the entertainment of customers or other non-employee guests.

The test that HMRC uses to assess this is to consider whether the employer would still have paid for the event if the non-employee guests had not been present. If the employer would not have paid without the presence of other guests, the staff entertaining is merely incidental and none of the cost is allowable.

Hence, for example, inviting a member of staff to join you and a customer for lunch will not turn the cost of the meal into allowable staff entertaining – it will remain non-deductible business entertaining (there would be no PAYE charges though).

Alternatively, you might have already arranged to take some staff out for lunch when a visitor arrives unexpectedly. So, you ask them to join you for lunch – now you only need to disallow the cost of the visitor's meal.

Better still, why not invite some customers to your annual staff party? You would still need to disallow an appropriate proportion of the cost, but this will often be more cost effective than having to disallow the cost of separately entertaining each customer.

Look at it this way: you and two business partners have a party and invite twelve staff and five customers. You will need to disallow a quarter of the cost (5 out of 20). If you had taken each customer to lunch separately, the whole cost of all five lunches would have been disallowable.

Travel and Incidental Costs
Incidental costs related to business entertaining, such as travel expenses, must generally also be disallowed. This would apply, for example, where you invited a customer to dinner and paid their taxi fare. The travel costs for employees attending their employer's own business entertaining event are allowable, however.

As for sole traders and business partners' own travel expenses when attending a business entertaining event, the position is not totally clear. However, such costs should be allowable where an event also includes a business element, such as where a business meeting is followed by dinner afterwards. In fact, where an event does have such a mixed purpose, the travel costs of all attendees should be allowable.

Inclusive Costs
In many businesses, it is customary to provide customers with basic hospitality, such as tea or coffee and perhaps a few biscuits. This is effectively basic office etiquette and may also apply in other situations, such as hairdressers' salons, for example.

Where such basic hospitality can be regarded as a normal part of the service being provided, the cost should be allowable.

Meals, accommodation and other entertaining expenses may also sometimes be included as part of a 'package' of services provided to customers. If so, the cost of these items is allowable. This might apply, for example, where a business sells residential training courses which include meals and accommodation.

Promotional Events

In principle, the cost of a promotional event arranged to publicise your business or its products is allowable. This includes the cost of any of your own products or services provided free as part of the event. However, the cost of any food, drink or other hospitality provided as part of the event is usually disallowable.

For example, a car dealer could have a 'track day' at which potential customers could drive its cars on a racetrack. The cost of renting the track, providing the cars and the no doubt astronomical insurance for the event would all be allowable, but the cost of any food or drink provided would be disallowable.

If, however, the dealer charged for the event as a commercial venture in its own right (i.e. not subsidised), or provided the event to actual customers only on a contractual basis as part of their purchase, then the whole cost of the entire event would be fully allowable.

Chapter 14

Travel Abroad and Claim the Cost

How do you get the taxman to pay for part of the cost of trips abroad?

At one end of the spectrum there is the pure business trip. You may need to travel to some far-flung location to meet customers, suppliers or business colleagues, or to view sites for some new venture abroad.

Just because your trip takes you far away doesn't prevent it from being a business trip and the travel, subsistence and accommodation costs involved remain fully allowable for tax purposes under the general principles which we have explored in the previous chapters.

Many business trips will, however, have some 'leisure' element to them. Your foreign host might take you to dinner, for example. Such minor, incidental, personal elements to the trip should not make any difference and the whole cost of the trip should still be allowable.

It would be slightly different if you paid for that dinner yourself though. Your own meal would represent allowable subsistence expenditure, but the cost of anyone else's meal (other than an employee of your own business) would usually represent entertaining expenditure and hence not be allowed as a tax deduction.

For longer trips abroad, the 'leisure' element of the trip often becomes more significant. At this point, we have to start separating out the business and private elements of the trip in order to establish how much is allowable. A lot will depend on the circumstances surrounding the trip. The most important factor in many cases will be your initial rationale for taking the trip in the first place.

Example

James is self-employed and has his own import-export business. He needs to visit Hi Fat, one of his suppliers, in Bangkok. Hi Fat organises a meeting on Monday, a factory tour on Tuesday and another meeting on Wednesday.

There are no available flights arriving in Bangkok on Sunday, so James has to travel on Saturday, leaving him a free day on the Sunday. James spends the day sightseeing and goes to a Thai boxing match in the evening. He spends £100 on entry fees (for museums, etc, and the boxing match) and £60 on food and drink during the day. His accommodation also costs £200 per night.

Although James has spent the day sightseeing, he is in Bangkok purely for business reasons, so he is able to claim the cost of his food and drink and his accommodation on Saturday and Sunday nights. The cost of James's flights also remains fully allowable, as his sole purpose for taking the trip was to meet Hi Fat. The only costs James cannot claim in these circumstances are his £100 of entry fees.

So, simply occupying your free time abroad in a pleasurable way still leaves you able to claim the vast majority of the cost of your trip.

So far, I'm assuming that James flew back home as soon as possible after concluding his business with Hi Fat, but what if he extended his trip?

Extending Your Trip

By Wednesday night, James's business in Bangkok is finished. However, he does not fly home until Saturday morning and spends all of Thursday and Friday sightseeing.

The position now will depend on the reason behind James's decision to not book a flight home until Saturday.

If Saturday was the earliest available return flight, or the cost of any earlier flight was significantly greater, then the extension to James's trip was purely business-driven. He would then be able to continue to claim all subsistence and accommodation costs in full, as well as the cost of his flights.

'Subsistence', for this purpose, would generally include all non-alcoholic drinks at any time and alcoholic drinks taken with meals. James would have to disallow any purely personal costs incurred, such as entry fees to museums, shows, etc.

If, however, James could have flown home on Thursday, but decided to extend his trip for personal reasons, then the situation is quite different. Here there are several potential scenarios to consider.

Firstly, let's suppose that James genuinely needed to visit Hi Fat for bona fide business reasons and then subsequently decided that, as he was going all the way to Bangkok, he might as well extend his trip to give him a chance to see the city.

The primary purpose for James's trip is therefore still business and he can continue to claim full relief for the cost of his flights and all his subsistence and accommodation costs from his arrival on the first Saturday until Wednesday night, plus any subsistence costs during his journey home.

In other words, James will only need to disallow the additional costs incurred due to extending his trip by an extra two days (as well as all purely personal costs such as entry fees for shows, etc).

James will have spent seven nights in Bangkok so a simple way to look at his accommodation costs would be to disallow two sevenths of the total bill (his first night's accommodation remains allowable as he had no choice but to fly in a day early).

However, he only needs to disallow the additional costs of extending his trip, so it may sometimes be worth 'digging a little deeper'. Suppose, for example, that it would have cost £1,000 to stay for five nights but that the hotel only charges £1,300 for seven nights. James's disallowable accommodation cost would then be just £300.

James could also improve his position by planning his dining habits carefully. Meal costs incurred up to Wednesday night (the business part of his trip) will be allowable but his meals on Thursday and Friday are a personal expense. Hence, if there are any more expensive restaurants which James would like to try out, he should do so by Wednesday night!

Mixed Purpose for Trip

In our second scenario, let's suppose that James's reasons for travelling to Bangkok were mixed. Visiting Hi Fat was useful, but not essential, and James also fancied a few days' break in Thailand.

Now we have to take a completely different approach to apportioning James's expenditure. We start by separating out any elements which are purely business (like a taxi fare from James's hotel to Hi Fat's office) or purely personal (like James's entry fee to the Thai boxing match).

Subsistence costs should be allocated according to whether they were incurred during a 'business day' (Monday to Wednesday) or a 'leisure day' (Sunday, Thursday and Friday).

The remaining costs, including flights, accommodation and subsistence costs on James's 'travel days' (both Saturdays), have a 'mixed' purpose. A self-employed person like James could then claim a reasonable proportion of these costs. In this particular case, James had six full days in Bangkok and spent three of these on business, so he could reasonably claim three sixths, or 50%.

For a self-employed person, the costs allowed for a 'mixed' trip like this are not too dissimilar to an extended business trip like our first scenario. James does, however, lose the ability to claim full relief for the cost of his flights and his allowable accommodation costs would reduce from £1,000 to £650 (£1,300 x 50%). He is also unable to claim subsistence costs on Sunday, as he can no longer argue that he was only in Bangkok for business reasons.

Lastly, let's suppose that James had actually already booked a holiday in Bangkok and then decided to visit Hi Fat while he was there. This is pretty much the 'mirror image' of our first scenario. The primary purpose of the trip is personal, so it is only the additional costs incurred in visiting Hi Fat which can be claimed.

This means James would not be able to claim any relief for his flights or his accommodation. All that he could claim would be additional travel costs (e.g. taxi fares) and subsistence incurred while visiting Hi Fat. This may sound ridiculously unfair, but remember James is basically on holiday. You can't turn a holiday into a business trip just by popping in on a business acquaintance while you're there!

To avoid this fate, you should arrange the business part of your trip first before you book your flights or accommodation.

Internal Travel

The treatment of internal travel costs, such as taxi or train fares, incurred whilst abroad on business, depends on the reason for the internal trip. A purely business journey will be fully allowable and a journey made for personal reasons, such as sightseeing or going to a show, will be fully disallowable. Travel costs incurred when going out for meals may be allowable, depending on the circumstances. For a self-employed person on a purely business trip, or a 'business day' during a 'mixed' trip, these will be allowable.

Business Conferences

For many people, their main experience of foreign business travel is the business conference. In theory, the principles for claiming tax relief for the costs of attending a conference are exactly the same as for other business trips. In practice, however, conferences do seem to give rise to a few problems!

A typical business conference will involve some lectures or presentations, meals, refreshments, accommodation and some business networking activities. It's that last category that causes the problems because 'networking' often involves some form of leisure activities.

For example, a conference in Florida might include an afternoon's golf. Is it still a business trip? If the golf is an integral part of the conference and the only people involved are conference delegates and organisers, I would argue that this is a pure business networking activity and the entire cost of attending the conference remains allowable. HMRC has been known to disagree with this view in similar situations however.

Chapter 15

Travelling Abroad with a Spouse or Partner

In the previous chapter we looked at foreign travel costs and how much of them can be claimed for tax purposes. In this chapter we will take a look at the tax position for trips taken together with a spouse, partner, or other family member.

For ease of illustration, I'm actually just going to talk about being accompanied by your spouse. As far as the tax treatment is concerned, however, being accompanied by an unmarried life partner or any other member of your family has much the same effect.

The first thing to consider is: what is the main reason for taking the trip? Is your spouse accompanying you on a business trip, or are you simply fitting some business into a holiday or other private trip?

In the former case, you are likely to be able to claim a significant proportion of the cost of the trip, in the latter you will generally only be able to claim any additional costs arising as a direct result of the business element of the trip.

The mere fact that your spouse accompanies you on a trip does initially tend to suggest there is at least some private element. This can be overcome in some cases, but it is necessary to show your spouse's presence was required for business purposes.

In some cases your spouse will actually work in your business, perhaps as a fellow partner or employed as your personal assistant, or in some other capacity. Whatever their role, there could be a genuine business reason for them to accompany you on the trip. This makes it a business trip for each of you and a suitable proportion of the travel, accommodation and subsistence costs for both of you can be claimed following the same principles as we looked at in Chapter 14.

Note, however, this generally only covers situations where your spouse has a permanent role in your business that is consistent

84

with the need to take them on the business trip. Hiring your spouse as a clerical assistant for a couple of weeks while you're abroad will not usually be enough!

Social and Networking Requirements
Sometimes you might need to take your spouse on a business trip in order to meet the cultural or social expectations of a foreign host or business contact.

Let us suppose, for example, that, in order to secure a large contract in South America, the managing partner of a UK-based partnership flies to Rio for some business meetings and is also invited to dinner at their opposite number's home. The South American host clearly expects the UK partner to take their spouse with them and, although this is ostensibly a social occasion, the contract rides on meeting those expectations.

In this situation, the travel costs in respect of the UK partner's spouse are wholly and exclusively incurred for business purposes and are therefore fully allowable.

The great difficulty in many cases though is in establishing exactly what the main reason for the spouse to go on the trip is. Imagine you take your spouse to Rio for three days so they can accompany you to that business dinner and help you win that contract. The dinner takes up one evening, leaving your spouse with two and a half days of free time while you attend other business meetings, etc.

If your spouse stayed in your hotel room for two and a half days and only emerged to go to the business dinner then it would be easy to demonstrate they had come to Rio purely for business reasons. But that would be ridiculous. Whatever the initial reason was for the trip, most people are going to make the most of any free time they have. This should not change the underlying nature of the trip although, of course, any additional expenses incurred in sightseeing, going to shows, visiting friends and relatives, etc, will all be disallowable private expenses.

The problem is the fact that your spouse will naturally want to occupy their free time in a pleasurable way will make it very difficult to establish that there was a clear business motive for taking them on the trip in the first place. Any documentation recording the rationale for your spouse's presence on the trip will be helpful: especially in the case of a partnership where the other partners' approval might be required. It would also be wise to ensure the business elements of the trip are arranged first before adding on any private elements like a visit to the theatre or a boat trip.

Where there is a mixture of business and private reasons for a sole trader or business partner to take their spouse with them, it may be possible to claim part of the spouse's travel costs in a similar way to the costs of the mixed purpose trips we looked at in Chapter 14. The stronger the business case for taking your spouse, the greater the proportion of the costs you are likely to be able to claim.

Purely Private Spouses

Where the business owner has simply taken their spouse with them on a business trip for purely personal reasons, the owner's own travel costs will be allowable on the same basis as we looked at in Chapter 14, but the spouse's costs will be a personal expense.

It would, however, only be necessary to disallow any additional costs incurred as a result of the spouse's presence on the trip. For example, there may not be any additional accommodation costs to disallow, as the room charge might have been the same whether the spouse was there or not. The same might apply to taxi fares or the costs of hiring a car.

That Special Person

If the spouse has some special skill which is relevant to the business owner's trip then the cost of taking them along might then become allowable. A good example might be a spouse who speaks the local language and can therefore act as an interpreter.

The spouse's expenses might also be allowable where the business owner is in such poor health that they must accompany them.

Finally, a business owner might claim the cost of taking their spouse where this was essential to their personal safety. This would be particularly relevant in the case of a female business owner travelling to a developing country but might also apply to a businessman whose wife has a black belt in karate!

Part 5

Investing in Your Business:
Capital Allowances

Chapter 16

Capital Allowances: The Basics

When your business spends money on most things like rent, wages, or stationery, the cost is instantly tax deductible in full.

In other words, if you spend £10,000 on rent during the year, your taxable profits will be reduced by £10,000 and your tax bill will typically fall by £4,200 if you are a higher-rate taxpayer (£10,000 x 42%).

When your business buys *assets* – things that are not used up during the year but last for several years – you may not be able to claim a full tax deduction in the year of purchase. Instead, you may only be able to claim, say, 18% per year. This 18% deduction is known as a capital allowance and is designed to compensate your business for asset depreciation due to wear and tear.

To help you understand some of the terminology used in this chapter, here is a quick overview of the capital allowances regime:

Capital allowances consist of:
>The structures and buildings allowance, and
>Plant and machinery allowances, which consist of:
>>The annual investment allowance
>>Enhanced capital allowances
>>Writing down allowances
>>Balancing allowances and charges

In the March 2021 Budget the Government introduced a temporary 130% super tax deduction for companies (not sole traders or partnerships). For more information, see the Taxcafe guide *The Company Tax Changes*.

Capital allowances are given by reference to your accounting period. The forthcoming changes to the way accounting periods are taxed (see Chapter 37) will not affect the amount of capital allowances available to you: unless you choose to change your accounting date.

Land and Buildings

The position for capital allowances on land and buildings is somewhat complex, but may be briefly summarised as follows:

- Land: no allowances are available (although the cost of altering land may sometimes qualify for either plant and machinery allowances or the structures and buildings allowance: see further below)
- Residential property: allowances are generally not available except in the case of integral features and certain other fixtures (see below) within qualifying furnished holiday lets or 'communal areas' within other rental properties that are not part of any individual 'dwelling' (e.g. a utility room or common stairwell in a block of flats)
- Commercial property: plant and machinery allowances are available on integral features and certain other fixtures (see below); the structures and buildings allowance is generally available on property constructed after 28th October 2018, or improvement or renovation expenditure incurred after that date. Further details are given below.

The Structures and Buildings Allowance
In 2018, a new allowance called the 'structures and buildings allowance' was introduced to provide tax relief when money is spent on *non-residential* property (i.e. commercial property).

The allowance is given at the rate of 3% per year on the cost of the construction, renovation, improvement or conversion of qualifying commercial property. (The rate was increased from 2% to 3% in 2020.)

The cost of land does not qualify. Where a new qualifying property is purchased from a developer, the allowance can be claimed on the purchase price, but with an appropriate exclusion for the cost of the land.

The allowance cannot be claimed on spending that qualifies for plant and machinery allowances, including 'integral features' and other qualifying fixtures (see below).

The structures and buildings allowance is also available when there are renovations or improvements to existing commercial property.

The allowance is available to landlords renting out non-residential property, as well as businesses using commercial property in their own trade or profession. It is limited to the 'net direct costs relating to physically constructing the asset'. This includes demolition costs, the costs of land alterations or preparations necessary for the construction, and other direct costs of bringing the structure or building into existence. However, in addition to excluding the cost of land, the structures and buildings allowance does not cover:

- Stamp Duty Land Tax and other purchase costs
- Costs of obtaining planning permission
- Other land alterations beyond what is necessary for the construction (e.g. most landscaping)
- Land reclamation and remediation (a separate relief is sometimes available, but only for companies)

The allowance claim generally commences on the later of the date the expenditure is incurred, and the date the building is first brought into qualifying use. For more information on the structures and buildings allowance, see the Taxcafe guide *How to Save Property Tax*.

Integral Features and Other Qualifying Fixtures
Certain 'integral features' and other qualifying fixtures inside commercial properties, qualifying furnished holiday lets, and communal areas within residential rental property (see above), qualify for plant and machinery allowances.

Integral features include all the existing wiring, lighting, plumbing, heating and air conditioning in any property you buy for your business. (Chapter 32 takes a detailed look at spending on integral features.) Other qualifying fixtures include fitted bathrooms, toilets, showers, and kitchens.

Plant and Machinery

Spending on 'plant and machinery' qualifies for the highest levels of capital allowances, generally referred to as 'plant and machinery allowances'. Plant and machinery is a somewhat old-fashioned term and there is no definition of it in the statute books (except in respect of fixtures).

For a typical business in the service sector, plant and machinery includes things like:

- Computers and office equipment
- Office furniture
- Cars and other vehicles

Businesses that 'make things', for example those in the manufacturing sector or construction sector, usually own specialist equipment and tools. These assets also attract plant and machinery allowances, although there are far too many different types of asset to mention.

Some assets do NOT attract plant and machinery allowances, the most notable ones being:

- Stock-in-trade
- Buildings and land (although integral features and certain other fixtures sometimes qualify: see above)

Stock in trade is simply the inventory or merchandise belonging to the business: the stuff it sells! Not all businesses sell goods but, for those that do, the tax treatment is covered in Chapter 39.

The Annual Investment Allowance
UK tax legislation contains a generous annual investment allowance ('annual investment allowance'), which provides 100% tax relief for spending on most types of qualifying plant and machinery. It is available for purchases of both new and second-hand assets.

The level of the Annual Investment Allowance has been changed repeatedly over the years. It is currently £1 million per year and the Government has announced that it will remain at £1 million permanently (although, of course, they don't really understand what 'permanently' means, so let's call it indefinitely, i.e. for the foreseeable future).

This means businesses can spend up to £1 million per year on qualifying equipment and other capital items and enjoy 100% tax relief in the year of purchase.

Most small businesses don't spend anywhere near this amount and will thus enjoy full and immediate tax relief on all of their qualifying capital spending.

It Doesn't Usually Matter When You Buy Assets

Plant and machinery allowances are not usually reduced if you buy assets part way through your accounting period. This means a sole trader could generally spend, say, £20,000 on qualifying business assets on the last day of their accounting period and reduce their taxable profits by up to £20,000.

One quirk to watch out for though, is that assets bought on hire purchase must actually be brought into use in the business by the end of the accounting period in order to qualify for allowances in that period (see Chapter 17 for more points on the timing of expenditure for capital allowances purposes).

Short Accounting Periods

The maximum annual investment allowance limit, and the rates of other capital allowances available, are all reduced proportionately if the business has an accounting period of less than 12 months. This mostly affects new businesses in their first year of operation.

Tax Relief for Cars

Most capital spending on plant and machinery is eligible for the 100% annual investment allowance. One notable exception, however, is cars. (Chapter 21 takes a detailed look at the capital allowance treatment of cars.) This is a great shame because cars are the only expensive assets many business owners purchase!

Although cars don't qualify for the annual investment allowance, vans and motorbikes do qualify (see Chapter 26).

Furthermore, certain new cars with zero CO_2 emissions qualify for 'enhanced capital allowances' which also provide 100% tax relief.

Enhanced Capital Allowances

Certain types of spending are eligible for 100% enhanced capital allowances. The most relevant for most small businesses are:

- Cars with zero emissions (until 5th April 2025)
- Goods vehicles with zero emissions (until 5th April 2025)

The vehicles must be new and unused to qualify for the allowance.

Enhanced capital allowance claims do not use up your annual investment allowance and are not generally subject to any limit.

The ability to claim 100% tax relief when you buy a car could prove extremely valuable. As mentioned earlier, most cars do not qualify for the annual investment allowance. Instead they usually attract much less generous writing-down allowances (see below).

So if your business buys a qualifying zero emission car for £30,000, the entire £30,000 expense can be offset against this year's taxable profits, with a suitable reduction for private use.

There is also a 100% first-year allowance for the installation of electric vehicle chargepoints until 5th April 2025 (previously 2023).

Writing-Down Allowances
Cars that do not have zero CO_2 emissions are only eligible for so-called 'writing down allowances'. Similarly, if your capital spending for the year exceeds the annual investment allowance, you are only entitled to claim writing down allowances on the excess. Of course, it is highly unlikely that the annual investment allowance will be exceeded by most small businesses now that it has been set at £1 million indefinitely.

The writing down rate on most plant and machinery is currently 18% per year. The remaining 82% – the 'unrelieved balance' – is carried forward to your next accounting period. You can then claim further capital allowances equal to 18% of this balance.

Writing down allowances operate on the so-called 'reducing balance basis'. In other words, if you buy an asset for £10,000, your capital allowance claim is calculated as follows:

Year 1:	£10,000	x	18%	=	£1,800
Year 2:	£8,200	x	18%	=	£1,476
Year 3:	£6,724	x	18%	=	£1,211
Year 4:	£5,513	x	18%	=	£993
Year 5:	£4,520	x	18%	=	£814
Year 6:	£3,706	x	18%	=	£668
Year 7:	£3,038	x	18%	=	£547
Year 8:	£2,491	x	18%	=	£449
Year 9:	£2,042	x	18%	=	£368
Year 10:	£1,674	x	18%	=	£302

Clearly, it can take many years to claim all your tax relief. In this example, the full amount of tax relief has not been recovered even after a whole decade! This demonstrates the value of the annual investment allowance and enhanced capital allowances. A £302 tax deduction in ten years' time is worth a lot less than a £302 tax deduction today.

Capital Allowance Pools
You do not have to calculate individual writing down allowances for every asset you own. Assets that qualify for writing down allowances are generally lumped together into something known as the 'main pool'. The main pool is effectively just a number expressed in pounds.

The Special Rate Pool
Some types of capital spending are only eligible for an even stingier 6% writing down allowance. These assets form what is known as the 'special rate pool'.

Most small businesses only have to worry about this writing down allowance if they buy a business car with CO_2 emissions of more than 50g/km. The 50g/km threshold has applied since 6th April 2021. (You can check your car's CO_2 emissions on a variety of websites such as *https://carfueldata.direct.gov.uk*)

Certain other types of expenditure must be allocated to the special rate pool instead of the main pool. These include:

- Certain defined categories of 'integral features'.
- Expenditure of £100,000 or more on plant and machinery with an anticipated working life of 25 years or more.
- Expenditure on thermal insulation of an existing building used in a qualifying trade.

Tax Tip
If your investment spending exceeds the annual investment allowance, it is better to receive the main 18% capital allowance rate on the remainder, rather than the 6% special rate.

Fortunately, the annual investment allowance can be allocated to spending on special rate items (except cars) instead of spending that qualifies for the normal writing down allowance rate.

This makes it more likely that any spending in excess of the annual investment allowance will fall into the main pool and enjoy an 18% writing down allowance.

Small Pools
Where the balance on either the main or special rate pool is £1,000 or less, the full balance can be written off for tax purposes.

Selling Assets
Where any asset on which capital allowances have been claimed is sold, a deduction is made from the pool equal to the *lower* of the sale proceeds or the original cost. If this results in a *negative* pool balance, a balancing charge arises. A balancing charge is added to your income and taxed.

Example
Susan, a sole trader, sells an old computer on eBay for £300. The computer was used 100% for business purposes, originally cost £1,000, and qualified for the 100% annual investment allowance.

The balance in Susan's main pool is currently £0 because all her previous asset purchases have already been written down to £0 thanks to the annual investment allowance.

Deducting the £300 sale proceeds from the £0 balance results in a negative balance of -£300. This is added to Susan's income and taxed.

Using Business Assets Privately
Where an asset is also used *privately* by the owner of an unincorporated business, capital allowances remain available BUT are reduced to reflect the private use.

For the vast majority of business owners the most important asset used both privately and for business purposes is their car (see Chapter 21). Other assets used both privately and for business purposes include computers and mobile phones. All such assets must each be placed in their own capital allowances pool, or 'puddle', as we like to call them.

The great advantage (or occasional disadvantage) is that a balancing allowance (or charge) will arise when each asset is sold.

Balances of £1,000 or less in 'puddles' cannot be written off like similar small balances in the main or special rate pools.

The annual investment allowance is available on assets (other than cars) with an element of private use. The allowance is, however, restricted to reflect the private use.

Assets purchased for a business proprietor's own use can only attract allowances if genuinely used in the business. Where the asset is provided to an *employee* of an unincorporated business, capital allowances are available in full but the employee may be subject to a taxable benefit in kind in respect of the private use.

Chapter 17

Maximising Your Capital Allowances Claim

Capital allowances can generate considerable tax savings, so you should give careful consideration to the timing of your capital spending.

All plant and machinery allowances are given in full for the year in which the qualifying expenditure occurs, even if on the final day!

In most cases, therefore, businesses will usually benefit by accelerating qualifying capital expenditure so that it falls into an earlier accounting period. Naturally, this is only worthwhile if the expenditure was going to be made fairly soon anyway. It would not be worth making speculative purchases of plant and machinery which may not be needed for some time to come.

Example
Betty's business has enjoyed bumper sales this year and she expects to make a taxable profit of £80,000. On the last day of her accounting period, Betty buys five new computers, three new printers, and some new furniture and filing cabinets. The total cost is £6,000.

This spending qualifies for the annual investment allowance and reduces Betty's taxable profits by £6,000, thereby reducing her Income Tax and National Insurance bill for the year by £2,520 (£6,000 x 42%).

Delaying Your Spending
In a few cases, a business may benefit by delaying qualifying capital expenditure. Where a business has already used up the annual investment allowance for the current accounting period but may not do so in the next accounting period, it could be worth deferring any further qualifying expenditure to the next period.

Changes in Income

If you expect your income to change significantly, you may be able to save tax by either delaying or accelerating your capital spending.

If you expect your income to *rise* you should consider *delaying* capital spending. If you expect your income to *fall* you should consider *accelerating* capital spending.

For example, business owners who expect their income to be below the £50,270 higher-rate threshold this year (£43,662 in Scotland) but above the higher-rate threshold next year, may benefit by delaying capital spending until next year.

Provided that the expenditure will be covered by the annual investment allowance, this will generally mean they obtain tax relief at 42% instead of 29.73%. In Scotland they could obtain tax relief at 44% and possibly 51% instead of 30.73% or less.

Those who expect to be in the same tax bracket next year as this year may be able to enjoy a small additional tax saving (0.73%) by spending money this year instead of next year. This is because National Insurance rates will return to their previous lower levels next year.

High Income Earners

Anyone expecting to earn taxable income of between £100,000 and £125,140 this year should not generally delay capital spending. Those who fall into this income band face a marginal tax rate of 62.73%. As a result, every additional £1 of tax deductible spending will save them 62.73p in tax. In Scotland those who fall into this income band face a marginal tax rate of 64.23% this year.

Anyone expecting to earn taxable income of between £125,140 and £150,000 this year and next year may wish to delay capital spending until next year. This is because the additional-rate threshold will be reduced next year. As a result, this year tax relief will be available at 42.73%, compared with 47% next year (43.73% compared with 49% in Scotland).

In all cases, the commercial implications of any delay or acceleration in spending need to be weighed against the potential tax savings.

More Points on Timing
Capital allowances can be claimed on assets bought on hire purchase ('HP') from the earlier of the date payment is made or the date the asset is first brought into use in the business.

In many cases, this simply means the allowances can only be claimed when the asset is brought into use, but it can differ in a case where there is an up-front deposit.

Example
Lisa buys a piece of machinery to use in her business, which has a 31st March accounting date. The total price of the machinery is £10,000. On 30th March 2023, she enters a hire purchase agreement under which she pays an immediate deposit of £3,000 and then pays monthly instalments thereafter. She first uses the machine on 2nd April 2023.

Lisa can claim capital allowances on £3,000 in 2022/23 and on £7,000 (the balance being paid by instalments) in 2023/24.

In some cases (particularly cars) an old asset may be traded in for the new asset. In this cases, the trade-in price allowed for the old asset is effectively a deposit, and will be treated in the same way as described above (although, of course, if the new asset is a car, the amount of capital allowances available will be considerably less).

See Chapter 19 for more on hire purchase. Another point to note is that assets bought on credit terms where payment is due four months or more after the purchase may not produce an immediate right to capital allowances.

Capital Allowance Disclaimers
Most capital allowances (except balancing allowances) on plant and machinery or cars may be 'disclaimed'. In fact, any proportion of the available allowance from zero to 100% may be claimed in each tax year.

Any 'disclaimed' element of the annual investment allowance or enhanced capital allowances will fall into the main pool or special rate pool, as appropriate, and will attract writing down allowances of 18% or 6%.

Disclaimers of capital allowances are useful in a number of situations where the allowance might otherwise go to waste, such as in the case of a small business whose owner has insufficient income to use their Income Tax personal allowance.

Rather than claim an allowance which will effectively be wasted, a disclaimer means that greater allowances will be available in future years.

The following example shows that a capital allowance disclaimer is generally worthwhile when the allowance would have gone to waste otherwise, but is seldom beneficial in other cases.

Example
Joe has a business profit for 2022/23 of just £11,000 before capital allowances. He has no other income. During the year, he bought a new machine for £10,000 and could therefore claim an annual investment allowance of £10,000 which would reduce his taxable profit to just £1,000.

This would be pointless, however, as Joe's profit is less than both his personal allowance and his National Insurance earnings threshold and is therefore already tax free anyway. Joe therefore disclaims his annual investment allowance in 2022/23 which means he has no capital allowance claim for the current tax year.

His expenditure of £10,000 falls into his main pool and he will be able to claim a writing-down allowance of £1,800 (18%) in the next tax year: 2023/24. This may not be much, but it is better than wasting his allowance altogether.

Later, Joe realises that while he will be paying basic rate Income Tax at 20% for 2023/24, he is likely to make enough profit to push him into the higher rate tax bracket for 2024/25.

He wonders, therefore, if he should disclaim his £1,800 allowance in 2023/24 in order to benefit from greater tax savings in 2024/25. Joe speaks to his accountant, Sylvia, about this but her answer is an emphatic, "No!"

Sylvia explains that by disclaiming his £1,800 allowance in 2023/24, Joe will pay an extra £360 in Income Tax (at 20%) and £162 in National Insurance (at 9%).

"Yeah," responds Joe, "but surely I'll save much more next year when I'm paying tax at 40%."

"No, you won't," responds Sylvia. "If you claim your £1,800 allowance in 2023/24, you will still have unrelieved expenditure of £8,200 to carry forward and that will give you an allowance of £1,476 next year anyway.

"The disclaimer would therefore only give you an extra allowance of £324 next year, so you'd only save £136, even with a 42% combined rate of Income Tax and National Insurance. It's just not worth it."

"Oh," says Joe; "well, thanks for putting me straight, I don't know how I'd cope without you pulling the strings."

Chapter 18

How to Claim a Cashback on Capital Spending

As stated in the previous chapters, most businesses are entitled to immediate 100% tax relief for qualifying capital expenditure thanks to the annual investment allowance.

Most spending on machinery, equipment and furniture for business use qualifies for the annual investment allowance, although cars do not usually qualify (but vans usually do).

Example
Let's take Jamie, a sole trader drawing up accounts to 31st March each year. Since 1st April 2022, Jamie has bought a few small tools but has not bought any significant capital items. His forecast profits for the year ending 31st March 2023 are £80,000, which will push him well into higher rate Income Tax.

Jamie is thinking of buying some new equipment for his business at a cost of £20,000. If Jamie buys the equipment by 31st March 2023, he will be able to deduct the full cost of the equipment from his business profits, saving him £8,546 in Income Tax and National Insurance (at 40% and 2.73% respectively).

Jamie has a problem though. Having just paid his tax bill for the previous year on 31st January 2023, he doesn't have enough money left for the new equipment. "It's a vicious circle," he says to himself, "you pay your tax one year then can't afford the money you need to spend to avoid another big bill next year!"

Two little letters provide the answer to Jamie's problem: 'HP'. Jamie could buy his new equipment on hire purchase and, provided that he signs the purchase contract **and** brings the equipment into use in the business by 31st March 2023, he will be entitled to 100% tax relief this year for the entire capital cost of £20,000.

So, for a relatively small initial outlay, Jamie will achieve his full tax saving this year.

Furthermore, having reduced his taxable profits for 2022/23 by £20,000, Jamie may have grounds to apply to reduce his self-assessment payments on account: the one that was due on 31st January 2023 and has already been paid and the one that will be due on 31st July 2023.

You can apply to reduce payments on account using form SA303 which can be completed online at: https://tinyurl.com/y75punre

This will *retrospectively* reduce the tax he had to pay on 31st January 2023, as well as reducing the instalment due on 31st July.

If Jamie's current year profits are less than last year's, he is likely to be able to claim an immediate tax repayment or, if you like, a 'cashback', of £4,273:

£20,000 x 42.73% tax = £8,546

£8,546/2 = £4,273 reduction in the first payment on account

That should sort out the HP payments on the equipment for a few months!

(See Chapter 19 for a detailed discussion of hire purchase.)

Part 6

Leasing vs Buying Business Assets

Chapter 19

Hire Purchase:
How to Maximise Your Tax Relief

An important choice that many business owners face when acquiring new machinery, equipment, or other assets for use in their business is whether to lease or buy.

The decision gets further complicated by additional choices, such as whether to purchase outright or through hire purchase (HP) or, if leasing, what form of lease to take.

Cashflow is usually a major factor and this will often rule out an outright purchase, leaving the business owner to choose between HP and leasing.

In this chapter we take a look at HP: how it's treated for tax purposes and how to get the most out of the deductions available.

What Is Hire Purchase?

Under an HP agreement, you technically only hire the equipment for the term of the agreement and then have an option to buy it at the end of that period.

Typically, there will be a small additional charge added to your last payment which is the fee for exercising your purchase option and gives you legal ownership of the asset.

For tax purposes, you are treated as if you had purchased the asset at the beginning of the HP agreement. This has the advantage of providing tax relief via the capital allowances system.

Finance agreements relating to asset purchases come in many varieties and the credit industry has an annoying habit of constantly inventing a bewildering array of new names for them. For tax purposes, however, any agreement which gives you legal title to an asset at the end of its term, or which gives you an option to purchase the asset at that time for a modest additional fee, is treated as HP, regardless of what the agreement is actually called.

Conversely, an agreement which allows you to use an asset for a defined period, but which either confers no right to obtain legal title to the asset, or which only confers a right to purchase the asset for something more than, or close to, market value (or the current estimate of what the asset's market value will be) at the end of the lease period, is not treated as HP for tax purposes. For tax purposes, such an agreement, whatever it is called, is treated as a lease.

As well as claiming capital allowances on the purchase price of an asset acquired under HP, you will also be able to claim a tax deduction for the interest charges arising under the agreement.

There used to be several acceptable methods for calculating the interest charges arising in each period, including:

- The actuarial method
- Straight line
- The 'Rule of 78'

Changes in accounting rules mean the actuarial method should now be used whenever possible. This is the most accurate method and reflects the true allocation of the interest costs arising. It is, however, extremely difficult to calculate so, in practice, it will generally only be possible to use this method where the finance company provides the appropriate details.

Failing the actuarial method, the 'Rule of 78' will now be the correct method to use for accounting purposes as it provides a good approximation of the true interest cost arising in each period. This is good news since, when compared with the simple, but crude, straight line method, it accelerates tax relief quite considerably.

Example
Moffat buys a new machine under HP. The cash purchase price of the machine is £12,300 and the total interest charge is £3,000. The business pays 36 monthly instalments of £425 (total £15,300) plus an administration charge of £50 which is added to the first instalment and an option fee of £50 which is added to the last instalment.

Being small amounts, I would generally simply claim each of the two additional fees of £50 as an additional finance cost when they are paid. The business allocates the interest cost using the 'Rule of 78', as follows:

i)   Allocate a number to each instalment in reverse order. Hence, in this case, the first instalment is allocated 36; the second is allocated 35; and so on until the last instalment is allocated 1.

ii)   Add up all these numbers (36+35+34+...+2+1). In this case, this comes to a devilishly intriguing total of 666.

iii)   For each instalment, you multiply the total interest charged under the agreement by the number allocated under (i) above and then divide it by the number you got at (ii) above. This gives you the interest charge within that instalment.

The interest charge within the first instalment is:
$$£3,000 \times 36/666 = £162.16$$

The interest charge within the second instalment is:
$$£3,000 \times 35/666 = £157.66$$

Continuing in this way for the first twelve instalments, we get total interest charges of £1,648.65 in the first year of the agreement. In other words, using the 'Rule of 78' provides 65% more tax relief for interest arising in the first year than the simple straight line method.

(Just in case you are wondering why it is called the 'Rule of 78', it is because the numbers 1 to 12 add up to 78. It is not, as I thought when I was a student, because it was invented in 1978!)

Accrued Interest
Most businesses remember to claim the interest charges within the HP instalments paid during the period but it is also perfectly legitimate to claim a further amount for accrued interest within the next instalment. I will explain this further by returning to our example.

Example Revisited

Moffat has a 31st March year end and actually purchased his new machine on 4th April 2022. His HP payments are due on the 4th of each month, commencing 4th May 2022. For the year ending 31st March 2023, he therefore claims all the interest within his first 11 instalments (total £1,536.04 using the 'Rule of 78'). He can also claim accrued interest of £98.08, representing 27/31sts of the interest charge within his 12th instalment due on 4th April 2023.

In summary, Moffat is able to claim the following amounts in the year ending 31st March 2023:

Annual investment allowance	£12,300 (purchase price)
Interest paid	£1,536.04
Interest accrued	£98.08
Finance charge	£50.00
Total	£13,984.12

HP and Capital Allowances

One critical point about an asset acquired under HP is that it is generally only eligible for capital allowances if it is brought into use in the business before its accounting date (see Chapter 17 for further details).

In one case a few years ago, a haulage firm with a 31st March year end purchased some new trucks on HP just before its year end but only bought road fund licences (tax discs) for them from 1st April.

HMRC pounced on this apparent error and stated that capital allowances could not be claimed in the year of purchase as the trucks were clearly not yet in use in the business as at 31st March.

Fortunately, however, the firm's accountant was able to point out that the trucks had been used internally, within the firm's own site, on 31st March, so the capital allowances were due in the earlier year after all.

The lesson is clear: make sure you bring HP assets into use before your year end.

Chapter 20

Leasing Assets

In the previous chapter we looked at the tax treatment of assets bought on hire purchase (HP). In this chapter, we will take a look at the tax considerations applying to finance leases and then take a look at the comparative merits of each method.

What Is a Finance Lease?

As discussed in Chapter 19, the leasing/credit industry creates many different terms for finance agreements and these can cause a great deal of confusion.

However, as far as we are concerned in this guide, where an agreement allows a lessee to use an asset, broadly as if it were their own, for a defined period, but without conferring any beneficial rights to acquire legal title to that asset at the end of that period, we will call it a finance lease.

In practical day-to-day terms, holding an asset under a finance lease is very much the same as buying an asset on HP. The lessee is treated as if they owned the asset (for the period of the lease), is generally free to use it as they please (subject to any restrictions under the lease) and is usually responsible for repairs, maintenance and running costs. (Repairs and maintenance may sometimes be covered by a separate, additional payment under the contract.)

The key difference between a finance lease and HP is that the lease does not include an option or right to purchase the asset at the end of its term or, if it does, it is at a more commercial price and not the notional £50 or so found in a typical HP agreement.

In other words, it is far from certain that the lessee will purchase the asset at the end of the lease. (While it is not absolutely certain that a hirer will buy an asset under a HP agreement, it is pretty likely, in view of the negligible size of the option price in most cases.)

Under a finance lease, you are not treated as owning the asset for tax purposes during the period of the lease and cannot claim capital allowances on it during that time (except in the case of some leases of five or more year's duration, known as 'long funding leases').

Instead you can claim your lease payments, including any finance element, as a tax deductible expense (but see further in Chapter 27 regarding cars held under finance leases).

As with the interest element of a HP agreement, you will also often be able to include an accrual for part of the next lease payment due after your accounting date (e.g. if the next payment is due 10 days after a 31st December accounting date, you could claim 21/31sts of that payment as an accrual).

Apart from this, you can generally simply claim your lease payments as they are made. However, you may have to spread them more evenly over the life of the lease if there are any 'balloon payments' (a larger payment at either the beginning or end of the lease).

Example
Bilbo takes out a finance lease over a new piece of machinery which has a purchase price of £20,000. He has an option to purchase the machine for £5,000 at the end of his three year lease (but he has no intention of doing so as, in his view, it will not be worth that much by then).

Bilbo has to make an initial, up front, balloon payment of £3,000, followed by payments of £425 per month over the life of the lease: a total of £18,300.

For tax and accounting purposes, Bilbo will be required to spread his total lease payments evenly over the life of the lease, giving him an allowable tax deduction of £6,100 each year (£18,300/3 = £6,100).

HP v Finance Leases

So, now that we have looked at the tax treatment of both financing methods, we come back to our original question: 'lease or buy', what is better, HP or finance lease?

At this point, we need to distinguish cars from other assets used in the business. We will come back to cars in Chapter 27. For the moment we will concentrate on other assets, such as computers, furniture, equipment, machinery, vans and trucks.

Where expenditure on these items qualifies for capital allowances, it will probably qualify for immediate 100% tax relief thanks to the annual investment allowance. This makes buying these assets under HP extremely attractive from a tax perspective.

Example Revisited

Let's now say that, instead of taking out a finance lease, Bilbo purchases the same piece of machinery under a HP agreement. Let's also say the agreement broadly reflects the same commercial reality as the finance lease.

Hence, the total payments under Bilbo's HP agreement will amount to £23,300: the purchase price of £20,000, plus the same finance cost of £3,300 which Bilbo suffers under both agreements. His total payments are £5,000 more than under the finance lease because he is actually purchasing the asset this time, so we must include its estimated value at the end of the period of the agreement.

Under the annual investment allowance, Bilbo is able to claim an immediate deduction of £20,000 as soon as he brings the machinery into use in his business. He can also claim his finance cost of £3,300 under the 'Rule of 78' method (see Chapter 19).

For the sake of illustration, to limit our comparison to tax factors only, we will assume Bilbo is able to sell the machinery three years later for £5,000. This gives him the same overall economic cost of £18,300 over three years as under the finance lease we looked at earlier.

Bilbo may only have to deduct his £5,000 sale proceeds from his main pool. However, we will assume the worst case scenario, meaning he will have a balancing charge of £5,000 to be added to his taxable income.

In summary, Bilbo's tax position will be as follows:

	Year 1	**Year 2**	**Year 3**	**Total**
Annual investment allowance	*20,000*			*20,000*
Interest under 'Rule of 78'	*1,814*	*1,100*	*386*	*3,300*
Total deductions	*21,814*	*1,100*	*386*	*23,300*
Balancing charge			*-5,000*	*-5,000*
Net deductions	*21,814*	*1,100*	*-4,614*	*18,300*

Naturally, the total net deductions under both HP and the finance lease eventually work out the same (since we fixed it so that both agreements had the same economic cost for the purposes of our comparison).

However, if we compare the timing of the deductions Bilbo obtains under HP with the simple £6,100 per year deduction he enjoyed under a finance lease then, assuming he is paying the same top rate of tax each year, HP comes out the clear winner from a tax perspective: with £15,714 more tax relief in the first year.

This, of course, is based on the assumption that the annual investment allowance was available. However, since the allowance has now been fixed indefinitely at £1 million, we can expect it to be available to most small business owners. (Remember we're not talking about cars here, we'll return to cars in Chapter 27.)

Where an asset purchase is not covered by the annual investment allowance then, in most cases, it would attract a writing down allowance at the rate of just 18%. In Bilbo's case, this would have given him a tax deduction of just £3,600 in the first year. Adding his interest claim would give him total relief of £5,414 (£3,600 + £1,814); £686 less than he would have obtained under a finance lease

In Summary
From a tax perspective alone, it is generally better to purchase machinery and equipment under HP rather than lease it under a finance lease, provided the purchase price will be covered by the annual investment allowance.

In practice, of course, there are also many non-tax considerations to take into account: including the fact that you get to keep an asset bought on HP, but a leased asset usually has to go back to the leasing company. Bilbo might get several more years out of his machinery if he buys it under HP, but he can only have it for three years under the finance lease.

On the other hand, someone like Bilbo is bearing the economic risk that the asset purchased under HP may not hold its value as anticipated. His costs under the finance lease are more certain, whereas there is more risk attached to buying the asset under HP.

Generally, in reality, there is a premium to pay for that certainty and the business owner will have to bear this in mind.

Finance Lease v Operating Lease/Contract Hire
Finance leases differ from operating leases or contract hire where you simply hire a piece of equipment for a pre-determined period and have none of the risks or rewards of ownership (e.g. you are not responsible for maintenance). Rent paid under an operating lease is simply allowed as it is paid (assuming it is for business purposes).

Part 7

Motoring Expenses

Chapter 21

Capital Allowances - Cars

The capital allowance rules for cars are quite complex but we are confident that you will have a solid grasp of them once you have finished reading this chapter.

The more you understand, the more tax you will possibly save. Remember capital allowances reduce your taxable profits and therefore reduce your tax bill.

As we shall see, the capital allowance rules for cars used by *self-employed* business owners (sole traders and partnerships) are far more generous than the rules for cars owned by *companies*. This is because the self employed are usually entitled to a much bigger tax deduction when they sell or trade-in their old cars.

The focus of this tax guide is the self-employed business owner, so we will not spend too much time discussing the capital allowance rules for companies.

However, the company rules are still worth mentioning because when a sole trader or partnership provides a car to an *employee* (i.e. someone who works in the business but is not an owner), the car is treated like a company car.

So in businesses owned by sole traders or partnerships the capital allowance treatment varies according to whether the car is used by:

- The self-employed business owner, or
- An employee of the business

Furthermore, it is also important to understand the company car rules if you are thinking about converting your business from sole trader or partnership status into a company. If you form a company you will no longer be self employed. Instead, you will become a company employee and, if the company provides you with a car, it will then be taxed as a company car.

'Purchase' and 'Sale'

Note that, throughout this chapter, when we talk about the date a car is 'purchased' what we are really talking about is the date you start to use the car in your business.

In other words, if you purchased a car in 2020, but only started using it for business purposes on 1st April 2022, the car will be treated as if it had been purchased on 1st April 2022 for its market value on that date.

Similarly, if you cease to use a car in your business, but do not actually dispose of it, then it must also be treated as if it had been sold for its market value on the date you ceased to use it in your business.

A car which is 'written off' is treated as sold for the amount of insurance proceeds received.

Cars Used by the Self-Employed Business Owner

The size of your capital allowance claim depends on the car's CO_2 emissions, measured in grams of CO_2 per kilometre (g/km). From 1st April 2021 the emission thresholds for capital allowances are as follows:

- Over 50g/km   6% per year
- 1 to 50g/km   18% per year
- Zero emissions   100%

The average car has CO_2 emissions of well over 50g/km, so most business owners will only be able to claim capital allowances of just 6% per year on 'regular' petrol or diesel cars.

You can check car CO_2 emissions easily using websites such as www.*carfueldata.direct.gov.uk*.

The CO_2 emission thresholds were higher in previous tax years. In other words, it has become harder and harder to qualify for the better capital allowance rates.

Note that a car which qualified for the 18% rate under a higher CO_2 emission threshold which applied when it was first purchased in the past will continue to enjoy that rate, as long as it is still used in the business, even if its CO_2 emissions now exceed the current threshold.

Future Changes
The 100% first year allowance for zero-emission cars will not be around forever. It comes to an end on 5th April 2025.

What Can Be Claimed?
For newly acquired cars your capital allowance claim is based on the cost of the vehicle, plus any extras. The car can be new or second hand – unless you are claiming the 100% enhanced capital allowance which only applies to new electric cars.

You cannot recover any VAT paid when you buy a car, even if your business is VAT registered. VAT can only be recovered on vans and motorbikes (see Chapters 24 and 26).

This means your capital allowance claim is based on the total cost, including VAT.

When you introduce a car into your business that was purchased at some point in the past, your capital allowance claim is based on the market value of the vehicle on the date it is introduced into your business.

Personalised number plates can also qualify for capital allowances in certain circumstances. Whether the number plate is acquired to promote the business or you personally is the key factor. For example, Bill Gates might claim relief for 'M1 CRO' but not for 'BG 1'.

Private Use Tax Tip
If a car used by a self-employed business owner has NO private use, it is treated like a company car for capital allowance purposes. The rules for company cars are generally much less generous than the rules for cars used by self-employed business owners.

Cars with no private use are rare but, if your car really has no private use, you should consider taking it to the shops once a year, claiming 99% business use and avoiding company car tax treatment!

(But, before you do, see also Chapter 24 regarding the VAT position on a car used exclusively for business purposes if you are VAT-registered.)

If your car has some private use its capital allowance claim will be reduced to reflect the vehicle's private use. However, when the car is eventually sold, you will usually be entitled to a special balancing allowance (a tax deduction). Company cars are not eligible for this special tax deduction.

Before we explain what happens when the car is sold, let's take a look at how your capital allowance claim is calculated when your car is used privately. This is best illustrated with an example.

Example
Gordon is a sole trader and buys a new car for £25,000 in 2022/23. The car has CO2 emissions of over 50g/km and 75% business use. In year 1 Gordon will be entitled to a capital allowance of £1,125:

£25,000 x 6% writing down allowance = £1,500
£1,500 x 75% business use = £1,125

The amount carried forward to year 2 (the unrelieved balance) is £23,500:

£25,000 – £1,500 = £23,500

The amount carried forward is £25,000 less £1,500; not £25,000 less £1,125. The amount carried forward (£23,500) is also sometimes known as the car's 'tax written down value'.

Example Continued
In year 2 Gordon will be entitled to a capital allowance of £1,058:

£23,500 x 6% writing down allowance = £1,410
£1,410 x 75% business use = £1,058

The amount carried forward to year 3 is £22,090:
£23,500 – £1,410 = £22,090

... and so on

It is important to point out that cars used privately by self-employed business owners are treated as separate, stand-alone assets. They are not lumped together with other assets in the main pool or special rate pool. This allows them to enjoy special tax treatment when they are sold.

Selling the Car
When the car is sold, a balancing allowance is available if the car is sold for less than its tax written down value (which is often the case).

A balancing allowance essentially makes up for any shortfall in the car's capital allowances. The balancing allowance reduces your taxable profits and therefore reduces your tax bill.

For cars purchased after 5th April 2009, a balancing allowance is only available if the car has both business AND private use.

Example Continued
Gordon's unrelieved balance carried forward to year 3 is £22,090. Towards the end of year 3 Gordon sells the car for £15,000. This gives rise to a balancing allowance of £5,318:

£22,090 - £15,000 = £7,090
£7,090 x 75% business use = £5,318

This means Gordon can claim a tax deduction of £5,318 in year three, saving him £2,234 in tax (at 42%) if he is a higher-rate taxpayer.

Key Result
This is a key difference between sole traders/partnerships and companies. Even though Gordon, a sole trader, is only allowed to claim a capital allowance of 6% per year for this type of car, he can claim a big catch-up tax deduction when he sells the car. Gordon would not be able to claim this balancing allowance if he was operating a company. Instead, the company would have to continue claiming tax relief at just 6% per year on the shortfall in the car's capital allowances (£7,090 in this case).

Sole traders and partnerships are also not able to claim these big catch-up tax deductions for cars given to their employees or if their own cars have no private use.

Balancing Charges

It's important to point out if a sole trader or partner's car (with private use) is sold for *more* than its tax written down value, a balancing *charge* arises. This charge is added to the business's taxable profits and is then subject to Income Tax and National Insurance at the usual rates.

A balancing charge is designed to compensate for the excess capital allowances given on the car. The amount of the charge is the difference between the car's sale proceeds and its tax written down value, with a proportionate reduction to reflect private use.

Given the strength of the used car market in recent times, it's quite possible that a car initially purchased second hand will be sold for more than its tax written down value.

Balancing Charges on Electric Cars

Electric cars currently qualify for a 100% first-year allowance and will thus almost certainly give rise to a balancing charge when they are sold. It's possible that you will pay tax on this balancing charge at a higher rate than you enjoyed on your original capital allowance claim.

Example

Elon is a sole trader who normally makes pre-tax profits of £75,000 per year. He buys a new electric car for £50,000 in 2022/23. The car has 75% business use.

Elon will be entitled to a capital allowance of £37,500 in 2022/23:
£50,000 x 100% first-year allowance = £50,000
£50,000 x 75% business use = £37,500

His capital allowance claim will reduce his taxable profits from £75,000 to £37,500. He will enjoy 42.73% tax relief on the first £24,730 of his claim. This takes his profits down to the £50,270 higher-rate threshold. He will enjoy just 29.73% tax relief on the final £12,770. In total, the car purchase will reduce his tax bill by £14,364.

A few years later (in 2025/26) Elon sells the car for £25,000. This will result in a balancing charge of £18,750 (£25,000 x 75% business use).

This will be added to his taxable profits and taxed at 42% if he is a higher-rate taxpayer, producing a tax bill of £7,875.

In summary, Elon has enjoyed a total tax saving of £6,489 (£14,364 less £7,875) by purchasing the electric car. He paid tax as a higher-rate taxpayer on all of his balancing charge but enjoyed tax relief as a basic-rate taxpayer on a big chunk of his original capital allowance claim.

Could Elon have done better? In Chapter 17 we saw that most capital allowances can be 'disclaimed'. Any unclaimed capital allowances can be carried forward to provide writing down allowances to utilise against future profits of the business, or simply not claimed at all.

Example Revisited

Let's say Elon decides instead to claim a first-year allowance on £33,000 instead of £50,000. His capital allowance claim for the year will then be reduced to £24,750 (£33,000 x 75% business use).

This will reduce his taxable profits to £50,250 and he will enjoy 42.73% tax relief on almost the whole amount. His tax bill will be reduced by £10,574.

The car will now have a tax written down value of £17,000 (£50,000 less £33,000) and writing down allowances can be claimed on this amount in future tax years. However, to keep the example simple we will assume that no further allowances are claimed.

When he sells the car for £25,000 this will result in a balancing charge of £6,000:

£25,000 less £17,000 = £8,000 x 75% business use = £6,000

This will be added to his taxable profits and we will assume it will be taxed at 42%, producing a tax bill of £2,520.

In summary, the electric car purchase now saves Elon a net total of £8,054 in tax (£10,574 less £2,520). He saves an extra £1,565 (£8,054 less £6,489) by disclaiming some of his first-year allowance.

Although this strategy worked for Elon, it will not necessarily produce similar tax savings for other taxpayers. There are lots of factors to consider, including the level of your taxable income both now, and when you sell the asset.

But there will be many cases where a full first-year allowance claim on the purchase will, at least partly, attract tax relief at a lower rate than you will suffer on your eventual balancing charge, meaning that restricting your initial claim could save more tax in the end.

Of course, someone like Elon, who is selling an electric car, may well intend to reinvest the proceeds in a new electric car. At present this would mean the balancing charge on the old car would effectively be wiped out by the first-year allowance on the new car. But this will not be the case after 5th April 2025 when the first-year allowance for new electric cars comes to an end. So it's definitely worth considering whether you might eventually save more tax overall by restricting your first-year allowance claim now.

Your accountant should be able to make the optimal capital allowance claim each year when completing your tax return.

Calculating Business Use

In the above examples the car had 75% business use. How do you calculate a car's business usage? This will depend on the number of miles travelled on 'business journeys' versus the total miles travelled.

In Chapter 11 we explain what is meant by the term business journey. This is an important topic if you want to maximise your tax relief when you travel by car, train, taxi or by any other means.

For capital allowance purposes an estimated *average* proportion tends to be used as accurate business mileage figures differ from one year to the next. The proportion claimed should be reviewed if there is a major change in the car's general usage pattern.

Cars Used By <u>Employees</u> of the Business

Cars used by employees are not treated as separate stand-alone assets. Cars entitled to an 18% writing down allowance are added to the main pool. Cars entitled to a 6% allowance are added to the special rate pool (See Chapter 16).

If the car is sold for less than its tax written down value, there will not be a balancing allowance. Instead, the outstanding balance remaining after deducting the car's sale proceeds will continue to attract capital allowances at 6% or 18%, along with any other assets inside the pool.

Chapter 22

Motor Vehicle Running Costs

In Chapter 11 we explained what a tax-deductible business journey is. If some of your business journeys take place in your own motor vehicle (e.g. a car, van or motorbike), then your motoring expenses will be tax deductible.

Motoring expenses come in two forms:

- The cost of the vehicle itself
- The running costs (fuel, insurance, etc)

Tax relief is available for the cost of the vehicle in the form of capital allowances. These are discussed in detail in Chapter 21 for cars and Chapter 26 for other vehicles.

In this chapter, we focus on the tax relief available for vehicle running costs. Almost all the costs of running the vehicle are tax deductible:

- Fuel
- Repairs and maintenance (servicing, MOT, oil, tyres, etc)
- Insurance
- Vehicle tax
- Breakdown cover (AA, RAC, etc)
- Warranty cover
- Interest on a loan or other finance to purchase the vehicle

Warranty cover needs to be spread over the life of the warranty but still ranks as an 'annual cost'. For example, for a three year warranty costing £900, claim £300 a year for three years.

How Much Can You Claim?
As a self-employed business owner you can claim the business element of the cost of running a car. The business element is found by comparing the number of miles of business travel with the total miles travelled in the year. (See Chapter 11 for a detailed explanation of 'business travel'.)

Example
Patrick drives a total of 12,000 miles during the year, 7,000 of which are business travel. The total annual running costs of his car are £3,000, so he is able to claim £1,750: 7,000/12,000 x £3,000 = £1,750.

Mileage Logs
The recommended method for determining your business mileage is to keep an accurate record, i.e. a 'mileage log'. For each journey you should record:

- The date
- The purpose of the journey (business or private)
- Your start point
- Destination
- Miles travelled and the car's total mileage at the end of the journey.

In practice, the same level of detail is not required for your private journeys, as long as you know your total annual mileage and have the details of your business journeys.

As we know from Chapter 11, normal home to work commuting is not classed as business travel for tax purposes.

Does Everyone Keep A Mileage Log?
A mileage log is strongly recommended and is usually the only approach HMRC is happy to accept in the event of an enquiry.

In practice, however, many people find it difficult to keep an accurate log (you've just driven 50 miles in pouring rain, you're already half an hour late for an important meeting and HMRC expects you to stop and fill in your mileage log first).

In these cases, a reasonable estimate of the car's proportionate business mileage is often used and is usually acceptable. However, if you do not keep a log you have to accept that, in the event of an enquiry, HMRC will often seek to reduce the business proportion.

Note, these days there are apps that may make keeping a record of your business journeys easier.

Fixed Mileage Rates

As an alternative to claiming a suitable proportion of running costs, sole traders and business partners can instead claim fixed mileage rates for business travel in their own motor vehicle.

For cars, the mileage rates applying are 45p per mile for the first 10,000 business miles per year and 25p per mile thereafter. (See Chapter 26 for the rates applying to vans and motor cycles.)

This alternative method is available to all sole traders and business partners (except for partnerships which include a company or other 'non-natural person' as a member).

A mileage log is essential to support a claim for business mileage (although a log is always advisable in any case).

If you use the fixed mileage rates you cannot also claim capital allowances, although relevant loan interest may still be allowed, where applicable.

The business owner may choose whether to adopt this approach or not but, once the decision has been taken whether to claim actual costs or business mileage rates, the same approach must then be used throughout the life of that car. We look at the pros and cons of this approach in Chapter 23.

Employees

If your business has employees, the basic choices are:

i)   The employer owns the car and pays for everything
ii)   The employer owns the car, the employee pays for fuel
iii)   The employee owns the car and claims business mileage from the employer

Under options (i) and (ii), the car is always referred to as a 'company car', even when the employer is a sole trader or partnership.

The best choice depends on the facts of each individual case and needs to be reviewed on a 'car by car' basis.

Under option (i), the business obtains tax relief for all the car's running costs. The employee is taxed on a benefit in kind. For 2022/23, this is generally equal to somewhere between 2% and 37% of the car's original list price, depending on the car's CO_2 emissions. A further benefit in kind equal to the same percentage of £25,300 is charged in respect of fuel. The business must also pay Class 1A National (normally at 13.8% but 14.53% this year) on both charges.

Note that electricity may be provided to charge an employee's electric, or hybrid, company car without giving rise to the additional fuel benefit. (But petrol or diesel provided to a hybrid driver gives rise to the full fuel benefit, as outlined above.)

Under option (ii) the employee is still subject to the benefit in kind charge on the car itself, but avoids the further charge for fuel.

The business may claim tax relief for all the running costs which it continues to incur and may also claim relief for any business mileage payments which it makes to the employee in respect of fuel used on business journeys.

The employee is not taxed on the business mileage payments they receive from the employer – provided that these do not exceed the approved rates published by HMRC. Any payments in excess of these approved rates will be subject to Income Tax and National Insurance in the same way as additional salary payments: unless the employer can demonstrate that the actual cost of business travel is genuinely higher than the approved rates.

The approved mileage rates in this case are somewhat lower than those for a small business owner using their own car for business, as they are only intended to reimburse the fuel cost, rather than the car's total running costs.

The current mileage rates (effective from 1st December 2022) applying to the reimbursement of fuel costs incurred by an employee driving a company car on business are as follows:

Engine size	Petrol	LPG
1,400cc or less	14p	10p
1,401cc to 2,000cc	17p	12p
Over 2,000cc	26p	18p

Engine size	Diesel
1,600cc or less	14p
1,601cc to 2,000cc	17p
Over 2,000cc	22p

The rate for fully electric cars is currently 8p per mile. Hybrid cars are treated as either petrol or diesel cars, as appropriate.

These rates are reviewed quarterly: on 1st March, 1st June, 1st September and 1st December each year. Employers may continue to operate the previous rates for up to a month after the date of change if they wish. The current rates can be found at: *www.gov.uk/guidance/advisory-fuel-rates*

Where the employer makes business mileage payments at a lower rate than these approved rates, the employee may claim tax relief for any shortfall.

Option (iii) is significantly different in that the employee owns the car personally. As such, the business has no running costs to claim (nor capital allowances), except for any business mileage payments which it makes to the employee.

The employee may receive tax-free business mileage payments of up to 45p per mile for the first 10,000 business miles in each tax year and 25p per mile thereafter.

Where the employer makes business mileage payments at a lower rate than these approved rates, the employee may again claim tax relief for any shortfall.

Employers may also make an additional payment of up to 5p per mile where an employee undertaking a business journey in their own car carries another employee of the business as a passenger (the journey must also qualify as a business journey for the passenger). However, unlike the main 45p or 25p rates above, the employee may not claim tax relief for any shortfall.

Employees Repaying Private Fuel Costs
In some businesses where option (ii) is being used, the business will pay the full cost of fuel in the first instance and then require the employee to repay the cost of private travel (rather than the employee paying for all fuel and then claiming business mileage payments from their employer).

While this is often more convenient, and is better cashflow for the employees, it is essential that the full cost of private fuel is accurately identified and reimbursed by the employee. Otherwise they will be subject to the fuel benefit charge: which could amount to as much as £9,361 (£25,300 x 37%) at 2022/23 rates.

HMRC will usually accept that the employee has borne the full cost of private fuel where they reimburse private mileage at the up to date advisory fuel rate, or greater. Exceptions may arise in the case of cars with engine capacities in excess of three litres.

Parking Charges

Parking charges may be claimed as part of travel costs in the normal way, provided incurred wholly and exclusively for the purposes of the business. For the reasons explained in Chapter 11, however, the cost of parking at home, or at your main, permanent business base, cannot be claimed. Parking at other business destinations, such as when visiting customers or suppliers, or as part of a longer business journey, is generally allowable, and may be claimed in full. This is unaffected by whether you are claiming the fixed mileage rates discussed above.

The cost of providing employees with parking at their main place of work is allowable and is not taxed as a benefit in kind.

The position regarding parking fines and other civil penalties imposed by the authorities is different, and varies according to who owns the vehicle, and whether it is being driven by the business owner, or an employee.

Private vehicles, owned and driven by the business owner
Fines and civil penalties relating to these vehicles cannot be claimed under general principles.

Employee's vehicles
Where the vehicle is registered in the name of the employee, but the business pays the fine, or reimburses the cost to the employee, the cost is allowable for tax purposes. However, the payment represents a taxable benefit in kind for the employee.

Vehicles owned by the business, or the business owner, but driven by an employee

Where the vehicle is registered in the business or business owner's name, there will be no benefit in kind charge on the employee. In this case, it is important to ensure the penalty notice is affixed to the vehicle and not handed to the employee.

As far as whether the cost may be claimed for tax purposes, the position is the same as for other business vehicles, as described below.

Business vehicles

The question of whether a parking fine on a business vehicle can be claimed is a controversial one. Here, we are talking about either a vehicle owned by the business (or business owner) and driven by an employee; or a vehicle owned by the business, driven by the business owner, and used predominantly for business purposes (e.g. a plumber's van).

Many people in the tax profession would argue there are circumstances where a parking fine for a business vehicle is wholly and exclusively incurred for the purposes of the business and should therefore be allowed, and we have a huge amount of sympathy for this view. Take, for example, an electrician working on a job for their employer at a city centre location where the only practical place to park the van is on double yellow lines. Many people would argue, under these circumstances, the fine is wholly and exclusively incurred for the purposes of the business and therefore represents an allowable expense.

However, we are sorry to say HMRC disagrees with this view and, sadly, their opinion is backed up by case law: although it is worth remembering case law always depends on the facts of the case and your circumstances may differ enough to enable you to mount a better argument than Group 4 Security did when they lost that particular case. It won't be easy though.

Commercial Charges

All of the above relates to fines and civil penalties imposed by the authorities. The position is different in the case of a so-called 'penalty charge' issued by a commercial organisation (Home Bargains in Galashiels do this to some of their customers, for example). Here, we need to look at basic principles: the cost is allowable if incurred by a business, or business owner, wholly and exclusively for the purposes of the business. The same applies if the cost is incurred in respect of a vehicle driven by an employee but owned by the business, or business owner.

Where a commercial penalty charge is incurred by an employee on their own vehicle, but paid or reimbursed by the business, this will be an allowable cost for the business. It is unlikely that a benefit in kind charge would arise under these circumstances, although it does depend on the facts of the case.

Chapter 23

How to Increase Tax Relief on Motoring Costs

Small self employed business owners have an important tax planning decision to make when it comes to motoring costs. If you make the right choice you could enjoy thousands of pounds of additional tax relief.

As we know self-employed individuals who use their cars for business purposes are entitled to claim tax relief on a percentage of their motoring expenses.

Motoring expenses come in two forms:

- The cost of the vehicle itself
- The running costs

Tax relief is available for the cost of the vehicle in the form of capital allowances. Running costs include fuel, repairs, insurance etc.

The percentage of motoring expenses on which self-employed business owners can claim tax relief is found by comparing the number of business miles travelled during the year with the total miles travelled.

The Alternative Route

As explained in Chapter 22, most business owners can alternatively choose to ignore their actual motoring expenses and claim tax relief at the following fixed business mileage rates instead:

- 45p per mile (first 10,000 miles)
- 25p per mile thereafter

Example

Patrick is a self-employed consultant. He travels 12,000 miles per year on business and 20,000 miles per year in total. Instead of claiming 60% of his actual motoring costs, Patrick can claim tax relief as follows on his 12,000 business miles:

- *10,000 x 45p = £4,500*
- *2,000 x 25p = £500*

Patrick's total tax deduction for the year will be £5,000.

If you want to calculate your motoring tax deduction using these business mileage rates, you cannot then claim either your actual running costs or capital allowances for the vehicle.

Whichever approach you adopt, you must apply it throughout the life of the car. So the content of this chapter may only become relevant when you buy your next car and can choose a new tax calculation method.

Simplicity versus Tax Savings

So which approach is best: mileage rates or actual expenses?

Many self-employed business owners may opt to calculate their tax deduction using the 45p and 25p business mileage rates because this method is supposedly simpler: you don't have to type up all your petrol receipts and other running costs or calculate capital allowances.

However, the amount of time saved may be exaggerated because you will still have to keep a log of your business mileage recording the date, purpose of the journey, start point, destination and miles travelled.

Maximising Tax Relief

The more important question is: Which method produces the biggest tax deduction, i.e. the most tax relief?

Sometimes your actual motoring expenses will produce the biggest tax deduction, sometimes the mileage rates – it all depends on your personal circumstances.

The amounts at stake are potentially significant and could amount to thousands of pounds per year.

The two most important factors influencing your choice are arguably:

- The cost of your car
- The amount of business mileage

The more expensive your car is, the more important it is to claim capital allowances, which means you will also claim your actual motoring costs.

The more you travel on business, however, the more likely you are to benefit from using the fixed mileage rates.

Example
Arthur is a sole trader and buys a new car for £40,000. He only drives 5,000 miles per year, half of which is business travel. His total running costs are £2,000 per year. He sells the car three years later for £24,000.

If he uses the fixed mileage rates the total tax deduction over the three year period will be: 5,000 miles x 50% business x 45p x 3 years = £3,375.

If he claims his actual motoring costs, his capital allowances claim will be £8,000 over the three year period: £40,000 – £24,000 x 50%; and his tax deduction for running costs will be £3,000: £2,000 x 3 years x 50%. His total motoring tax deduction will therefore be £11,000.

By claiming his actual motoring costs, Arthur will increase his tax deduction by £7,625.

However, claiming your actual motoring costs will not always produce the most favourable tax outcome, especially if you drive a modestly priced car and do a lot of business mileage.

Example

Terry is also a sole trader and buys a car for £10,000. He drives 25,000 miles per year, 75% of which is business travel. His total running costs are £5,500 per year. He sells the car three years later for £4,000.

If he uses the fixed mileage rates the total tax deduction over the lifetime of the car will be £20,063:

10,000 miles x 45p x 3 years = £13,500
8,750 miles x 25p x 3 years = £6,563

If he claims his actual motoring costs, his capital allowances claim will be a paltry £4,500 over the three year period: £10,000 – £4,000 x 75%; and his tax deduction for running costs will be £12,375: £5,500 x 3 x 75%. His total motoring tax deduction will therefore be £16,875.

By using the 45p and 25p mileage rates, Terry will increase his tax deduction by £3,188.

Chapter 24

How to Save VAT on Your Motoring Costs

If your business is VAT registered it's essential to understand the special VAT rules for motoring costs so that you maximise your tax relief.

Reclaiming VAT on the Purchase Price

Cars

When you buy a car for use in your business the general rule is that you cannot reclaim any VAT. There are exceptions, however, including taxis, driving school cars and hire cars.

You can also, in theory, recover the VAT if your intention is to use the car exclusively for business purposes and it will not be available for any private use. How do you convince the taxman that a car is not available for private use? With difficulty!

It has been argued that if there is insurance for business use only, this acts as a legal restraint on any private use, so it should be possible to reclaim VAT.

Although VAT generally cannot be recovered on cars it's interesting to note that several taxpayers have taken the taxman to court on this issue and won.

In one case (*Shaw v Revenue & Customs*) a farmer was able to reclaim VAT on a BMW X5.

The taxman argued that because the farmer's insurance also covered use for social, domestic and pleasure purposes, the vehicle was available for personal use and VAT should not be reclaimed. However, the farmer pointed out that even his combine harvester was covered for social domestic and pleasure use because it was cheaper than a policy covering business use only!

The farmer had actually purchased a second BMW X5 for private use and although the BMW bought for business use could be used privately it was very unlikely that it would be.

In another case won by the taxpayer (*Jane Borton TC05224*), a Land Rover was purchased with the intention to use it exclusively for business purposes, transporting tools and materials to and from building sites. The vehicle was insured for business use only. The tribunal decided that, taking account of all the evidence, the taxpayer had no intention when buying the car to make it available for anyone's personal use. As a result VAT of £4,913 was allowed.

In summary, it is not impossible to reclaim VAT on a car but the odds are stacked very heavily against you. The vast majority of business owners should NOT make a claim for VAT when they buy cars for use in their business.

Commercial Vehicles

If you are VAT registered, you can reclaim VAT on certain commercial vehicles. Note that if you are a sole trader or partnership business you cannot automatically reclaim the VAT: the vehicle also has to be used for business purposes.

If the vehicle is used 75% for business purposes, you can reclaim 75% of the VAT, and so on. Most smaller commercial vehicles, like vans, have at least some private use. If you claim 100% business use the taxman may not believe you!

A vehicle is a commercial vehicle if it has:

- a payload of 1 tonne or more, or
- an unladen weight of 3 tonnes or more

Obvious examples include tractors, lorries and most vans. Many double-cab pickups also fall into this category: the likes of the Volkswagon Amarok, the Mitsubishi L200 or the Ford Ranger. The manufacturer's website will tell you if the payload is more than one tonne.

Motorbikes

You can reclaim VAT on a motorbike used for business purposes. Again for self-employed business owners there has to be a suitable reduction in the VAT claim if the bike also has private use.

Accessories

You generally cannot reclaim VAT on accessories (e.g. satnavs or car phone kits) that are fitted when the car is purchased. If, however, you buy an accessory later on you can reclaim all VAT if the accessory is used for business purposes.

Running Costs

Self-employed business owners normally have to reduce their VAT claims if there is any private use of an asset. However, when it comes to vehicle servicing and repair costs, there is an important exception:

You can reclaim 100% of the VAT paid on vehicle servicing and repairs, even if the vehicle is also used privately.

Example

Fiona is a VAT registered sole trader. She sends her car to the garage for its annual service and ends up with a bill of £1,000 + £200 VAT. She uses her car just 5% of the time for business purposes. She can recover 100% of the VAT (£200) and then claim 5% of the net cost for Income Tax purposes (£1,000 x 5% = £50).

Parking Costs

There is no VAT levied on the use of on-street parking meters. However, some parking charges do attract VAT, e.g. multi-storey car parks.

The VAT can be recovered if the expense is incurred when you are out and about on business, e.g. visiting customers or leaving your car at the airport.

Leasing and VAT

If you lease a vehicle and use it exclusively for business purposes all the VAT on the lease payments can be reclaimed.

If the leased vehicle is used for both business and private purposes, you can reclaim 50% of the VAT, regardless of whether the business use is 1% or 99%.

When you are shopping around for the best deal you should ask whether the cost includes VAT or not and factor your 50% VAT reclaim into your calculations.

VAT on other charges such as servicing costs are not included in the 50% restriction and can be recovered in full.

Leasing does NOT include hire purchase – you generally cannot recover VAT on hire purchase if there is any private use (there is no VAT on the interest element in any case).

With short-term hire car contracts of up to ten days in duration, the VAT can be recovered in full provided the car was hired for one or more specific business trips and this is unaffected by whether there is some private use of the car in the evenings or at the weekend. This concession does not apply where a car is hired as a replacement for another car that is temporarily off the road.

For hire contracts of more than ten days, only 50% of the VAT can be recovered unless there is exclusive business use of the vehicle.

Number Plates

You can reclaim the VAT on a personalised number plate, providing the number plate was purchased for business purposes, for example to advertise the business or to create the impression of success.

Your chances of successfully reclaiming VAT are probably greater if the number plate is similar to the name of the business, rather than your own name. For example, Richard Branson would be better off going for V1 RGN, rather than RB1.

In many cases this distinction is not necessary, however, because the business's name and the owner's name are one and the same.

Your claim may be assisted by the fact that:

- Your business is trying to attract publicity locally (i.e. where the vehicle will be seen)
- The business name is readily identifiable (some number plates are too cryptic)
- The amount paid for the number plate is modest in relation to other costs of the business

VAT on Fuel

If a vehicle is used exclusively for business purposes all the VAT on fuel can be reclaimed. If a car is used for both private and business travel, there are two main choices when it comes to reclaiming VAT on business fuel. We take a closer look at which method is best in the next chapter.

Chapter 25

VAT on Fuel: How to Claim a Bigger Refund

If your business is VAT registered and your car is used for both private and business travel, you have two main choices when it comes to reclaiming VAT on your business fuel:

- Reclaim the VAT on **all** your fuel, but pay the Fuel Scale Charge, or
- Only claim back VAT on fuel used for business purposes

Choosing the correct method could save you many hundreds of pounds over the life of your car.

Note: Van owners cannot use the Fuel Scale Charge method. They can only claim back VAT on fuel used for business mileage.

Method #1
Fuel Scale Charge
With this method you can claim back all the VAT on your fuel, even fuel used for private, non-business travel. In return, you have to pay a Fuel Scale Charge – an amount is added to the VAT bill of the business.

The Fuel Scale Charge is a fixed charge based on your car's CO_2 emissions. If you do a lot of private mileage and reclaim all the VAT on private fuel using this method, you could save a lot of tax!

The accompanying table contains the full range of charges applicable from 1st May 2022 for businesses that submit quarterly VAT returns.

VAT – Quarterly Fuel Scale Charges

CO2 Band (g/km)	VAT £
120 or less	29.00
125	43.67
130	46.50
135	49.33
140	52.33
145	55.33
150	58.17
155	61.17
160	64.17
165	67.00
170	69.83
175	72.83
180	75.67
185	78.67
190	81.67
195	84.50
200	87.50
205	90.50
210	93.17
215	96.17
220	99.17
225 or more	102.00

For example, if you have a car with CO_2 emissions of 150g/km the VAT due is £58.17. This amount is added to the VAT your business pays HMRC (Box 1 on your VAT return).

The actual VAT you have paid on your fuel is then reclaimed just like any other business expense (Box 4 of your VAT return).

If your car's CO_2 emissions are not a multiple of 5, you should round down to the nearest emission figure, e.g. 153g/km rounds down to 150g/km.

Method #2
Claim VAT on Business Mileage Only

With this method you simply claim back VAT on fuel that is actually used for business mileage. If you have driven 3,000 miles during the VAT quarter and 1,000 are business miles, you can recover one third of the VAT on your fuel.

If you have quite low private mileage, you may be better off using this method.

If you use this method you must keep a detailed log of your business mileage. (Remember, without an accurate mileage log HMRC will often seek to reduce your tax claim in the event of an enquiry, leading to additional tax and possibly penalties too.)

Publicly, HMRC states you cannot use the advisory fuel rates (see Chapter 22) to calculate the VAT on fuel used for business mileage. In practice, they generally accept this method. Nonetheless, we will stick with actual costs for the purpose of the example below.

Example
Keeley, a VAT-registered sole trader, drives an executive saloon with CO2 emissions of 232g/km. The car does 28.5 miles per gallon and she does 16,000 private miles and 4,000 business miles per year.

Method #1 Fuel Scale Charge
Keeley pays extra VAT of £102 per quarter – £408 per year. Her overall VAT position is as follows:

Private mileage	*16,000*
Business mileage	*4,000*
Total Mileage	*20,000*
Total fuel cost	*£5,264*
VAT reclaimed	*£877*
Less: Scale charge	*£408*
Total VAT Relief	*£469*

Method #2 Claim VAT on Business Mileage Only
Business mileage	*4,000*
Business fuel cost	*£1,053*
Total VAT Relief	*£175*

Overall, method one (Fuel Scale Charge) delivers £294 more VAT relief per year than method two (claiming VAT relief on business mileage only).

More comparisons, based on different amounts of private mileage, are contained in the table below. A negative number means Keeley is better off claiming actual business mileage rather than paying the Fuel Scale Charge.

Fuel Scale Charge Savings

Private Mileage	VAT Saving
1,000	-£364
3,000	-£276
5,000	-£189
8,000	-£57
10,000	£31
13,000	£162
16,000	£294
20,000	£469

The above figures are based on an estimated average fuel cost of £1.65 per litre over the course of the year.

If Keeley's private mileage is less than around 9,300 miles she enjoys more VAT relief by basing her claim on her actual business mileage (method two).

It's interesting to note that the savings are purely dependent on the amount of private mileage. Business mileage is totally irrelevant – as long as there is *some* business mileage, that is!

Cars with Lower CO2 Emissions

Melody, a VAT-registered sole trader, drives a car with CO2 emissions of less than 120g/km. It does 60 miles per gallon. If she pays the Fuel Scale Charge she will pay £29 per quarter – £116 per year. The table below shows her savings from using the Fuel Scale Charge instead of reclaiming VAT on her business mileage.

Private Mileage	VAT Saving
1,000	-£95
3,000	-£53
5,000	-£12
8,000	£51
10,000	£92
13,000	£155
16,000	£217
20,000	£301

The above figures are again based on an estimated average fuel cost of £1.65 per litre over the course of the year.

Company Cars

Cars provided to employees are usually called 'company cars': even when the business is not a company.

Where the business pays for all the fuel used in a company car, either of the same two methods for claiming VAT relief may be used. The employee will, however, be subject to a benefit-in-kind charge.

Where the business instead pays a mileage allowance in respect of business travel, the business can claim VAT relief on the allowance paid (i.e. one sixth of the payment at the current 20% VAT rate).

Where an employee uses their own car for business travel and is reimbursed by the business, the business can again claim VAT relief on the fuel element within the mileage allowance paid.

HMRC publishes advisory fuel rates every quarter, which businesses can use for reimbursing fuel costs incurred by employees and as the basis for the calculation of the fuel element within mileage allowances for private cars. See Chapter 22 for further details.

HMRC will also accept rates published by motoring organisations, such as the AA and RAC, as the basis for the calculation of the fuel element within mileage allowances.

Summary

The Fuel Scale Charge produces greater VAT savings if you have high private mileage. If your private mileage is quite low, paying the Fuel Scale Charge is not worthwhile.

The amounts saved may appear quite small, but remember:

- They are *annual* amounts. If you make the right choice now, you could save many hundreds of pounds over a number of years.
- They are calculated for just one car. If you have more than one business car, your savings are multiplied accordingly.

Chapter 26

Become a Van Man and Claim the Full Monty of Tax Reliefs

When most of us think of vans, we probably picture something like a battered old Ford Transit – not really suitable for taking the kids to school or popping down to the golf club (you might even get black-balled).

But when we tell you that many of the vehicles classed as 'vans' under tax legislation are every bit as comfortable and convenient as the average modern 4 x 4, you might start to look at them in a different light.

Add in the fact that, when it comes to saving tax, vans have several major advantages over cars, and most people really sit up and take notice. Over half the cost can often be recovered in tax relief, effectively making it a much cheaper alternative to a car.

VAT

First, there's the VAT. If your business is registered for VAT, you can claim back VAT on a van purchased for business use.

Example
Let's take two vehicles, both costing £30,000: one's a car and one's a van. Vanessa buys the van and claims back £5,000 in VAT. Carlos pays the same amount of VAT on his car but can't reclaim a penny, no matter how much he uses the car in his business.

Capital Allowances

The second big advantage is capital allowances. Vans are eligible for the annual investment allowance which currently provides immediate 100% tax relief for up to £1 million of capital spending.

Most cars currently attract writing-down allowances at either 6% or 18%, depending on the car's CO_2 emissions (see Chapter 21 for further details).

Zero emission cars currently attract a 100% enhanced capital allowance but, in general, we can say that the capital allowance treatment of vans is more generous than the capital allowance treatment of cars.

Example continued

Let's suppose that Vanessa and Carlos are both sole traders using their vehicles 100% for business purposes, both are higher-rate taxpayers, and both purchase their vehicles during an accounting period of 12 months ending on 31st March 2023.

After recovering her VAT, Vanessa can claim the remaining cost of £25,000 against her profits for tax purposes. This saves her a further £10,683 (at 42.73%: 40% Income Tax and 2.73% National Insurance).

Including her VAT reclaim, Vanessa has recovered a total of £15,683, or 52% of the cost of her van. The taxman has paid over half!

Carlos's car has CO2 emissions of 150g/km. Because this is more than 50g/km he can only claim capital allowances at 6% this year. This gives him a claim of just £1,800 in the first year, saving a mere £769 in Income Tax and National Insurance.

Carlos will be able to claim further capital allowances in later years but at this point he is £14,913 worse off than Vanessa despite the fact that they bought similar vehicles for similar purposes. Vanessa's just happened to be classed as a van.

Private Use of the Vehicle

The capital allowances on both vans and cars bought by sole traders or business partners for their own use must be restricted to reflect any element of private use.

The VAT reclaim on a van with an element of private use will also need to be restricted. Even so, most of the van's advantages still remain.

Example continued

Let's suppose that Vanessa and Carlos both use their vehicles privately 25% of the time. Vanessa's VAT reclaim will be reduced to £3,750, giving her a net purchase cost for the van of £26,250.

Her capital allowances claim will then be as follows:
Annual investment allowance (75% business use)
£26,250 x 75% = £19,688

Vanessa's Income Tax and National Insurance saving will be £8,413 (£19,688 x 42.73%) and her total tax savings on the van will be £12,163 (£3,750 VAT plus £8,413 Income Tax and National Insurance).

Carlos's capital allowances claim will be reduced to £1,350, saving him just £577 in Income Tax and National Insurance.

Both business owners have lost some of their tax relief, but Vanessa is still more than £11,000 better off than Carlos simply because she bought a van instead of a car.

Employees

There are no restrictions for private use when a vehicle is bought by a self-employed business owner for use by an employee.

Instead there is an Income Tax benefit-in-kind charge on the employee using the vehicle privately. The employer must also pay employer's National Insurance on the same charge.

Cars almost always have some private use and the annual benefit-in-kind charge is currently usually somewhere between 2% and 37% of the car's original list price, depending on its fuel type and CO_2 emissions level.

Example continued

Let's now suppose that Carlos's car has a petrol engine and was bought for a higher-rate taxpayer employee. For the sake of illustration, we will assume that the car's list price was £30,000. With CO2 emissions of 150g/km, the benefit-in-kind charge on the car for 2022/23 will be £10,500 (£30,000 x 35%). Carlos's employee will pay Income Tax of £4,200 (at 40%) and Carlos has to pay £1,526 in employer's National Insurance (at 14.53% this year).

By contrast, the annual benefit-in-kind charge for private use of a van is currently just £3,600, resulting in Income Tax of £1,440 if the employee is a higher-rate taxpayer and employer's National Insurance of just £523 this year.

The benefit-in-kind charge on a car applies whenever there is any private use, even if it is simply *available* for private use and even if it is merely used for home to work travel.

Vans score again here because an employee who is only permitted to use the van for home to work travel is not subject to the benefit-in-kind charge.

Minor and incidental private use, such as stopping to buy a paper on the way home without making a significant detour, is also permitted.

Private Fuel for Employees

Further benefit-in-kind charges apply where fuel is provided to employees of the business for private use. For cars, the charge for 2022/23 is £25,300 multiplied by the car's taxable percentage. So the charge can be as high as £9,361 (£25,300 x 37%).

This will cost a higher rate taxpayer employee £3,744 in Income Tax (at 40%) and the employer £1,360 in National Insurance (at 14.53% this year).

Once again, a van proves better: the private fuel charge is just £688, costing a higher rate taxpayer employee £275 a year in Income Tax and costing the employer just £100 in National Insurance.

What is a Van?

The definition of a van varies from one tax to another.

For **capital allowances**, a van is effectively a vehicle which is:

i)   Primarily suited for the conveyance of goods or burden of any description, or

ii)   Of a type not commonly used as a private vehicle and unsuitable to be so used.

A vehicle only needs to meet one of these criteria to qualify as a van and be eligible for 100% relief immediately thanks to the annual investment allowance.

For **VAT** purposes, a van is generally a vehicle which:

i)   Can carry a maximum payload of at least one tonne, or

ii)   Has no accommodation to the rear of the driver's seat fitted, or capable of being fitted, with side windows.

For benefit-in-kind purposes, a van is simply defined as a vehicle primarily suited for the conveyance of goods or burden.

Vehicles with a maximum laden weight over 3.5 tonnes are not classed as 'vans', but could provide even greater advantages. Not many people will want to use them for the 'school run' though!

Double-Cab Pick-Ups

One type of 'van' which has become popular in recent years is the so-called 'double-cab pick-up'. An attractive alternative to a large car, they have enough seating space for the average family and often have removable canopies which effectively make them just like a large '4 x 4' with a lot of extra storage space in the back.

Several manufacturers produce these vehicles specifically designed to carry a payload of one tonne and thus meet the VAT definition of a van.

HMRC has also confirmed it will accept double cab pickups with a payload of one tonne or more as vans for both benefit-in-kind and capital allowances purposes.

Where the payload area has a hard top canopy, the weight of the canopy must be deducted from the payload weight. For this purpose, HMRC will deem the weight of any hard top canopy to be 45kg. Many double cab pickups have a payload of 1,045kg to allow for a canopy to be fitted without reducing the payload below the one tonne threshold.

Broadly speaking, however, as long as this rule is met, a double-cab pickup attracts all the tax advantages of a van while providing the comfort of a car.

Changes Ahead?

Some types of 'van', which have side windows behind the driver and which can be fitted with additional seating, may be treated as cars for some tax purposes.

In one recent tax case between Coca-Cola and HMRC, the Court of Appeal decided two types of modified 'crew-cab' vehicle were cars and not vans for benefit-in-kind purposes.

The vehicles in question were VW Transporter T5 Kombis and a Vauxhall Vivaro. They were ruled to be cars because they were not primarily suitable for carrying goods but were equally suitable for carrying passengers.

The court's ruling is in line with HMRC guidance, which states that if a vehicle has side windows behind the driver and passenger doors, it is unlikely to be a vehicle primarily suited for the conveyance of goods or burden of any description.

This is particularly so if it is fitted, or is capable of being fitted, with additional seating behind the row that includes the driver. This remains true whether or not those additional seats are in the vehicle at the time.

Where does this leave double-cab pickups?

The court case dealt specifically with crew-cab vehicles that had a panel van shape, but the case has led some tax commentators to speculate that, at some point, HMRC may turn its attention to double-cab pickups. The argument is that some double-cab pickups are not primarily suited for carrying goods but are equally suitable for carrying passengers.

For the time being, HMRC guidance still states a double-cab pickup with a payload of one tonne or more is accepted as a van for benefit in kind purposes.

Motorbikes

If there's not enough room on your driveway for a double-cab pickup, you might fancy a motorbike instead. Motorbikes attract many of the same tax advantages as vans but take up a lot less space.

VAT can be reclaimed on the purchase of a motorbike used for business purposes and businesses can also claim the annual investment allowance on this expenditure – generally providing immediate 100% tax relief in most cases.

Sole traders and business partners using a motorbike personally must restrict their claims to reflect private use.

Motorbikes purchased for the use of employees will not be subject to any private use restrictions but may give rise to benefit-in-kind charges.

The annual benefit-in-kind charge is equal to 20% of the *market value* of the motorbike when first provided to the employee plus any running costs borne by the employer, including fuel.

Unlike cars and vans, however, the charge is proportionately reduced to reflect any business use. It is also worth noting that the charge is based on the motorbike's market value when first provided, not on list price, and can be reduced considerably by buying a second-hand bike.

Mileage Rates

As with cars, it is possible for sole traders and business partners to claim fixed mileage rates for business travel in their own van or on their own motorbike as an alternative to claiming the actual running costs.

The rate for vans is the same as cars: 45p per mile for the first 10,000 business miles per tax year and 25p per mile thereafter. For motorcycles, a single flat rate of 24p per business mile may be claimed.

When claiming mileage rates it is important to remember that:

- Keeping a mileage log is essential (although a mileage log is advisable in any case)
- You cannot also claim any running costs or capital allowances for the vehicle; although you could still claim a suitable proportion of any finance costs, where relevant
- Once you have chosen one method or the other (i.e. either fixed mileage rates, or a proportion of actual running costs and capital allowances), you must stick to that method throughout your ownership of the vehicle

Chapter 27

Cars: Lease or Buy?

In Chapters 19 and 20, we looked at the pros and cons of buying equipment for your business under HP or leasing it under a finance lease. We also looked at how HP and finance leases are defined for tax purposes, including the fact that this is based on the terms of the agreement and not on what that agreement is called. Those definitions apply equally in the case of cars.

Up to now, we have looked at the general principles applying to most types of assets, such as machinery, computers, furniture and vans. Cars, however, are subject to some additional rules, which mean we need to take a slightly different approach when considering the 'lease or buy' question.

VAT

The first significant difference between cars and other business assets is the fact that businesses are generally unable to recover any of the VAT on the purchase of a car: whether under HP or not.

Where cars are held under a finance lease, the business may generally recover 50% of the VAT on the lease payments (assuming the business is registered and fully taxable for VAT purposes). This represents a major advantage for VAT registered businesses leasing cars rather than buying them.

As with most other things in the tax world, however, there are many other factors to take into account: such as the comparative merits of the finance deals available and, of course, the fact that a leased car will have to go back to the leasing company one day.

Lease Payments

Where a business asset is held under a finance lease, the business may usually claim a tax deduction for the lease payments (see Chapter 20 for further details).

For cars with CO_2 emissions in excess of 50g/km, a 15% disallowance must be applied to the lease payments (in other words, only 85% of the payments may be claimed). The 50g/km threshold applies to leases commencing after 31st March 2021 (previously it was 110g/km).

Capital Allowances

Where a car is purchased under HP it will be eligible for capital allowances. It will not, however, be eligible for the immediate 100% deduction provided by the annual investment allowance, as cars are not eligible for this allowance. However, new cars with zero CO_2 emissions are currently eligible for an immediate 100% tax deduction.

For cars purchased after 31st March 2021, only those with CO_2 emissions of 50g/km or less are eligible for writing-down allowances of 18%. Cars with CO_2 emissions above 50g/km are eligible for writing-down allowances of just 6%.

You Keep What You Get

The rate of capital allowances available on a car is set when you buy the car and not reduced later simply because the CO_2 emissions thresholds change (although the Government has been known to reduce the rate of writing down allowances in other ways).

Similarly, the question of whether or not your finance lease payments are subject to the 15% disallowance is also determined on the date you enter into the contract. Hence, existing contracts for cars with CO_2 emissions of more than 50g/km, but no more than 110g/km, which were entered into before 1st April 2021, are not subject to the 15% disallowance, even in respect of payments made on or after that date.

Private Use by the Self-Employed

Where any asset is used privately by a self-employed business owner, all of the relevant Income Tax deductions must be restricted accordingly, including capital allowances, lease payments, and HP interest. For example, where the asset has 30% private use, only 70% of the relevant deductions may be claimed.

This is equally true for any assets subject to private use but applies most commonly to cars owned by the self-employed.

No such adjustments are required in the case of assets used privately by employees, although benefit-in-kind charges will apply instead.

Private use does not affect the recovery of VAT on car lease payments, since the standard flat-rate restriction of 50% is deemed to cover this already.

Making the Decision

As with any other asset, the 'lease or buy' question for a car is dependent on a number of factors, including the relative merits of the deals available at the time. From a tax perspective, however, the factors outlined above mean the decision is also dependent on:

- Whether the business is registered and fully taxable for VAT purposes
- The level of the car's CO_2 emissions
- The amount of private use by the proprietor

For the sake of illustration, I will now look at a 'like with like' situation where the car can either be purchased under HP or held under a finance lease at the same overall cost before considering tax.

To start off with, we'll also assume the car will have 25% private use by a sole trader who is registered and fully taxable for VAT purposes and that the car has CO_2 emissions over 50g/km.

Example
Prianka is interested in a car that costs £30,000 to buy outright. She expects to run it for four years and it will have an estimated market value of £6,000 at the end of that time.

Prianka draws up accounts to 31st March each year and will acquire the car on 1st April 2023.

Prianka could enter an HP agreement to buy the car over four years at a total cost of £36,000. Assuming she then sold it for £6,000 on 31st March 2027, her allowable deductions for Income Tax purposes would be as follows:

Year to 31stMarch:	2024	2025	2026	2027
Capital allowances	1,800	1,692	1,590	18,918
Interest	2,602	1,868	1,133	398
	4,402	3,560	2,723	19,316
Private use (25%)	-1,101	-890	-681	-4,829
Deductions	3,301	2,670	2,042	14,487

The interest charges included above have been calculated using the 'Rule of 78' (see Chapter 19 for details).

The total deductions claimed over the four year period amount to £22,500, which is equivalent to 75% of Prianka's total cost of £36,000 less the car's sale proceeds of £6,000.

Alternatively, Prianka could hold the car under a four-year finance lease at a total cost of £30,000. The lease payments would amount to £7,500 each year but Prianka would be able to reclaim 50% of the VAT arising, reducing her actual cost to just £6,875.

For Income Tax purposes, she would then need to disallow 15% of the net payment due to the car's CO_2 emissions, and a further 25% of the remaining 85% due to her private use of the vehicle. This would leave her able to claim a deduction of £4,383 each year, or a total of £17,532 over four years.

In this example, I have chosen Prianka's acquisition date for the car on the basis of simplicity. Buying the car on HP and bringing it into business use before the end of her previous accounting period would accelerate some of her capital allowances, but would not significantly alter the overall outcome (apart from the fact that allowances claimed in 2022/23 would attract slightly greater tax savings: by 0.73%).

Weighing it Up
Buying the car under HP would give Prianka total Income Tax deductions of £22,500 over four years. This would save her £6,525 in Income Tax and National Insurance as a basic rate taxpayer or £9,450 as a higher-rate taxpayer.

Leasing the car would give rise to VAT repayments totalling £2,500 and Income Tax deductions of £17,532. Prianka's total savings would then amount to £7,584 as a basic rate taxpayer, or £9,863 as a higher-rate taxpayer.

So, from a purely tax-driven point of view, we can see Prianka would usually expect to be better off leasing her car rather than buying it under HP. Not only are the total tax savings greater, but tax relief is also obtained much earlier on average.

The same considerations will usually apply to most other sole traders or business partners acquiring a car for their own use, but there are some potential exceptions to be aware of.

It could sometimes be better to buy the car under HP if the business owner expects to be a basic-rate taxpayer in the first few years they own it, but a higher-rate taxpayer when they sell it.

A higher-rate taxpayer with no more than 10% private use of the car would be slightly better off overall if they bought it under HP. However, the slight overall saving must be weighed against the fact that most of the tax relief only arises when the car is sold.

Non-VAT Registered Traders
The position would be different if Prianka had not been registered for VAT. She would then have been unable to recover any of the VAT on her finance lease payments and would simply have claimed an Income Tax deduction of £4,781 each year (85% of £7,500 less the 25% private use adjustment).

The total deduction over four years would then be £19,124 – 15% less than the £22,500 available under HP. It is, however, important to remember the majority of the deductions available under HP only arise when the car is sold, whereas the deductions arise evenly over the period of a finance lease.

Low Emission Cars
Where the car has CO_2 emissions of 50g/km or less, there are two important changes to take into account: a higher rate of capital allowances will be available where the car is purchased under HP, but there will be no 15% disallowance of finance lease payments.

Keeping the other facts the same as for Prianka, a car with some CO_2 emissions, but no more than 50g/km, would give rise to the following deductions when purchased under HP:

Year to 31st March:	2024	2025	2026	2027
Capital allowances	5,400	4,428	3,631	10,541
Interest	2,602	1,868	1,133	398
	8,002	6,296	4,764	10,939
Private use (25%)	-2,001	-1,574	-1,191	-2,735
Deductions	6,001	4,722	3,573	8,204

As before, the total deductions available over the four year period amount to £22,500.

If the same car was held under a finance lease, the trader would again be able to reclaim 50% of the VAT arising, reducing their annual cost to £6,875. They could then claim an Income Tax deduction for 75% of this sum: £5,156 per year, or £20,624 over the four year period.

Hence, taking account of the £2,500 of VAT repayments, for cars with this level of emissions, finance leases again appear more beneficial in most cases for VAT-registered traders.

Where the business is not registered for VAT, the Income Tax deductions available under a finance lease would simply amount to £7,500 per year less the 25% private use adjustment, i.e. £5,625. The total deductions claimed over four years would thus amount to £22,500. While this is the same total as for a similar car purchased under HP, it must again be remembered that tax relief is generally available sooner under a finance lease.

The position for second-hand electric cars is the same as other low emission cars, as detailed above. New electric cars are different, however.

New Electric Cars
Businesses purchasing new, fully electric cars, with zero CO_2 emissions are eligible for an immediate 100% deduction for the cost of the car (subject to a private use adjustment).

This completely switches the timing of the available tax relief for cars purchased under HP: most of the relief will be available in the year of purchase, rather than the year of sale. (A balancing charge equal to the sale proceeds, less any applicable private use adjustment, will usually arise on the sale of such a car.)

However, we must also remember there is again no 15% disallowance of finance lease payments for these cars. So, what does this do to the 'lease or buy' question?

For VAT-registered businesses, finance leases are probably still more beneficial in most cases but, for non-VAT registered businesses, it would generally be more beneficial to buy these cars under HP.

In Conclusion
From a pure tax perspective alone, many businesses, including most VAT registered businesses, will be better off holding cars under finance leases rather than purchasing them under HP.

Potential exceptions include:

- Non-VAT registered businesses purchasing cars with CO_2 emissions of more than 50g/km
- Non-VAT registered businesses purchasing new, fully electric cars with no CO_2 emissions
- Sole traders or business partners buying cars for their own use who expect to have private use of 10% or less, or who expect to be paying a higher rate of tax when they sell the car

Remember, however, all of this is based on tax considerations alone and takes no account of any other differences that may arise. In practice, it is essential to take account of the commercial aspects of the deals on offer, including the effective interest rates and other terms applying.

Proprietors Making Mileage Claims
Some sole traders and business partners claim business mileage rates rather than the actual cost of their cars (see Chapter 23). Where the fixed mileage rates are being claimed, no other costs related to the proprietor's car can be claimed: apart from finance costs. Hence, while the interest element of payments under a HP agreement could still be claimed, lease payments could not.

If we take Prianka by way of example, if she were claiming the fixed mileage payments on her car, her only other claim would be an Income Tax deduction of £4,500 (in total) in respect of her interest payments under the HP agreement (£6,000 x 75%). This would save her £1,305 as a basic rate taxpayer or £1,890 as a higher rate taxpayer.

If she held the car under a finance lease, she could not claim any Income Tax deduction for her lease payments but would be able to reclaim a total of £2,500 in VAT. Hence, in Prianka's case, she will be better off holding the car under a finance lease if she is VAT-registered, but better off purchasing it under HP if she is not.

In practice, of course, the decision whether to lease or buy the car should be made first and then, following that decision, the business owner can decide whether or not to claim the fixed mileage payments in place of actual costs.

Cars for Employees
Where a car is provided to an employee of any business, we call it a 'company car'.

There are no private use adjustments for company cars. For VAT registered businesses, this has the effect of increasing the value of the tax deductions available under HP relative to the value of the VAT repayment available under a finance lease. However, despite this, many VAT registered businesses will still enjoy a greater overall saving by holding employees' cars under finance leases.

It is only in the case of a higher-rate taxpayer sole trader (or partnership made up of higher-rate taxpayers) acquiring a car with CO_2 emissions in excess of 50g/km, for use by an employee, that the ultimate savings available under HP may eventually exceed those available under a finance lease.

Even then, the fact there will be no balancing adjustment on the sale of the car means it will usually take a very long time before the tax deductions available under HP outweigh the combined VAT, Income Tax and National Insurance savings provided by a finance lease.

In fact, taking the same facts as in Prianka's case, but assuming instead that the car will be provided to an employee by a VAT-registered higher-rate taxpayer sole trader (or a partnership made up of higher-rate taxpayers), it could take up to 57 years before the savings available under HP exceed those available under a finance lease!

For non-VAT registered businesses acquiring company cars, the considerations are much the same as for a non-VAT registered business acquiring a car for the proprietor's use. However, the fact there is no balancing adjustment on the sale of the car means there will usually be a considerable delay in obtaining full tax relief for the cost of a car purchased under HP.

For low emission cars (those with CO_2 emissions more than zero, but not exceeding 50g/km) and second-hand electric cars, this delay means a finance lease will usually be preferable.

For cars with CO_2 emissions in excess of 50g/km, the delay in tax relief must be weighed against the 15% reduction in allowable finance lease payments. However, it would usually still take 27 years for the tax relief available under HP to exceed the 85% allowance under a finance lease (based on a car similar to the one acquired by Prianka); unless the business ceased trading in the meantime.

Based on tax considerations alone, it therefore seems fairly clear that all businesses will generally benefit more by holding company cars under finance leases.

The one major exception is in the case of a non-VAT registered business providing new, fully electric cars to its employees. Thanks to the immediate 100% deduction for the cost of purchasing these cars, it will generally be more beneficial to buy them under HP: until 5th April 2025, that is!

Part 8

Maximising Tax Relief on Borrowings

Chapter 28

How to Maximise Your Interest Tax Deduction

Interest is one of the most important tax deductions for businesses and their owners. The way we structure our finances can make an enormous difference to the amount we can claim.

The theory behind interest relief is often far more generous than most people realise. In practice, however, keeping track of every potential interest deduction can be a bit of a nightmare. As a result, many business owners do not claim anything like as much as they are theoretically entitled to.

The principles set out below generally apply to all types of business. However, residential property rental businesses are now subject to harsh restrictions on the tax relief they can claim. We will examine these diabolical restrictions later in this chapter. For now it is important to emphasise these restrictions only affect the *rate* of tax relief and do not affect *how much* interest may be claimed in the first place, which continues to be determined under the same general principles as any other type of business.

Sole Traders
Interest arises when we borrow money. We can borrow money in many different ways: a mortgage, a bank loan, an overdraft, a credit card or a personal loan.

In principle, it does not matter how we have borrowed the money: whether the interest is tax deductible depends on what we use that money for.

To make life easier, throughout this chapter I will generally refer to any form of borrowing as an 'account'. The interest on any account used exclusively for business purposes is fully tax deductible and this is equally true whether we are talking about an overdraft, a credit card, or any other form of borrowing.

Hence, if you buy an asset for your business on a credit card and this is the only transaction you ever make on that card, then all the interest on that card will be tax deductible.

Using an account for business purposes means buying business assets with the money from that account or otherwise using the account to fund the business – such as by paying staff or rent for the business premises.

The problem is that very few accounts held by sole traders are used exclusively for business purposes. At this point we need to distinguish between a business account with some private use and a private account with some business use. This distinction may sound rather artificial, but it can make a huge difference to the amount of interest relief available.

Business Accounts with Private Use
Many sole traders operate a separate business bank account and some also have a business credit card. These have the advantage of being recognised as business accounts for tax purposes, although the drawback is that you usually have to pay the bank for the privilege in the shape of bank charges, overdraft arrangement fees, etc.

Where these accounts are only ever used for business purposes then all of the interest and other charges on the account are fully deductible.

The problem with most business accounts, however, is that they are also used to pay the proprietor's personal drawings. They may also sometimes be used to meet personal expenses.

Technically, therefore, it should be necessary to track every single transaction going through the account in order to calculate the amount of interest relating to the business transactions.

Thankfully, this mind-boggling level of complexity can usually be avoided as HMRC generally accepts that all of the interest and charges on a business account can be deducted as a business expense.

There is one major proviso, however: the proprietor must not have an overdrawn capital account.

What is a Capital Account?

A proprietor's capital account is a measure of the amount of money they have put into the business. It is made up of money invested plus profits less drawings and other private expenditure met from business resources. If this measure comes out as a negative figure, they have an overdrawn capital account.

Example

Matt starts up a new business on 1ˢᵗ April 2022. He pays £100,000 to buy business premises, £40,000 for equipment and deposits £10,000 into a business bank account. At this point his capital account stands at £150,000.

In the year ending 31ˢᵗ March 2023, the business makes a profit of £12,000 and Matt draws out £80,000 in cash, as well as using the business bank account to meet private expenditure of £17,000. By this point, the business bank account is overdrawn by £70,000.

Matt's capital account now stands at £65,000 (£150,000 + £12,000 - £80,000 - £17,000). As this is still positive, he may claim a full deduction for all the overdraft interest on his business bank account.

The profit used to calculate the balance on a proprietor's capital account is the profit before tax. However, where a proprietor's Income Tax liability is paid from a business account, this must be counted as private expenditure.

Many sole traders do not draw up balance sheets for their business, so the capital account exists only in a notional sense. Nevertheless, it still remains an important concept in determining their interest deduction.

Where a balance sheet is prepared for the business, the capital account will appear on it and will be based on general accounting principles. For the purposes of interest deductions, however, the capital account must be adjusted to eliminate any non-cash items included for accounting purposes, such as depreciation and asset revaluations.

Example Continued

In the year ending 31ˢᵗ March 2024, Matt makes a profit of £150,000, draws out £170,000 in cash and uses his business bank account to meet private expenditure of £55,000, including paying his own Income Tax.

He also obtains a valuation of £125,000 on his business premises and adopts this new value in his accounts. The business bank account is now overdrawn by £140,000.

Matt's balance sheet now includes a balance of £15,000 on his capital account. This, however, includes the revaluation of £25,000 on his business premises: a non-cash item. Without this, his capital account is £10,000 overdrawn.

Thankfully, however, Matt's accounts also include £16,000 of accumulated depreciation on the equipment he bought in 2022. Adjusting for this non-cash expense, his capital account becomes positive again by £6,000. Once again, therefore, Matt is entitled to claim a full deduction for the interest on his business bank account.

Capital Introduced

As we can see, by using a business bank account, Matt has obtained unrestricted tax deductions for his interest costs, even though the account has effectively funded his private expenditure. This is because the capital he introduced into the business, plus the profits he has made to date (as adjusted for non-cash items) still exceeds the amount of private expenditure and drawings to date. This is called the 'capital introduced principle'.

Overdrawn Capital Accounts

All is not lost if the proprietor's capital account is overdrawn, but things do become a little more complicated since an apportionment of the interest costs generally becomes necessary.

Example Part 3

By 31ˢᵗ March 2025, Matt's business bank account is overdrawn by £100,000 and his capital account, as adjusted for non-cash items, is overdrawn by £30,000. This year, Matt will not be entitled to a full deduction for his interest costs and some sort of adjustment will be required. If the bank and capital account balances had been the same all year, he would need to disallow 30% (£30,000/£100,000).

In reality, both balances will have fluctuated over the course of the year, so the apportionment calculation will be more complex than the simple 30% suggested above.

Any reasonable and consistent basis will usually be acceptable. For example, Matt could calculate the apportionment on a month by month basis, using the actual overdraft balance at each month end and assuming that his capital account balance had reduced evenly over the course of the year.

This more detailed calculation will generally be beneficial in a period where the capital account balance is reducing. In Matt's case it would reduce the disallowable proportion of his overdraft interest to around 11.5% instead of the original crude calculation of 30% (assuming that his overdraft was also reducing evenly over the course of the year). To be consistent, however, the same approach would have to be used in a year when the capital account balance was increasing.

Mitigating Factors

The restriction in interest relief where there is an overdrawn capital account is only necessary if, or to the extent that, the overdrawn balance has been caused by personal drawings or private expenditure. Where part of the overdrawn balance is caused by trading losses or other business factors, the restriction can be amended accordingly.

Example Part 4

On 1st April 2027, after a couple of years of successful trading, Matt's capital account, as adjusted for non-cash items, is £10,000 overdrawn, and his business overdraft stands at £200,000. During the following year, he relocates to new premises. Due to the ensuing disruption, the business makes a trading loss of £50,000 and a capital loss of £10,000 on its old trading premises (based on the original cost of £100,000, not on the later valuation).

As a result, by 31st March 2028, Matt's business bank account is £300,000 overdrawn and his capital account, as adjusted for non-cash items, is £100,000 overdrawn. However, £60,000 (£50,000 + £10,000) of the overdrawn balance on Matt's capital account is due to trading and business factors; meaning that only £40,000 arises due to his drawings and personal expenditure and this is the relevant figure for the purposes of restricting his interest relief.

As before, there are many ways to calculate the restriction in Matt's interest relief for the year ending 31st March 2028. The two key points are to be reasonable and consistent. However, if we take the average of the relevant opening and closing balances then:

The average overdrawn capital account balance, as adjusted for non-cash items, and as amended to reflect personal drawings and private expenditure only, is (£10,000 + £40,000)/2 = £25,000

The average amount of the business overdraft is (£200,000 + £300,000)/2 = £250,000

And this would give rise to a restriction in interest relief of £25,000/£250,000 = 10%.

As we can see, taking these 'mitigating factors' into account may reduce the interest relief restriction caused by an overdrawn capital account quite considerably.

Private Accounts with Business Use

If a personal current account were used exclusively for business purposes then any overdraft interest would remain fully allowable. Furthermore, if a business proprietor had two or more personal accounts and used one of them predominantly to run their business, the treatment should be much the same as for a business bank account.

Sometimes, however, a business proprietor will use their only or main personal current account both to run their business and for all their private expenditure.

In this case, it will usually only be possible to claim a deduction for interest costs that can be directly allocated to specific business expenditure. In practice, this is not only horrendously complicated, but may also mean no deduction is available.

Example Revisited

Let's go back to Matt's first year of trading but assume, instead, that he ran his business through his own personal bank account. His profits of £12,000 would be paid into that account, but he would have paid out £97,000 for private expenses (assuming he spent all the drawings he took out in the original version of the example). Any interest arising must therefore be a personal cost, for which no deduction is available.

As we can see, in Matt's case, he was much better off using a business bank account (assuming his tax relief outweighed any additional charges arising).

The position would be very different, however, if Matt only went into overdraft in order to fund the purchase of business assets or other business expenditure. Here, the position would be similar to that for other personal accounts with some element of business use, such as credit cards or loan accounts.

Two main issues arise: how to allocate the interest charges and how to allocate repayments.

Example 2

On 1st May 2022, Julie has a brought forward balance of £3,000 on her credit card, made up of accumulated interest and private expenditure. She now uses the card to buy equipment for her business costing £4,000. At the end of the month, she is subject to an interest charge of £105. Of this, she can claim a deduction for £60 (£4,000/£7,000 x £105).

Julie makes the minimum repayment of £130 leaving a balance of £6,975 on the card. But what has she repaid?

Clearly, the first part of Julie's repayment covers her interest charge but, after this, she is free to allocate the rest of the repayment as she wishes. To maximise her tax deduction, she therefore allocates it (in her own accounting records) to the private expenditure on the card.

The next month, Julie is subject to an interest charge of £104 and can claim a deduction for £59.64 (£4,000/£6,975 x £104).

Where there are both business and private elements within the same account, the borrower can allocate repayments in the most beneficial way unless there is any agreement with the lender stipulating a different allocation.

By allocating repayments to the private element first, the interest deduction for the business expenditure will be preserved. The payment of the interest itself will generally need to be accounted for first, however, as it is only the capital element of the repayments that can be allocated in this way.

The position is different where the original expenditure was itself for a mixed purpose, as it is not possible to repay only the private element in this case.

Disposals of Business Assets

Where funds have been borrowed to purchase a business asset that is later sold, the interest deduction for those borrowings may continue but this depends on the amount of any disposal proceeds and on what these funds are used for.

Example 2 Continued

In 2024, Julie scraps the equipment she originally purchased on her credit card and receives disposal proceeds of £50, which she puts into her business bank account. As Julie has kept these proceeds in her business, she can keep claiming a deduction for the interest.

If Julie had kept the disposal proceeds personally, she would have to reduce the business element of her credit card balance by £50 in her interest deduction calculations from that point onwards.

Partnerships

Most of the same principles apply equally to partnerships. Interest on the partnership's business accounts can be claimed in full as long as the partners' capital accounts are not overdrawn.

However, to claim a trading deduction for any interest borne on partners' personal accounts which have been used for business purposes, it is essential that the interest cost is reflected in the partnership accounts.

Alternatively, a partner may make a personal claim for interest on sums borrowed to invest in the partnership, either to purchase a partnership share, lend money to the partnership, or purchase equipment for partnership use (including cars). This is known as 'qualifying loan interest' and is deducted from the partner's personal income rather than the profits of the partnership.

Qualifying loan interest carries the advantage of being deductible from any of the partner's personal income, not just their partnership profit share. However, where it is deducted from their partnership profit share, it will generally also be allowed for

National Insurance purposes, unless the loan was used to purchase a share in the partnership.

Where the interest arises on an account that has also been used for private purposes the qualifying element is calculated using the same principles that apply when a sole trader uses a private account for business purposes.

However, a loan to buy equipment for use in the partnership generally ceases to be eligible for relief when that equipment is disposed of.

Qualifying loan interest is subject to the annual tax relief 'cap', which is explained in Chapter 53.

Members of LLPs that have an investment business (rather than a trade or profession) cannot claim qualifying loan interest. This includes property investment, or letting, businesses.

Spouses and Civil Partners: Bear It and Grin
Generally speaking, you can only claim a deduction for interest on an account in your own name. You can, however, also claim interest on a joint account with your spouse or civil partner or in their name alone: provided you personally bear the interest cost. This applies both to sole traders claiming a direct deduction and to partners claiming qualifying loan interest.

Personal Loans
Interest on funds borrowed for business purposes remains tax deductible, regardless of who you borrow it from. Personal loans from friends, family or private investors are subject to the same basic rules as any other form of borrowing.

It is important to ensure that any interest is paid under a formal loan agreement. Where the lender and borrower are connected (e.g. close relatives), the rate of interest must not exceed a normal commercial rate. The interest rate can, however, reflect the specific circumstances, such as being unsecured and repayable at any time.

Remember also that the person lending you the money will be subject to Income Tax on the interest they receive (subject to the personal savings allowance discussed in Chapter 2).

Residential Property Businesses

Owners of residential property businesses can no longer claim tax relief on their interest and finance costs in the same way as other business owners. Tax relief for their interest and finance costs is now restricted to basic rate only. This restriction does not apply to commercial property, qualifying furnished holiday lets, or properties held inside companies.

However, the restriction *does* apply to:

- Individual landlords
- Joint owner individuals
- Trusts
- Partnerships
- Partners claiming qualifying loan interest (see above) on funds invested in a partnership that runs a residential letting business

Full details of this dreadful restriction are included in the Taxcafe guide *How to Save Property Tax*.

Further Points for Property Businesses

Subject to the restriction in the *rate* of relief for interest and finance costs incurred by residential property business owners, it is widely accepted within the tax profession that the 'capital introduced' principle discussed earlier in this chapter should apply equally to property businesses. In this context, mortgages over rental properties should effectively be treated the same as business bank accounts.

Hence, the *amount* of interest eligible for relief should be calculated following the same principles discussed throughout this chapter, it is only the way in which relief is given, and the rate of relief available, which will need to be restricted as discussed above.

These principles are generally accepted by HMRC, although some occasional resistance to the application of the 'capital introduced' principle may be encountered. For more details, plus guidance on what to do if you encounter problems, see the Taxcafe guide *How to Save Property Tax*.

Chapter 29

How to Make Interest on <u>Personal</u> Loans Tax Deductible

The general rule is that interest is a tax deductible expense if the borrowed money is used for business purposes.

It doesn't matter if you use a personal credit card or business overdraft facility to buy that new computer for the business. It also doesn't matter if you borrow against your own home to buy your business premises.

In each of these cases the interest on the borrowed money will be tax deductible because the money was used for business purposes.

The fact that the money was borrowed using personal accounts or personal assets is irrelevant.

Example
Harry, a sole trader, buys a new office for £100,000 using a mortgage of £70,000. To fund the deposit, as well as his legal fees and the cost of furnishing the new property, Harry borrows a further £40,000 against his own home.

The extra £40,000 has also been invested in the business, so Harry may also claim interest relief for this element of the mortgage on his home.

If, for example, Harry previously had a mortgage of £80,000 on his home, he will now be able to claim £40,000/£120,000 (one third) of his home's mortgage interest, as well as all the interest on the business property's mortgage.

Harry can make a direct claim for one third of his home's mortgage interest as a direct expense. If he is also making a 'use of home' claim (see Chapter 3) he should only include the remaining two thirds of his home's mortgage interest in that calculation.

Finally, please note that not all money borrowed for business purposes is fully tax deductible. Residential property businesses are now subject to a restriction in tax relief on their interest and finance costs (see Chapter 28).

Part 9

Business Property

Chapter 30

Business Premises: Rent or Buy?

Is it better to rent or buy your business premises? There are both tax and non-tax issues to consider:

Tax Relief

Rent paid for business premises is generally fully tax deductible, whatever type of business you have.

If you buy business premises, capital allowances may be available on some of the fixtures, fittings and equipment within the property (see Chapter 32).

Up until recently it was not possible to obtain tax relief for the cost of the building itself. However, a new structures and buildings allowance provides tax relief for new commercial properties and renovations and improvements to existing properties.

Tax relief is given at the rate of 3% per year on the straight-line basis. In other words, if a project's costs come to £100,000, an allowance of £3,000 per year can be claimed for 33 years.

The interest paid on any mortgage or other loan to buy business premises is generally fully tax deductible, with one important exception. Tax relief for interest paid by residential property businesses (typically on buy-to-let mortgages) is now restricted.

If a residential landlord takes out a loan to buy a commercial property which they use as their premises for the residential property business, the tax relief on the interest will also be restricted.

Capital Gains Tax

If you buy your own trading premises, you may qualify for several Capital Gains Tax reliefs that other property investors do not enjoy. Note the word 'trading'. This means investment businesses (e.g. property investment businesses) do not generally qualify.

Rollover relief allows you to roll over your capital gains into the purchase of new trading property. You can buy the new property between a year before and three years after selling the original property.

This effectively defers any Capital Gains Tax liability on the original property until the new property is eventually sold and gives your business flexibility to change premises and grow without adverse Capital Gains Tax consequences.

All of the old property's sale proceeds must be reinvested. Any shortfall is deducted from the amount of gain eligible for rollover. Relief is also restricted if there is less than full trading use of the property.

Business Asset Disposal Relief
Entrepreneurs' Relief has a new name: Business Asset Disposal Relief. Most people will struggle to remember such a drab name, so it will probably continue to be called Entrepreneurs' Relief – a good example of pointless fiddling with the tax system.

Business Asset Disposal Relief allows individuals to pay Capital Gains Tax at just 10% when they sell their business premises, but generally only if they sell their business as well.

Remember if you sell your premises without selling your business, you may not have to pay Capital Gains Tax immediately anyway, as you can defer the gain using rollover relief.

In partnerships, Business Asset Disposal Relief may also be available where a business partner personally owns the partnership's trading premises. Relief is restricted where rent has been paid for the use of the property since April 2008.

Business Asset Disposal Relief allows each individual to have £1 million of capital gains during their lifetime taxed at just 10%. In the March 2020 Budget the lifetime limit was reduced from £10 million to £1 million with immediate effect.

Property Pensions

Commercial property is one type of direct bricks and mortar property investment you can put inside your self-invested personal pension (SIPP).

Investing via a pension allows rental income from the property to roll up tax free and has a number of other tax advantages.

The problem with SIPPs is the severe borrowing restriction – generally no more than 50% of net assets. Even if you have £100,000 sitting in your SIPP account, you can only borrow an extra £50,000.

Nevertheless, for those with large pension savings, who can afford to make big pension contributions, or can team up with business associates, this is still a viable option.

In summary, buying your own trading premises could produce additional tax benefits not enjoyed by other property investors.

Non-Tax Benefits & Drawbacks

When you buy business premises using a mortgage, you generally swap having to pay rent for having to pay interest. Effectively the bank becomes your landlord! These are the pros and cons:

- Depending on the level of interest rates, property prices and rental values, one route will always be cheaper than the other and the disparity will change over time. Every property is different.
- If you rent you will never be exposed to falling property values... and likewise you will never benefit from rising property prices.
- Rents can be more predictable than interest payments and can be agreed many years into the future. Interest payments can be fixed but not usually for long periods.
- A long lease could bind your business and harm its growth.
- Tenants do not enjoy the same security as owners, having less control over the long-term location of their businesses.
- You continue to be liable for rental payments under a lease even if you cease trading. If you own the property, you could sell it, although this process can take time.

Chapter 31

Repairs Save More Tax than Improvements

Repairs expenditure is generally eligible for immediate and full Income Tax relief. Thanks to the new Structures and Buildings Allowance, spending on improvements to non-residential property can qualify for Income Tax relief... but at just 3% per year.

Example
Gwen has an old office block with a damaged wall. If Gwen spends £50,000 to have the wall repaired, she will be able to claim full tax relief for this expenditure. If she has the wall demolished and has an extension built for £100,000, the spending may qualify for the new Structures and Buildings Allowance, providing Income Tax Relief at 3% per year.

Note that most improvement expenditure is an eligible deduction for Capital Gains Tax purposes when the property is sold. If the Structures and Buildings Allowance has been claimed then the cost of the asset will be reduced by the total amount of relief claimed (thereby increasing the taxable capital gain).

What is a Capital Improvement?
Judging whether something is an improvement is not a question of aesthetics or taste. Whenever you add something 'extra' to an asset which wasn't there before, you've made a capital improvement and it means you cannot deduct the cost as a repair expense. If you built a new extension on the side of a Victorian building, it would be an 'improvement' for tax purposes – whatever Prince Charles might think!

Alterations will generally also be capital improvements, even if nothing is actually added. If you demolish a wall to combine two rooms into one, you will not have added anything, but it will still be a capital improvement.

Like For Like
Replacing 'like for like' will generally be a repair, unless:

- You replace an asset in its entirety, or
- The replacement is of a significantly higher standard

Each building and all its fixtures is generally regarded as a single asset for this purpose. Moveable items like machinery or furniture are separate assets.

For example, let us suppose you have a property with a separate garage at the rear. If you demolish the garage and replace it, this will be a capital improvement. This is because the garage is a separate, stand-alone, asset and replacing it therefore constitutes capital expenditure.

Contrast this with replacing a staircase. As long as there is no improvement element to the expenditure, this would be allowable as a repair because the staircase is not a separate asset in its own right. If you widened the staircase at the same time, however, this would then be a capital improvement.

Where the replacement is of a higher standard, this will generally be regarded as a capital improvement. For example, replacing a porcelain bath with a marble one would be capital expenditure.

Where the replacement is simply the modern equivalent of the original item, this is not regarded as an improvement and can be claimed as a 'like for like' repair. The best example of this is replacing single-glazed windows with standard double-glazed units. HMRC has specifically confirmed this is accepted as a repair.

Integral Features
Certain items within commercial property are classed as 'integral features', including electrical systems, plumbing, heating, air conditioning, lifts and escalators. The good news is that these items qualify for capital allowances (see Chapter 32).

On the downside, however, expenditure on replacing part of an integral feature is classed as a capital improvement if such expenditure amounts to more than half of the cost of replacing the entire feature within any twelve month period.

Where significant repairs are taking place, it may therefore be worth staggering them over a longer period to avoid this problem.

New Properties

Generally speaking, any expenditure which restores an asset to its original condition will be regarded as a repair. When I say 'original condition' though, I am talking about the condition of the asset when you acquired it.

If you buy a property with a hole in the roof, the cost of repairing that roof will be capital expenditure because you are improving on the condition of the property when you bought it.

In practice, normal repairs and redecoration work on newly acquired properties is usually considered allowable. Such expenditure will generally be regarded as 'normal' if the work required is unlikely to have had any significant impact on the property's purchase price (or rent payable in the case of a leased property).

For example, let's suppose you buy office premises. The property could be occupied as it stands, but is really in need of redecoration. The cost of this redecoration work should usually be allowed as a deduction against your business profits.

If the property is severely dilapidated beyond normal 'wear and tear' however, the work may be so extensive that it has to be treated as a capital improvement.

In some borderline cases, it may be worth considering occupying the property first in order to ensure that the expenditure can be properly regarded as a repair.

Example
Owen buys an office that hasn't been decorated since the 1970s. He carries out some work to ensure the property meets the necessary health and safety standards (this work will be a capital improvement) and then occupies it for a year. After that, he has the whole place redecorated. The cost of the redecoration should now be an allowable deduction.

This approach will not help in extreme cases (like a hole in the roof), but could be worth considering where there is extensive redecoration work to be carried out.

Collateral Damage

Where repairs are merely incidental to a capital improvement, the cost will all be regarded as capital expenditure. For example, you might have an extension built and then need to redecorate the adjacent room – this will all be capital.

If, however, you can put up with the slightly damaged decor in that adjacent room for a while, redecorating it later, in say a year or two, should usually be allowed as a repair.

Splitting the Cost

Although you cannot claim for repair work which is merely incidental to a capital improvement, you can claim the repair element of any work which has both repairs and improvement elements.

This is particularly common where a kitchen or bathroom is replaced. All the 'like for like' replacements of units, worktops, sinks, etc, can be claimed as a repair. Only additional or higher standard items need to be treated as capital improvements. Incidental decorating work can be apportioned between the repairs and improvements on any reasonable basis.

Remember here that 'higher standard' doesn't mean just more modern. If the only 'improvement' is a more modern material, it's still a repair.

Splitting out your expenditure on an 'item by item' basis can yield significant benefits in the shape of deductible repairs expenditure. In this way, you can improve your property and still get immediate tax relief.

Chapter 32

Integral Features: Claiming Tax Relief on the Purchase Price

Thanks to the annual investment allowance, businesses buying commercial property may currently be entitled to an immediate tax deduction of up to £1 million.

In the November 2022 Autumn Statement, the Government confirmed that the annual investment allowance will be fixed at £1 million indefinitely.

Where the relief applies to qualifying expenditure on, or within, property, it is available both to those buying property for their own business and landlords acquiring commercial property to let out.

For many years, there was an ongoing battle to define the boundary between buildings and equipment within the buildings. The category of 'integral features' introduced in 2008 covers the borderline items and provides immediate tax relief for certain types of commercial property expenditure including:

- Electrical lighting and power systems
- Cold water systems
- Space or water heating systems, air conditioning, ventilation and air purification systems and floors or ceilings comprised in such systems
- Lifts, escalators and moving walkways
- External solar shading

In a nutshell: All the wiring, lighting, plumbing, heating and air conditioning in any commercial property qualifies for immediate 100% tax relief for spending within the annual investment allowance. Almost any type of commercial property will qualify, including shops, offices, hotels, doctors' and dentists' surgeries, workshops and garages.

The property does not need to be newly built – the integral features regime applies to any property purchased after 5th April 2008.

For property purchases taking place after 5th April 2012, the purchaser and seller now generally have to agree a value for the qualifying fixtures within the property and make a joint election to that effect (known as a 'Section 198 Election'), which the purchaser has to submit to HMRC within a fixed time period after the purchase in support of their claim.

For purchases taking place after 5th April 2014, the purchaser will not generally be able to claim capital allowances on any fixtures where the seller would have been entitled to make a capital allowances claim, but failed to do so. Such failures to make legitimate claims are commonplace, so it is vital to check the seller's capital allowances claims history.

This does not, however, include cases where the seller was unable to make a claim: such as where they had bought the property before April 2008 and were unable to claim capital allowances on some of the integral features.

Qualifying expenditure in excess of the annual investment allowance generally attracts writing down allowances at 18%, although the rate for 'integral features' is just 6%. This rather measly rate can sometimes be avoided by simply allocating the annual investment allowance to 'integral features' in preference to other qualifying expenditure.

Subject to the procedures for second-hand property discussed above, people buying commercial property will often be able to benefit from significant tax savings by allocating part of the purchase price to 'integral features' and other items of qualifying equipment within the property, such as white goods, sanitary ware and moveable partitioning. More than 30% of the price of a modern office could often qualify for allowances and even an empty retail unit could yield a claim of around 15%.

Purchase price allocations must be made on a reasonable basis and a surveyor can help you with this. Make sure you get a surveyor who knows about integral features though!

Where you are required to agree a value for qualifying items with the seller of the property, this will usually only bind you in respect of items on which they either have, or could have, made a capital allowances claim. If they held the property before April 2008, this will not generally include any cold water plumbing or electrical systems, so you will still be free to claim allowances on these.

If you want to replace any of the 'integral features' within a property (e.g. rewiring it, or putting in a new heating system) you can claim tax relief on that expenditure too: in addition to any tax relief claimed on the original integral features that you rip out. For this purpose, it is important to ensure the original integral features are used (i.e. the building is occupied) for some period before they are replaced.

Where the property was originally constructed after 28th October 2018, or was improved after that date, you may additionally be entitled to claim the structures and buildings allowance. Although the annual rate for this allowance is only 3%, it automatically passes to the purchaser of a non-residential property: although it is essential to obtain details of any available claim from the seller.

Chapter 33

Loan Arrangement Fees

From time to time most business owners consider re-financing: either to move to a fixed-rate loan or just to get a better deal.

But, as we all know, re-financing does not come cheap. Apart from interest on the new loan, there are always those 'extra' costs to be considered: loan arrangement fees, mortgage broker's fees, penalty fees on the redemption of the old loan and perhaps some legal fees or survey fees in the case of mortgages and other secured loans.

Loan arrangement fees are often all too easily forgotten as they are usually added to the new loan balance (often costing twice as much in the long run due to the interest charged as a result).

But these are a real cost and, where the loan has been taken out for business purposes, they can and should be deducted from business profits.

The loan arrangement fees, together with any other costs incurred as a result of the re-financing, are classed as 'incidental costs of raising loan finance' (let's call them 'loan finance costs' for short).

Generally accepted accounting practice states that these costs should be written off against business profits over the life of the loan and this is one of those cases where tax law follows the same principles.

Example
Jack is a sole trader running a small shop in Cardiff. He has an existing mortgage over the shop with Useless Bank plc. Jack decides to move his mortgage to Slightlybetter Bank plc. He incurs broker's fees of £500, legal fees of £400 and a loan arrangement fee of £2,000 which is added to the new mortgage. The new mortgage is for a ten year period.

Jack has incurred a total of £2,900 of loan finance costs and can therefore claim £290 as a deduction against his trading profits in each of the next ten years. The fact that the loan arrangement fees were added to his mortgage makes no difference to this.

Accelerating Relief

Spreading these costs over the life of the loan is based on accounting practice rather than tax law. We can therefore look to accounting practice to provide some possible means to accelerate relief for these costs.

Firstly: materiality. Accounting practice does not require absolute precision but only requires that accounts are not materially misstated. Hence, where the loan finance costs are very small in comparison to the total size of the business, it would be reasonable to deduct the whole cost in the period the loan is taken out.

Secondly, where a cost has been incurred but has outlived its usefulness, it is appropriate to write off any remaining balance. Hence, if Jack were to re-finance his shop again after a few years, any remaining part of the original £2,900 costs in the example which had not yet been claimed could then be deducted in full.

Taking this a step further, it is worth considering the fact that the modern trend is to re-finance loans at fairly frequent intervals, every few years.

Where the business has a strategy of refinancing at frequent intervals, say every five years, it is reasonable for it to deduct its loan finance costs over this period, rather than the whole term of the loan. In Jack's case, this would give him a deduction of £580 each year for five years instead of £290 each year for ten.

Penalty Fees

As we all know, banks don't let go so easily and will usually charge a penalty for the early repayment of the old loan. If a company or partnership incurs such a cost it can be treated as a business cost and a full deduction can be claimed straight away.

For sole traders, HMRC takes the view that such costs are a personal cost and hence not allowable. We regard this view as fundamentally flawed and would argue that, if re-financing has been carried out for sound business reasons, the costs arising should be deducted from business profits.

Saving money is a pretty sound business reason, so a lot of re-financing carried out by business owners would meet our criterion!

It is important to note HMRC's view on this issue is simply that: a view. It is not the law. Where the law itself (set by Parliament and the Courts) states something is not allowable, there is no argument!

Other Qualifying Loans

Sole traders, partnerships and companies carrying out re-financing should all be able to claim the costs incurred under the principles set out above. This would include a sole trader who re-mortgaged their own home to invest funds in their business or to replace a mortgage previously used for the same purpose.

Directors, shareholders and business partners who borrow money to invest in, or lend to, a company or a trading partnership are generally able to claim tax relief for their interest costs. This is known as 'qualifying loan interest'. Sadly, this relief does not extend to loan finance costs. It is worth bearing this in mind when weighing up the comparative merits of different mortgage deals.

Buying New Properties

When you buy a new property, most of the incidental costs arising (Stamp Duty Land Tax, legal fees, etc) have to be treated as part of the capital cost of the property.

Where the purchase is financed with a mortgage, however, part of the legal fees you incur will relate to arranging the loan (dealing with the charge over the property, etc.).

When the property is a business property, you should therefore arrange for the lawyer to charge the costs relating to the mortgage separately. These can then be claimed against your business profits over the life of the loan. This also applies to other costs incurred specifically in order to obtain the mortgage, such as extra survey fees for example.

Residential Property Businesses

Owners of residential property businesses can no longer claim tax relief on interest costs in the same way as other business owners. This restriction also applies to loan arrangement fees and other finance costs. For more information, see the Taxcafe guide *How to Save Property Tax*.

Part 10

E-Commerce

Chapter 34

Websites, Domain Names and Other Internet Costs

Website Development Costs

These days you can make a living online even if you do not have your own website. Selling on Amazon and ebay are obvious examples.

If you do want a website for your business, is the cost of developing it tax deductible?

There is some debate as to whether such spending is "revenue" or "capital" in nature although, in tax terms, for most small businesses there is little practical difference.

Revenue expenses can always be deducted in full immediately when calculating the taxable profits of the business.

Capital spending used to be written off over many years but these days, thanks to the £1 million annual investment allowance, most capital spending is fully tax deductible in the year it is incurred. Hence, despite the uncertainty surrounding this revenue versus capital issue, most businesses should still be able to claim an immediate tax deduction for their website development costs.

In the unlikely event that your capital expenditure for the year exceeds the annual investment allowance, the excess will only qualify for writing down allowances. The writing down rate for most spending is currently 18% per year.

Capital versus Revenue
According to HMRC's *Capital v Revenue Expenditure Toolkit*, if a business spends money developing a website that creates an "enduring asset", the spending should be treated as capital expenditure:

"Application and infrastructure costs, including domain name, hardware and operating software that relates to the functionality of the website should normally be treated as capital expenditure.

"Design and content development costs should normally be treated as capital expenditure to the extent that an enduring asset is created. One such indication may be an expectation that future revenues less attributable costs to be generated by the website will be no less than the amounts capitalised.

"A website that will directly generate sales, subscriptions, advertising or other income will normally be regarded as creating an enduring asset and consideration should be given to treating the costs of developing, designing and publishing the website as capital expenditure.

"Whilst a revenue deduction would not therefore be allowable, this capital expenditure will generally qualify as expenditure on plant and machinery for capital allowances purposes."

According to HMRC, spending on initial research and planning, before the website is developed, is normally allowable as revenue expenditure.

Where you have a simple website used solely to advertise or promote your business, it should be acceptable to simply claim the development costs as revenue expenditure on the basis that the site has no 'enduring benefit'. It will be important to ensure that this treatment is also reflected in your accounts, as it is rare for a revenue tax deduction to be allowed for an item which is capitalised in the accounts.

The businesses that have to be careful are the ones developing fully functioning e-commerce websites (capital expenditure) that have already exceeded the annual investment allowance for the relevant period. However, now that the annual investment allowance has been set at £1 million indefinitely, this will be fairly rare for sole traders or partnerships, unless the business also has other major capital expenditure in the period.

Maintaining and Updating a Website

Once your website is up and running, the cost of maintaining and updating it (e.g. changing prices), including web hosting costs, should be classed as revenue spending and will be fully tax deductible.

Rental Payments

What HMRC's guidance seems to overlook is that the main cost of developing a website is paying for programmers and web developers. It usually does not involve buying 'hardware' or 'infrastructure'.

These physical bits are usually rented from a webhosting company and these monthly costs will therefore generally be revenue expenditure.

E-commerce Platforms

HMRC's view of the tax treatment of website development costs is very much based on what happened in the early days of the internet.

Back then if you wanted a sophisticated e-commerce website that sold products online you would typically have to go to a web developer and the cost could run to thousands of pounds.

These days for a modest monthly subscription of £20-£30 small businesses can set up a fully functioning online store using one of the e-commerce platforms such as Shopify.

These platforms will give you online tools to help you create your website (complete with shopping cart etc), host your website and process orders.

The monthly subscription cost will be fully deductible as a revenue expense.

Advertising

If you want to advertise your business online using Google Adwords, Facebook or some other website then, like most advertising costs, the cost is usually fully tax deductible.

Transaction Costs & Commissions

When you sell online, you will inevitably incur a variety of charges: credit card transaction fees, commissions to resellers, product listing fees, etc. All of these costs are deductible when calculating the taxable profits of your business.

However, sometimes these costs are a bit opaque – there is no invoice as such to pay, the costs are simply deducted from your balance (although an invoice should be available to download).

It is important not to forget these costs and give the details to your accountant when your accounts are being prepared, so that your taxable profits are not overstated.

Chapter 35

Tax Saving Opportunities for Internet Businesses

If you are starting a new dedicated internet business, you may be able to take advantage of the following tax-saving opportunities:

Working from Home

A major shackle for many new businesses is having to rent a shop or office to attract customers. This means overheads – rent to a landlord and possibly business rates to the local council. These have to be covered each month before you make a penny of profit.

However, if your business is wholly based on e-commerce, you may be able to work from home. The great thing about working from home is that, instead of incurring new premises costs, you can reduce your existing ones!

For example, let's say you use a room in your house as your office. If the house has five rooms in total (ignoring the kitchen, hallways and bathrooms), this means you could potentially claim up to one fifth of all your household costs for tax purposes

Costs that can be claimed include: mortgage interest, council tax, repairs, insurance, electricity, gas and cleaning. (See Chapter 3 for more information.)

Part-time Businesses

Possibly the best way to start any business is part time. Having a back-up income significantly reduces the risk and gives you breathing space to get things up and running. Many internet businesses are run permanently on a part-time basis to provide a second source of income.

The tax treatment of part-time businesses is much the same as for any business. Providing it is a genuine business, you should be able to claim all your expenses as normal, although some of these would have to be reduced to reflect the part-time nature of the business: e.g. your home office tax deduction.

If your part-time business makes a loss in the early stages you can generally offset this against your other income (e.g. salary income) and capital gains. However, you would have to be able to prove that you are in business with the intention of making a profit. Loss relief for part-timers is also usually restricted to a maximum of £25,000 per tax year if you spend less than ten hours per week working in the business. See Chapter 4 for further details of restrictions on loss relief for part-timers.

This type of loss relief is not available if you run your business through a limited company because company losses cannot be offset against the owner's personal income.

Further restrictions in this type of loss relief for all sole traders and business partners apply as part of the tax relief 'cap' explained in Chapter 53.

Living Abroad

The great thing about many internet businesses is they can be run from anywhere. So, if you fancy a complete lifestyle change you could move abroad and set up your internet business in another country.

There are many countries that have no or very low Income Tax and Corporation Tax. According to the Adam Smith Institute the average person has to work from January until roughly 7th June to pay their taxes, so it's easy to see why some consider moving abroad to save tax.

Having said this, it's extremely important to note that if you live and work in one country, but have customers or employees in a second country, you will very often be subject to taxes and compliance requirements in that second country. A good example of such a tax is VAT.

Part 11

Year-End Tax Planning & Pro-active Accounting

Chapter 36

Year-End Tax Planning Strategies

Most sole traders and partnerships are able to choose any accounting year-end date they wish. This is not going to change, but the effect of having a different year end to the tax year end on 5th April *is* changing as a result of new legislation, which we will look at in Chapter 37.

That new legislation will not affect businesses with a 31st March or 5th April accounting date (or any date in between). This means the year-end tax planning strategies we will examine in this chapter will remain just as effective in future for these businesses.

For businesses with other accounting dates, the strategies will remain worthwhile in future, but will generally have a lesser impact than they have in the past. We will look at the position for these businesses in Chapter 38, but the potential savings we will look at in that chapter will still be based on the strategies outlined in this chapter.

In this chapter, we will look at a variety of year-end tax planning strategies designed to defer tax or, in some cases, to produce absolute savings.

By deferring income for just one day, it may be possible to postpone tax for a whole year; by accelerating expenses, it is often possible to enjoy tax relief one year earlier.

Year-end tax planning is even more powerful if you expect your marginal tax rate to fall for the next year: you will not only be postponing tax, you will be saving it as well. In most cases, where your taxable income will be at a similar level in both 2022/23 and 2023/24, there will be a small, 0.73% reduction in marginal tax rates, due to the reduction in Class 4 National Insurance. In other cases, where your income level is changing, the reduction may be more significant.

Conversely, you may be expecting to pay tax at a higher rate next year than this year. We will look at the benefits of 'reverse year-end planning' in that scenario later. Remember, this will include cases where your taxable income is in the £125,140 to £150,000 bracket in both 2022/23 and 2023/24.

Business Year-End Planning

For business owners, there are effectively two types of year-end planning to be considered. Firstly, there's personal year-end planning: things like making pension contributions. The tax year end on 5th April is the key date for this type of planning. In this chapter, however, we are going to focus on business year-end planning: *where your own accounting date is the key date.*

For tax years up to and including 2022/23, most business owners pay tax on the profits for their accounting year ending during the relevant tax year. Hence, for example, a sole trader with a 31st December accounting date will pay tax for 2022/23 based on their profits for the year ended 31st December 2022. As this date has now passed, such a business owner is effectively already within the regime we will be covering in the next chapter. However, taking action by 31st December 2023, following the strategies outlined in this chapter, may still save them tax in 2023/24: we will look at how much in Chapter 38.

Alternatively, after reading Chapter 37, our sole trader with the 31st December 2022 year end may decide to change their accounting date to 31st March and hence draw up their next set of accounts for the fifteen months ending 31st March 2024. We'll look at year-end planning in that situation in Chapter 38 also.

But the principle to remember at this point is that, whatever your current or future accounting date is, year-end planning can still help you to defer, or reduce, your tax liabilities, and it is your own business's accounting date that you generally need to take action by.

Accelerating Expenses

Business year-end tax planning should generally only be about accelerating the expenditure you need, or plan, to make anyway: it's seldom worth spending extra money just to save tax.

Unless you are on the cash basis (see Chapter 49) liabilities incurred by your accounting date can reduce your taxable profits, even if you only pay the bill later. In a few instances, where there is a legal obligation to have work carried out, just getting a quote by your accounting date may be enough: repairs required to get an M.O.T. certificate on a van for example.

An easy way to reduce your tax bill is to buy large items that enjoy an immediate 100% deduction under the annual investment allowance. Examples include vans, computers, and office equipment. Integral features in commercial property also qualify, including wiring, lighting, plumbing, and heating.

Cars

Buying a car will probably not help most business owners cut their tax bills by much. If the car has CO_2 emissions of more than 50g/km you are only entitled to claim up to 6% of the cost as a tax deduction in the accounting year that you purchase the car (18% if the car has CO_2 emissions of 1-50g/km).

On the other hand, new zero emission cars (electric cars) currently qualify for an immediate 100% enhanced capital allowance.

For self-employed business owners these allowances do, however, have to be restricted to reflect private use.

If you are selling a car, you will often benefit by completing the transaction before your accounting date. Sales of cars often give rise to balancing allowances, which can sometimes significantly reduce your taxable profits. (Beware, however, that balancing charges can also sometimes arise: so do your sums first.)

Business Property

If you own your business premises, one of the best ways to save tax is to carry out repairs before your accounting date.

Anything classed as an improvement is less help, however, as Income Tax relief on this expenditure may only be given at 3% per year, thanks to the structures and buildings allowance (except 'integral features', which may attract 100% tax relief under the annual investment allowance).

Some types of property expenditure are often classed as repairs for tax purposes BUT may increase the value of your property: such as new (replacement) kitchens or bathrooms, double glazing, re-wiring, and decorating.

Many property owners think of these items as improvements, but they are often fully tax deductible repairs, providing you follow the rules. (See Chapter 31 for more information.)

Other Business Expenditure

As explained in Chapter 2, simply purchasing more trading stock before your accounting date will not generally alter your taxable profits (unless you are using cash accounting: see Chapter 49).

Utility bills, interest costs, and many other items are all effectively time-related, so it is not generally possible to accelerate these. It remains important to include accruals in respect of these costs, where appropriate, however. Again, the position is different if you are using cash accounting.

Nonetheless, there are some items of expenditure which can sometimes be accelerated in order to provide earlier tax relief. Naturally, this is only worth considering where funds are available and there are little or no adverse commercial implications to making the expenditure earlier. Subject to these points, items worth considering include:

- Repairs and maintenance
- Topping up business vehicles and company cars with fuel
- Making business journeys (such as visiting customers)
- Staff entertaining
- Advertising and promotion
- Staff recruitment (agents' commission will generally be a deductible expense)
- Legal and professional costs, such as business advice, or consultancy (provided these are not capital expenditure, or personal expenditure to benefit the business owner, and could not otherwise have been accrued at the accounting date in any case: such as accountant's fees for preparing your annual accounts)
- Employee bonuses (where these are discretionary or gratuitous, rather than contractual)

Deferring Income

For businesses supplying goods, it makes sense to consider delaying the completion of sales until after the accounting date, so that the profit falls into the next period. Commercial pressures will often dictate the opposite!

Sadly, for businesses supplying services, deferring income is not so easy. A few years ago, these businesses could defer income just by delaying issuing invoices. Unfortunately, you are now generally required to include all the income that has effectively been earned by the accounting date, whether invoiced or not. However, where commercial pressures allow, you could still consider putting off some work until after the year end, so that the income 'earned' by that date is less. Most people would agree that two half-finished jobs are worth less than one completed one.

Year-end Planning in Reverse

If you expect to pay tax at a higher rate next tax year, it may be better to do the opposite: accelerate income and defer expenses. Those who may wish to consider reversing their year-end tax planning include those expecting their marginal rate to rise from 29.73% to 42%; from 42.73% to 47%; or from 42.73% to 62%. (Remember the 42.73% to 47% rise will apply to anyone with taxable income in the £125,140 to £150,000 bracket in both 2022/23 and 2023/24.)

Of course, reverse year-end planning does mean deferring tax relief (or accelerating the tax cost) by a year. The comparison between the permanent, absolute saving and the cashflow disadvantage is something each business owner will need to consider themselves. However, the extra tax paid at the outset can be considered an 'investment' and some of the rates of return on that investment are quite impressive:

Paying £2,973 more in January 2024 to save £4,200 in January 2025 is equivalent to an investment providing a return of 41%.

Paying £4,273 more in January 2024 to save £4,700 in January 2025 is equivalent to an investment providing a return of 10%.

Paying £4,273 more in January 2024 to save £6,200 in January 2025 is equivalent to an investment providing a return of 45%.

How to Accelerate Income and Defer Expenses
If you expect your tax rate to rise next year, you may wish to consider accelerating income or deferring expenses in order to bring more taxable income into the current year. Some of the techniques you could consider include:

- Defer capital expenditure in order to claim the annual investment allowance next year instead of this year.
- Defer other non-essential/non-urgent business expenditure, including discretionary repairs and maintenance expenditure and other non-urgent items, as listed above.
- Defer gift aid donations and personal pension contributions to after 5th April.
- Complete orders and projects and bring billing up to date. Accounting rules often require part-completed work to be brought into account, but there is still a large element of profit dependent on completion and billing in many cases. For example, two half completed projects are, in accounting terms, likely to yield less profit than a single completed project of the same size.
- Connected businesses (e.g. wife has business, husband also has his own business): make extra sales to connected businesses in advance of year end.

Cash Accounting

Taxable profits may be deferred, or accelerated, by joining, or leaving, the cash accounting scheme. The effect on each business is different and this issue is covered in detail in Chapter 49. Note, however, that cash accounting is not just a question of timing and there are many pitfalls to be wary of!

Chapter 37

Planning with Accounting Dates

We looked at year-end tax planning for businesses in Chapter 36. Another thing you may be able to do is change the year-end itself. Now may not be a good time to do this in many cases: although in others, now may be a better time than ever!

New legislation will change the way business accounting periods for sole traders and partnerships are taxed in 2023/24 and later years. We will look at these changes later in this chapter, but first let's look at the current regime.

The current regime will not be obsolete for some time yet, as most business owners effectively have until 31st January 2024 to decide whether they want to change their accounting date in 2022/23.

And it's well worth assessing whether to change your accounting date in 2022/23 because, if doing so will save you some tax, this will be your last chance to benefit from the current regime.

The Current Regime (Up to 2022/23)

For tax years up to and including 2022/23, businesses are generally free to change their accounting date at least once every six years. This means they will either be shortening an accounting period, or extending it. The maximum permitted length for an accounting period is generally 18 months.

It's easier for sole traders to change their accounting date than it is for companies because they don't need to tell Companies House. The consequences of the change can be much more complex, however: although extremely beneficial in some cases.

The sole trader simply draws up accounts to their new accounting date and puts this date on their tax return. For the new date to be effective for tax purposes:

- The tax return must be submitted on time,
- The new accounting period must not exceed 18 months, and

- Unless the change is made for *commercial* (non-tax) reasons, there must not have been another earlier change in the previous five tax years.

If you've shortened your accounting period, you will have either one or two accounting dates falling in the tax year. Remember the tax year runs from 6th April one year to 5th April the next year.

If just one accounting date falls in the tax year, you will be taxed on your profits for the period of 12 months ending on your new accounting date. This means part of your profits for the previous accounting period will be taxed twice. Any profit that is taxed twice is known as an 'overlap profit'. This also frequently occurs when you start a new business.

Under the current regime, relief for your overlap profit is given when you cease trading, or sometimes on a subsequent change of accounting date. We'll come on to that in a minute but, before we do, it is worth pointing out the new legislation we will examine later in this chapter means all remaining overlap profits not yet relieved by 2022/23, will effectively be relieved either in 2023/24 alone, or over the five year period from 2023/24 to 2027/28.

It may seem like a bad idea to be taxed on the same profit twice, but sometimes you can generate future overlap relief, which could later save you tax at 42% or even more, without paying any extra tax now.

Example 1
Matt draws up accounts to 31st March. His profits for the year ended 31st March 2022 were £36,000. His profits for the rest of 2022 fell to just £300 per month.

Matt decides to shorten his accounting period and prepares accounts for the nine months ended 31st December 2022. Because just one accounting date will fall into the 2022/23 tax year, Matt will have to pay tax on his profits for the 12 month period to 31st December 2022.

This means his profits for January to March 2022 will be subject to tax twice: once when he submits his accounts to 31st March 2022 and again when he submits his accounts to 31st December 2022. However, because his profits to 31st December 2022 are so low, there is no extra tax to pay. His taxable profits for 2022/23 are:

Three months to 31ˢᵗ March 2022: 3/12 x £36,000 = £9,000
Nine months to 31ˢᵗ December 2022: 9 x £300   = £2,700
Total: £11,700

This is less than both the personal allowance and the National Insurance earnings threshold. Matt has thus created an overlap of £9,000 available for future use with no current tax cost. If he returns to his usual profit levels in future, this will save him £2,610 (£9,000 x 29%) or, if he becomes a higher rate taxpayer in future years, it will save him £3,780 (£9,000 x 42%).

If two accounting dates fall in the year, you will be taxed on the profits of both periods. This means you are taxed on more than twelve months of profit in one year, but it also means you may be eligible to claim overlap relief: the effect will be much the same as we shall see in Example 2 below.

If you extend your accounting period, you will either have one accounting date falling in the tax year or none. Where no accounting date falls in a tax year, there is scope to create overlap profits available for relief in the future. Sadly, it is now too late to benefit from this variation of planning with overlap relief. However, you may still be able to create broadly the same effect by having a short accounting period ending during 2022/23 in the way we saw in Example 1.

Using Overlap Relief Now

Under the current regime, if you extend your accounting period, but your new accounting date still falls in the same tax year, you are taxed on the profits of the whole period. As this is more than 12 months, you can claim relief for some or all of any overlap profit that arose in the past.

Most people whose existing accounting date is not 31ˢᵗ March or 5ᵗʰ April will have overlap profits from when they started trading, or from when the self-assessment system began in 1997. You can find your overlap profit in Box 70 on the (full) self-employment pages of your tax return. If there's nothing there, or you used the short version, check with your accountant: many of them neglect to complete this box as it only affects future periods.

The overlap relief available on a change of accounting date is based on the length of the extended accounting period in excess of twelve months as a proportion of the original period of overlap (but the relief cannot exceed the total overlap profit available).

This means extending your accounting period to a date falling later in the same tax year will be beneficial whenever your profits have fallen below their original level at the time the overlap was created.

Example 2
Catherine has overlap profits brought forward of £45,000 due to a previous overlap period of nine months. She therefore has overlap profits of £5,000 per month.

Her profits have now fallen to just £2,500 per month, so Catherine decides to draw up accounts for the eighteen months ended 31ˢᵗ October 2022. Her taxable profit for 2022/23 is:

Profit for period ended 31/10/2022: 18 x £2,500	*£45,000*
Less overlap relief for period in excess of 12 months	
6/9 x £45,000	*(£30,000)*
Taxable profit:	*£15,000*

If Catherine had stuck to her usual accounting date, her taxable profit would have been £30,000 (12 x £2,500). The change of accounting date has halved her taxable profit, saving her £4,460 in Income Tax (at 20%) and National Insurance (at 9.73%).

The only drawback here is Catherine has effectively 'cashed in' some of her overlap relief at an effective rate of just 29.73%. This could be disadvantageous if her marginal tax rate is higher in later years.

Partnerships
Partnerships can generally change their accounting date in much the same way as sole traders. The impact on each partner will differ, however, as each will have their own individual overlap profit and marginal tax rate. The same change of accounting date could be beneficial for one partner, but disastrous for another.

Limited Liability Partnerships ('LLPs') that change their accounting date need to advise Companies House using form LL AA01 and are subject to the same deadlines as a company. Generally, the change must be notified by the earliest of:

- Nine months from the new accounting date
- Nine months from the existing accounting date
- 21 months from the date of incorporation (for the LLP's first set of accounts)

And before the accounts for the relevant period have been filed!

Forthcoming Changes

New legislation is bringing radical changes to the way profits arising in a trading business's accounting periods are taxed. In a nutshell, from 2024/25 onwards, all trading businesses will be taxed on a tax year basis.

Twelve month accounting periods ending on a date between 31st March and 4th April will be accepted as a good enough approximation to the tax year.

Hence, we can quickly point out that the changes discussed throughout the rest of this chapter will generally have no impact on businesses with a 31st March or 5th April accounting date (or indeed any date between).

You will still be able to draw up accounts to any date you wish but, if that date is not between 31st March and 5th April, you will be required to apportion your results in order to match the tax year.

The results to be apportioned for this purpose will be after claiming capital allowances, where relevant, and hence, as noted in Chapter 16, the changes will not affect your capital allowances entitlement.

Example 3 Part 1
Zoe draws up accounts to 31st December each year. Her profits for the year ending 31st December 2024 are £60,000; her profits for the year ending 31st December 2025 are £80,000. Her taxable profits for the tax year 2024/25 will be:

£60,000 x 270/366 = £44,262
£80,000 x 95/365 = £20,822
Total £65,084

The apportionment is based on the number of days in each accounting period falling into the relevant tax year. Other apportionment methods will be permitted provided they are reasonable and used consistently. A common method is to use calendar months: 31st March will again be accepted as a reasonable approximation for the tax year end where this method is used.

The major practical problem for Zoe will be that her 2024/25 tax return will be due for submission by 31st January 2026: only a month after the end of one of the accounting periods required to calculate her taxable profit. In such cases, estimates will be allowed (with later amendments to correct the return to accurate figures), but it is far from a satisfactory way of going about things. In reality, many traders are likely to change their accounting date to either 31st March or 5th April.

Transitional Rules for 2023/24

Under the new legislation, 2023/24 is to be a transitional year. Sole traders and partnerships with an accounting date not falling between 31st March and 5th April will be taxed on:

i)   The profits of their normal accounting period, PLUS
ii)   The profits of the period commencing the next day and ending 5th April 2024, LESS
iii)   Any overlap profits they have (see above)

The normal accounting period for the purposes of (i) is the twelve months following your last accounting date falling into 2022/23, regardless of what period you actually draw accounts up for in 2023/24. This has important, and generally beneficial, consequences for traders who want to change their accounting date in 2023/24 in anticipation of the new rules, and we will look at this point further a little later.

In most cases, (ii) is likely to exceed (iii), thus creating additional taxable profit, known as the 'transition profit'. In some cases, however, (iii) may exceed (ii), meaning there is effectively a 'transition loss'.

Example 3 Part 2
Zoe started trading many years ago and has overlap profits of £5,500 brought forward. Her profits for the year ending 31st December 2023 are £40,000. Her taxable profits for 2023/24 will be:

Year ending 31ˢᵗ December 2023: £40,000
Period from 1ˢᵗ January to 5ᵗʰ April 2024:
£60,000 x 96/366 = £15,738
Overlap relief (£5,500)
Total £50,238

Zoe has a transition profit of £10,238 (£15,738 – £5,500). Under the new legislation, this can be spread over five years, with 20% of it being taxed each year from 2023/24 to 2027/28. In Zoe's case, this adds a further £2,048 (£10,238 x 1/5) to each year's taxable profits over that period. Hence, her final taxable profits will actually be:

2023/24: £40,000 + £2,048 = £42,048
2024/25: £65,084 + £2,048 = £67,132

However, traders can choose to accelerate any part of their transition profit and have it taxed in an earlier year. They might do this if they have a year in which they are a basic rate taxpayer, but would generally expect to be a higher rate taxpayer.

Example 3 Part 3
Zoe is reasonably certain she will be a higher rate taxpayer each year from 2024/25 onwards. She therefore decides to have all her transition profit taxed in 2023/24, when she is a basic rate taxpayer. This means all her transition profit is taxed at 29%, instead of four fifths of that profit being taxed at 42% or more, thus saving her at least £1,065 (£10,238 x 4/5 x 13%).

The downside for Zoe is that to achieve an ultimate absolute saving of £1,065, she needs to pay £2,375 more tax on 31ˢᵗ January 2025 than she otherwise might have done.

To put it another way, using the five year spreading relief, Zoe would pay an extra £594 for 2023/24 (£2,048 x 29%) and an extra £860 (at least) each year from 2024/25 to 2027/28 (£2,048 x 42%). By having all her transition profit taxed in 2023/24, she pays an extra £2,969 in one go (£10,238 x 29%).

Changing Your Accounting Date
If these proposals go ahead, the sensible thing for many traders to do would seem to be to change their accounting date to either 31ˢᵗ March or 5ᵗʰ April. This will not be compulsory and other accounting dates can be retained: they will just lead to the

practical difficulties of carrying out apportionments, as discussed above.

The sensible time to change your accounting date would appear to be in 2023/24. For example, Zoe could draw up accounts for the fifteen months ending 31st March 2024 and then adopt a 31st March accounting date thereafter.

Changing your accounting date in 2023/24 will still allow you to benefit from the five year spreading relief for transition profits. Hence, for example, Zoe will be able to claim spreading relief for her profits for the period from 1st January to 31st March 2024 (less her overlap relief), regardless of whether she changes her accounting date in 2023/24 (or later) or not.

However, if Zoe were to change her accounting date in 2022/23, she would still benefit from overlap relief but would have no transition profits in 2023/24 eligible for spreading relief.

In most cases, it will therefore make sense not to change your accounting date any earlier than 2023/24. However, as with everything in tax, there are exceptions, and we will look at these further below.

Transition Profits and Losses: Other Points
Transition profits will be subject to both Income Tax and Class 4 National Insurance, where applicable.

Generally speaking, transition profits will form part of your taxable income for most tax purposes. However, they will not be counted as part of your income for the purposes of: the Child Benefit Charge (see Chapter 2); basic rate tax relief for interest and finance costs on residential rental property; or other tax reductions, such as relief for investing in Enterprise Investment Scheme shares.

If the normal accounting period under (i) above produces a loss, this must be deducted in arriving at the transition profit eligible for spreading relief.

A transition loss will generally be set against the profits for the normal accounting period under (i). However, where the transition loss exceeds the profits for the normal accounting period, and there is thus an overall loss for 2023/24, any part of your overlap profit that has not yet been relieved may be carried back and set off against your total income in the previous three tax years, taking the more recent years first.

Impact on Planning with Accounting Dates
The key thing to remember is, generally speaking, transition profits will be a good thing because:

- Transition profits will be spread over five years
- There may be opportunities to accelerate profits into low tax years, thus making additional savings
- Transition profits will be exempt from the Child Benefit Charge

Hence, it will usually make sense not to do anything that might reduce your transition profit. There will, of course, be exceptions though, as we shall see a little later. Remember, your transition profit will be:

- Your profit for the period starting the day after your next normal accounting date after 5th April 2023 and ending on 5th April 2024, LESS
- Any overlap profits you have (see above)

For example, if you have a 31st December accounting date, your transition profit will be your profit for the period from 1st January to 5th April 2024, less any overlap profit brought forward.

Remember, however, if you change your accounting date in 2022/23, this will alter, or could even eliminate, your transition profit. Let's look at what this means for the planning strategies we covered earlier in this chapter.

Example 1: Matt created an overlap profit of £9,000 at no tax cost. He also now has the possibility of having some transition profit for the period from 1st January to 5th April 2024. This planning is likely to remain beneficial.

Example 2: Catherine saved £4,460 by using £30,000 of her overlap profit in 2022/23. However, this has shortened her transition period in 2023/24 from eleven months to five, thus restricting her opportunity to benefit from the potential savings on transition profits discussed above. Hence, it is possible Catherine may have been better off *without* the earlier planning.

Nonetheless, there are circumstances under which the net effect of the earlier planning will simply be to obtain a £15,000 reduction in taxable profit a year earlier: in 2022/23 instead of 2023/24 (£15,000 is the net of the overlap relief Catherine claimed in 2022/23 less the additional business profits brought into account by extending her accounting period).

Those circumstances arise in Catherine's case where:

a) Her profits for the period from 1st November 2022 to 5th April 2024 do not exceed £65,270 (meaning, after deducting her remaining overlap relief of £15,000, she will be a basic rate taxpayer for 2023/24); **and**
b) Her profits for the period from 1st May 2023 to 5th April 2024 do not exceed £45,000 (meaning she would not have had a transition profit, even if she had not carried out the earlier planning)

If (a) and (b) both apply, Catherine has simply made a saving of £4,460 in 2022/23 instead of a saving of £4,350 (£15,000 x 29%) in 2023/24. In this case, she has not only obtained relief a year earlier she has also saved an extra £110.

Furthermore, the earlier planning may actually be more advantageous if either:

c) Her profits for the period from 1st November 2022 to 5th April 2024 do not exceed £27,570 (meaning, after deducting her remaining overlap relief of £15,000, she will have no Income Tax to pay for 2023/24); **or**
d) While meeting conditions (a) and (b) above, her profits for the period from 1st November 2023 to 5th April 2024 are more than £15,000 (meaning, as a result of the earlier planning, she now does have a transition profit)

As we can see, there are a few potential outcomes where the earlier planning could remain worthwhile. In other cases, however, and particularly if Catherine is a higher rate taxpayer in 2023/24, the earlier planning would be disadvantageous.

Example 3: If Zoe was a basic rate taxpayer in 2022/23, she may have been in broadly the same position if she had changed her accounting date and drawn up accounts for the fifteen months ending 31st March 2023. As long as those accounts showed a profit of no more than £55,770 then, after claiming her overlap relief of

£5,500, she would have remained a basic rate taxpayer and the additional profit created by extending her accounting period would have been taxed at 29.73%.

So, if we assume the extra profit taxed in 2022/23 comes out at the same £10,238 as the transition profit arising in 2023/24 that we saw earlier, it will cost her an extra £3,044. That's £75 more than if she had kept the same accounting date and then elected not to claim spreading relief in 2023/24. It's also due a year earlier and there is no alternative option to spread the transition profits. Hence, overall I'd say this would have been a bad idea for Zoe.

Furthermore, if Zoe's profits for the fifteen months ending 31st March 2023 were more than £55,770 she would have been pushed into higher rate tax for 2022/23, meaning she lost out even more.

On the other hand, if Zoe had expected to be a higher rate taxpayer in 2023/24, the situation would have been quite different. In that case, she would have saved tax by changing her accounting date in 2022/23, provided that her profits for the fifteen months ending 31st March 2023 were less than £55,770. However (sticking with the same figure of £10,238 in additional profit we have used so far) she would have had to pay an extra £3,044 in January 2024 instead of an extra £860 each January from 2025 to 2029 (assuming her taxable income each year remained between £50,270 and £100,000). Hence, while she might eventually achieve an overall saving of £1,256, she would suffer a considerable cashflow disadvantage.

Whether an earlier change of accounting date is worthwhile for Zoe in this last scenario is debatable but there are some scenarios under which someone with rising profits would clearly be better off changing their accounting date earlier.

Example 4

Joseph has a 30th June accounting date and made a profit of £52,000 for the year ended 30th June 2022. Since then, he has been making a profit of £7,250 per month and he expects this to rise to £9,000 per month from April 2023. He has overlap profits of £17,500 brought forward from when he started business.

If he leaves things as they stand, he will have profits of £92,250 for the year ending 30th June 2023 (£7,250 x 9 + £9,000 x 3) and £108,000 each year thereafter.

His transition profit will be £63,500 (£108,000 x 9/12 = £81,000 – £17,500). He can use spreading relief to have this taxed at £12,700 each year for five years. Most years this will increase his tax bill by £7,874 as the highest marginal rate of 62% will apply, although in 2023/24 the cost will be slightly less, £6,324.

There are two ways Joseph could save tax. The first would be to pay the extra £6,324 for 2023/24 but then accelerate all of his remaining transition profits into 2024/25. The extra cost in 2024/25 would be a whopping £26,447 but he would save £5,049 in the long run.

But a better strategy for Joseph might be to change his accounting date in 2022/23 by drawing up accounts for the nine months ending 31st March 2023. This means he will be taxed in 2022/23 on an extra £47,750 (£7,250 x 9 = £65,250 – £17,500) BUT the extra tax he will suffer will all be at 42% and will amount to just £20,055.

Admittedly, this strategy will cost Joseph an extra £1,891 in 2023/24, but he will save £7,874 each year from 2024/25 to 2027/28. Hence, overall, he could save £9,550 (4 x £7,874 – £1,891 – £20,055) by changing his accounting date in 2022/23.

Note the calculations in Example 4 are based on HMRC's interpretation of the new legislation. There is, however, some controversy over whether transition profits are supposed to cause the withdrawal of an individual's personal allowance when they fall into the income bracket between £100,000 and £125,140, with some experts claiming this is not what the legislation says but HMRC saying that it does. Since HMRC are undoubtedly the biggest bully in the playground they usually win. But not always! Time will tell but, for now, I would tend to suggest planning on the basis that HMRC will win this one.

Weighing it All Up

Most sole traders and business partners who do not currently have a 31st March or 5th April year end are going to suffer extra tax over the next few years as the Government effectively forces them to catch up on those extra profits for the months between their accounting date and the end of the tax year. Most of them will have some overlap relief to deduct but, if they started business many years ago, the chances are this will be a lot less than the extra profits they're being taxed on.

The choice many will face is whether to change their accounting date in 2022/23 and pay extra tax in January 2024 **OR** leave things as they are and be taxed on their transition profits over the years from 2023/24 to 2027/28.

For the majority, it will be better to leave things as they are as the extra tax is deferred considerably and transition profits provide other advantages such as the planning opportunities created by the ability to accelerate them into a low tax year and the fact they are exempt from the Child Benefit Charge. But there are exceptions as we have seen. So how do you decide what is best for you? This is my suggested approach:

Step 1: Check whether you are able to change your accounting date in 2022/23 under the current regime (see above). If not, that's the end of the story.

Step 2: Establish what your marginal tax rate would be for 2022/23 *if* you were to change your accounting date this year.

Step 3: Compare the marginal rate you get at Step 2 with your probable future marginal tax rate in the years 2023/24 to 2027/28.

If the rate you get at Step 2 is *higher* than your expected marginal tax rates for 2023/24 to 2027/28, you will generally be better off not changing your accounting date in 2022/23. For the practical reasons discussed above you might want to change it in 2023/24 to make it easier to do your tax returns in future.

If the rate you get at Step 2 is *lower* than your expected marginal tax rates for 2023/24 to 2027/28, you will be able to save some tax by changing your accounting date in 2022/23. If it is only lower than your expected tax rate in some of those years, your saving will be less, and, if your expected rate for 2023/24 is lower than the rate from Step 2 there may even be no saving at all.

In most cases, the rate you get at Step 2 can't be the same as your expected marginal tax rates for 2023/24 to 2027/28, as taxpayers under state pension age will see their marginal tax rate fall by 0.73% after 2022/23 even if they stay in the same income bracket. And a fall of 0.73% is still enough to mean you will be better off not changing your accounting date in 2022/23.

For those already over state pension age, if you expect your marginal tax rates for 2023/24 to 2027/28 to be the same as the rate you get at Step 2, the advantages provided by transition profits mean you will again be better off not changing your accounting date in 2022/23.

Those reaching state pension age some time before 7th April 2027 should bear in mind this will lead to a reduction in their marginal tax rate as they will then be exempt from National Insurance (see Chapter 2).

Changing your accounting date in 2022/23 will usually mean accelerating at least some of the additional tax you're going to be suffering and it also means missing out on the other potential opportunities provided by transition profits. So, if you get this far and it looks like an early change of accounting date might be beneficial, it's time to take professional advice.

Finally, remember that preparing accounts for a period of less than a year will mean the annual investment allowance for that period is restricted: while it's £1 million for a year, it would only be £250,000 for a three month accounting period, and that might catch some people out.

For some my suggested exercise above will be simple, for others it may seem quite daunting. But, take heart: you have until 31st January 2024 to decide what to do.

Chapter 38

The Value of Year-End Planning

In Chapter 36, we looked at a variety of year-end planning strategies designed to defer or save tax by moving taxable income from one accounting period to another. However, in Chapter 37, we then saw that forthcoming changes mean business accounting periods will be taxed differently in future. We also saw that transition profits will, in general, be a good thing because of the five year spreading relief and other potential benefits.

So what does all this mean for the value of the year-end planning strategies in Chapter 36?

Well, firstly, if you have a 31st March or 5th April accounting date (and you don't change it), the value of the strategies in Chapter 36 is unaffected by the changes examined in Chapter 37.

What about other accounting dates? Let's look at an example to illustrate how this will work. Note, in this chapter, I am going to work in months, rather than days for all the calculations. Both methods are equally acceptable where applied consistently and, as things are complicated enough already, it makes sense to go for the simpler option. But you could find days work better for you.

Example 1
Maggie is a sole trader making an annual profit of around £75,000. She has a 30th April accounting date, overlap profits of £25,000 from when she started her business, and is planning to spend £20,000 on repairs to her business premises, although the work is not urgent and could be carried out any time over the next couple of years.

Let's say she has the work done during the year ending 30th April 2023. That will reduce her 'normal' taxable profits for 2023/24 (see Chapter 37) by £20,000, saving her £8,400 in Income Tax and National Insurance (at 42%).

If she has the work done during the year ending 30th April 2024, it will reduce her transition profits by £18,333 and her 'normal' taxable profits for 2024/25 by £1,667. This will produce savings of £1,540 in 2023/24, £2,240 in 2024/25, and £1,540 again in each of 2025/26,

2026/27, and 2027/28. The total saving is the same (£8,400) but it is spread over a much longer period. And that's a best case scenario: if Maggie's taxable profits drop beneath £50,270 in any of those years, the saving will be further reduced.

What if Maggie defers the work until the year ending 30th April 2025? Now there is no impact on her transition profits and the expenditure will reduce her taxable profits for 2024/25 by £18,333 and her profits for 2025/26 by £1,667. Assuming she keeps the same 42% marginal tax rate throughout, this will mean her cumulative position in tax paid, compared with incurring the expenditure in the year ending 30th April 2024, will be as follows:

January 2025: £1,540 more paid
January 2026: £3,920 less paid
January 2027: £3,080 less paid
January 2028: £1,540 less paid
January 2029: same amount paid

Overall then, deferring the expenditure until after 30th April 2024 has mostly accelerated Maggie's tax relief: the opposite of what year-end planning would normally be expected to do!

Furthermore, incurring the expenditure after 30th April 2024 has the added benefit that Maggie will have more transition profit with which she may be able to achieve additional tax savings, and she can probably be more certain of what marginal rate of tax she will obtain relief for her repairs expenditure at.

To summarise what this example tells us: where the business owner's marginal tax rate remains the same each year, year-end planning for accounting periods ending during 2023/24 is more valuable than ever, producing tax savings that last five years. But, for accounting periods ending during 2024/25, it may be better to defer expenditure in order to mostly obtain tax relief earlier.

BUT, it's important to point out that the impact of year-end planning on transition profits is most pronounced for accounting dates falling early in the tax year. The effect for other accounting dates will be quite different.

Example 2

Maggie's twin sister, Janet, is exactly like Maggie in every way except that Janet draws up accounts to 31ˢᵗ December each year.

If Janet spends £20,000 on repairs during the year ending 31ˢᵗ December 2023, it will save her £8,400 in tax for 2023/24, the same as Maggie. However, if Janet has her repairs carried out during the year ending 31ˢᵗ December 2024, it will reduce her transition profits by just £5,000 while her taxable profits for 2024/25 will be reduced by £15,000. This leads to tax savings of £420 in 2023/24, £6,720 in 2024/25 and £420 again in each of 2025/26, 2026/27, and 2027/28.

If Janet has the work done during the year ending 31ˢᵗ December 2025, there is no impact on her transition profits and the expenditure will reduce her taxable profits for 2024/25 by £5,000 and her profits for 2025/26 by £15,000. In this case, this will mean her cumulative position in tax paid, compared with incurring the expenditure in 2024, will be as follows:

January 2025: £420 more paid
January 2026: £5,040 more paid
January 2027: £840 less paid
January 2028: £420 less paid
January 2029: same amount paid

So, for a 31ˢᵗ December 2024 accounting date, the position is very different to the position we saw for a 30ᵗʰ April 2024 accounting date. While there are some nuances in the cashflow consequences, it would generally seem better to accelerate qualifying expenditure so that it falls before the end of the accounting period and mostly saves tax earlier.

The position will be different for each accounting date. The following table shows the cumulative percentage of additional, or reduced, tax relief obtained by each of the affected tax years where qualifying expenditure is accelerated so that it falls into an accounting period ending during 2024/25 instead of the following accounting period:

Year End	Cumulative Additional or Reduced Relief Obtained by Accelerating Expenditure			
	2023/24	**2024/25**	**2025/26**	**2026/27**
30-Apr-2024	18.33%	-46.67%	-36.67%	-18.33%
31-May-2024	16.67%	-33.33%	-33.33%	-16.67%
30-Jun-2024	15.00%	-20.00%	-30.00%	-15.00%
31-Jul-2024	13.33%	-6.67%	-26.67%	-13.33%
31-Aug-2024	11.67%	6.67%	-23.33%	-11.67%
30-Sep-2024	10.00%	20.00%	-20.00%	-10.00%
31-Oct-2024	8.33%	33.33%	-16.67%	-8.33%
30-Nov-2024	6.67%	46.67%	-13.33%	-6.67%
31-Dec-2024	5.00%	60.00%	-10.00%	-5.00%
31-Jan-2025	3.33%	73.33%	-6.67%	-3.33%
28-Feb-2025	1.67%	86.67%	-3.33%	-1.67%

Remember these percentages show the *cumulative* difference created by the timing of the expenditure. In every case, the same total relief is obtained by 2027/28. Negative percentages mean that less relief has been obtained by this point or there is a 'cumulative deficit' if you like. It is assumed that spreading relief is claimed where the expenditure is incurred in an accounting period ending during 2024/25 and thus reduces transition profits.

As we can see, the case for accelerating the expenditure gets stronger the further down the table you go, whereas the case for deferring it is stronger the closer to the top of the table we are.

By way of example, if a sole trader with a 31st July 2024 accounting date incurs £10,000 of qualifying expenditure by that point rather than later, they will enjoy £1,333 of relief in 2023/24 and a further £4,667 of relief in 2024/25: hence a total of £6,000 thus far, or 60%.

If that same sole trader incurred the expenditure after 31st July 2024, they would enjoy £6,667 of relief in 2024/25, or 66.7%.

Hence, cumulatively, by this point (2024/25), accelerating the expenditure has led to 6.67% less relief, as per our table. This cumulative deficit increases to 26.67% by 2025/26 before then falling back to 0% over the next two years: it takes until 2027/28 for everything to equalise.

It's fairly easy to translate the additional or reduced relief into the cumulative impact on your tax bills if your marginal tax rate is the same each year. For example, if our July year end trader is a typical higher rate taxpayer, we can easily work out that they will be £1,120 worse off by 2025/26 if they accelerate their £10,000 of qualifying expenditure (£10,000 spend x 26.67% cumulative deficit x 42% marginal tax rate).

Where the business owner's marginal tax rate is changing, however, the complexity goes up another notch.

Falling Tax Rate
An individual's marginal tax rate generally reduces where their taxable income falls, such as when it falls below £50,270 or £100,000. However, their marginal tax rate will also fall when their income rises above £125,140. As we saw in Chapter 36, these scenarios make year-end planning more valuable. But how do the changes we examined in Chapter 37 affect this?

Example 3
Priti has a 30th April accounting date. She plans to buy a new machine at a cost of £10,000, which will be immediately deductible in full by virtue of the annual investment allowance. Her profits for the year ending 30th April 2023 (before deducting the cost of the machine) will be £110,000 and she expects them to rise to £140,000 per year thereafter. She has overlap profits of £45,333 available.

If Priti had a March year end, accelerating her £10,000 of expenditure to before 31st March 2023 would create an absolute, permanent saving of £1,573 (62.73% - 47% = 15.73% x £10,000). But things will be quite different for Priti.

Is she buys the machine by 30th April 2023 she will have profits of £100,000 for that accounting period. She will also have a transition profit of £83,000 (£140,000 x 11/12 = £128,333 – £45,333 overlap relief). Spreading this over five years means she has extra taxable profits of £16,600 each year from 2023/24 to 2027/28. Her total taxable profit for 2023/24 is thus £116,600, rising to £156,600 for the next four years.

Alternatively, if she buys the machine during the year ending 30th April 2024, she will have taxable profits of £110,000 for the year ending 30th April 2023 and £130,000 for the year ending 30th April 2024. This gives her transition profits of £73,834 (£130,000 x 11/12 = £119,167 – £45,333) spread over five years at £14,767 per year. Her total taxable profit for 2023/24 is thus £124,767, rising to £153,933 for 2024/25 and then £154,767 for the next three years.

So, this is the difference that buying the machine by 30th April 2023 will make to Priti's tax bills:

2023/24: £5,064 saved (£124,767 – £116,600 = £8,167 x 62%)
2024/25: £1,253 extra tax (£156,600 – £153,933 = £2,667 x 47%)
2025/26 to 2027/28: £862 extra tax (£156,600 – £154,767 = £1,833 x 47%)

The overall, net saving is £1,225, or 12.25% of the cost of the machine, made up of a saving of more than 50% in the first year less costs of 12.5% in the second year and 8.6% in the following three years.

As we can see, where the business owner's tax rate is falling, year-end planning remains valuable for accounting periods ending during 2023/24. But let's look again at a different accounting date.

Example 4
Priti also has a twin sister, Jaswinder, who is exactly like her in every way except she has a 31st December accounting date and overlap profits of just £12,500.

For Jaswinder, buying her new machine by 31st December 2023 will give her profits of £100,000 for that accounting period but her transition profit will be £22,500 (£140,000 x 3/12 = £35,000 – £12,500 overlap relief), which will be spread over five years at £4,500 per year. Her total taxable profit for 2023/24 will thus be £104,500, rising to £144,500 for the next four years.

Alternatively, if she buys the machine during the year ending 31st December 2024, she will have taxable profits of £110,000 for the year ending 31st December 2023 and £130,000 for the year ending 31st

December 2024. This gives her transition profits of £20,000 (£130,000 x 3/12 = £32,500 – £12,500) spread over five years at £4,000 per year. Her total taxable profit for 2023/24 would be £114,000, rising to £136,500 for 2024/25 and then £144,000 for the next three years.

Now let's look at the difference that buying the machine by 31ˢᵗ December 2023 makes to Jaswinder's tax bills:

2023/24: £5,890 saved (£114,000 – £104,500 = £9,500 x 62%)
2024/25: £3,760 extra tax (£144,500 – £136,500 = £8,000 x 47%)
2025/26 to 2027/28: £235 extra tax (£144,500 – £144,000 = £500 x 47%)

This time, the overall, net saving is £1,425, or 14.25% of the cost of the machine, made up of a saving of 58.9% in the first year less costs of 37.6% in the second year and 2.35% in the following three years.

So, with an accounting date later in 2023/24, and a falling marginal rate of tax, year-end planning is even more valuable.

Rising Tax Rate

A business owner's marginal tax rate increases when their taxable income rises above key tax thresholds, the main ones being £50,270 and £100,000.

As we know, business owners in this position can benefit from the reverse year-end planning we looked at in Chapter 36. Once again, let's look at what the changes we saw in Chapter 37 mean for this type of planning.

Example 5

Serwaah has a 30ᵗʰ April accounting date and expects to be a basic rate taxpayer in 2023/24, even after including her transition profits. However, she is pretty certain she will be a higher rate taxpayer from 2024/25 onwards.

She is planning to buy a second-hand van for £12,000 and isn't sure whether to buy it before or after 30ᵗʰ April 2023. A purchase before her accounting date will produce an immediate saving for 2023/24 of £3,480 (£12,000 x 29%). However, a purchase after her accounting date will, instead, reduce her transition profit by £11,000. The overall effect on her taxable profits if she claims spreading relief would then be a reduction of £2,200 in 2023/24, £3,200 in 2024/25, and £2,200 again each year from 2025/26 to 2027/28. So, deferring the purchase by applying reverse year-end planning would change her tax bills as follows:

2023/24: £2,842 extra tax (£12,000 – £2,200 = £9,800 x 29%)
2024/25: £1,344 saved (£3,200 x 42%)
2025/26 to 2027/28: £924 saved (£2,200 x 42%)

Serwaah's overall, net saving is £1,274, or 10.6% of the cost of the van, but it takes until 2026/27 to achieve any saving and 2027/28 to get the full benefit.

Many business owners may consider the time taken to achieve a saving with this planning is too long and prefer to get immediate relief, albeit at a lower rate.

Furthermore, someone like Serwaah might be in a position to accelerate all her transition profit into 2023/24 and have it all taxed at 29%, in which case her year-end planning at 30th April 2023 will be largely irrelevant since only one twelfth of the van's cost would then provide relief at 42%.

Example 6
Guess what: Serwaah has a twin sister, Fremah, exactly like her in every way, except Fremah has a 31st December accounting date. So, what happens if Fremah defers her purchase of the van to after 31st December 2023? The van's cost now only reduces Fremah's transition profits by £3,000, but it reduces her 'normal' taxable profits for 2024/25 by £9,000. Assuming Fremah claims spreading relief so she pays tax on £600 less of transition profit each year (£3,000/5), this is the impact on her tax bills created by deferring the purchase:

2023/24: £3,306 extra tax (£12,000 – £600 = £11,400 x 29%)
2024/25: £4,032 saved (£9,600 x 42%)
2025/26 to 2027/28: £252 saved (£600 x 42%)

Fremah's overall, net saving is £1,482, or 12.35% of the cost of the van. Furthermore, not only does Fremah enjoy a greater tax saving than her sister Serwaah (Example 5), it only takes a year for her to start enjoying that saving.

But what if Fremah accelerates her transition profits and has them all taxed in 2023/24. Her reverse year-end planning would then work out like this:

2023/24: £2,610 extra tax (£12,000 – £3,000 = £9,000 x 29%)
2024/25: £3,780 saved (£9,000 x 42%)

The net saving is then reduced to £1,170, or 9.75% of the cost of the van (or 13% of the 9/12ths of the cost that provides relief in 2024/25), but it's all achieved in one year at less up-front tax cost.

So, we can conclude that reverse year-end planning where the business owner's marginal tax rate is increasing is more valuable for accounting dates falling later in 2023/24. This remains true even if they accelerate all their transition profits into 2023/24.

How does it stack up for other accounting dates? Where the business owner's marginal tax rate is rising from 29% in 2023/24 to 42% in all later years, assuming they claim spreading relief, the overall savings achieved as a percentage of the cost of the relevant expenditure are as given in the table below. Those full savings are not achieved until 2027/28 in every case. The time taken to achieve **any** net saving is as noted.

Year End	Final Net Saving	Net Saving Achieved By	
30-Apr-2023	10.62%	2026/27	three years
31-May-2023	10.83%	2026/27	three years
30-Jun-2023	11.05%	2026/27	three years
31-Jul-2023	11.27%	2025/26	two years
31-Aug-2023	11.48%	2025/26	two years
30-Sep-2023	11.70%	2025/26	two years
31-Oct-2023	11.92%	2024/25	one year
30-Nov-2023	12.13%	2024/25	one year
31-Dec-2023	12.35%	2024/25	one year
31-Jan-2024	12.57%	2024/25	one year
29-Feb-2024	12.78%	2024/25	one year

Remember, however, many people in this scenario may choose to accelerate all their transition profits into 2023/24. In this case, their saving will be similar to what we last saw for Fremah: a 13% saving on the proportion of the costs providing relief in 2024/25, all achieved in one year.

Where the business owner's marginal tax rate is rising from 42% in 2023/24 to 62% in later years, the overall savings achieved by 2027/28 and time taken to achieve **any** net saving are as follows:

Year End	Final Net Saving	Net Saving Achieved By	
30-Apr-2023	16.33%	2026/27	three years
31-May-2023	16.67%	2026/27	three years
30-Jun-2023	17.00%	2026/27	three years
31-Jul-2023	17.33%	2025/26	two years
31-Aug-2023	17.67%	2025/26	two years
30-Sep-2023	18.00%	2025/26	two years
31-Oct-2023	18.33%	2024/25	one year
30-Nov-2023	18.67%	2024/25	one year
31-Dec-2023	19.00%	2024/25	one year
31-Jan-2024	19.33%	2024/25	one year
29-Feb-2024	19.67%	2024/25	one year

The savings are greater here, but the timing is the same. Once again, business owners might choose to accelerate all their transition profits into 2023/24. This will provide a 20% saving on the proportion of the costs providing relief in 2024/25; all achieved in one year.

Changing Your Accounting Date

As discussed in Chapter 37, many business owners who currently have an accounting date other than 31st March or 5th April may choose to change their accounting date in either 2022/23 or 2023/24. Making the change in 2023/24 will generally be preferable but there are exceptions.

Those who change to a 31st March or 5th April accounting date in 2022/23 need to consider the impact of year-end planning in 2022/23 in the light of the principles for taxing profits under the current regime as set out in Chapter 37, including the impact on any overlap profits created for use in 2023/24.

Those who change their accounting date in 2023/24 may do so by either having a long accounting period up to 18 months, or a normal twelve month accounting period followed by a short accounting period ending on 31st March or 5th April 2024.

Long Accounting Periods in 2023/24

Where there is a single, long accounting period ending on 31st March 2024, the additional, or reduced, tax relief obtained in each tax year as a percentage of any qualifying expenditure which is accelerated so that it is incurred by that date instead of after it is as follows:

Length of Accounting Period	Additional or Reduced Relief Obtained by Accelerating Expenditure		
	2023/24	2024/25	2025/26 to 2027/28
13 months	93.85%	-98.46%	1.54%
14 months	88.57%	-97.14%	2.86%
15 months	84.00%	-96.00%	4.00%
16 months	80.00%	-95.00%	5.00%
17 months	76.47%	-94.12%	5.88%
18 months	73.33%	-93.33%	6.67%

Short Accounting Periods in 2023/24

Where there is a 'normal' accounting period of twelve months ending during 2023/24, followed by a short accounting period ending on 31st March 2024, the effect of accelerating any qualifying expenditure so that it is incurred by the end of the 'normal' accounting period ending on the old accounting date instead of in the subsequent short accounting period will simply be to ensure 80% more relief is obtained in 2023/24 and 20% less relief is obtained each year from 2024/25 to 2027/28 (where spreading relief is claimed).

Alternatively, if transition profits are accelerated so they all fall into 2023/24, year-end planning at this date becomes irrelevant.

For the short accounting period ending on 31st March 2024, the effect of accelerating any qualifying expenditure so that it is incurred by that date instead of in the following accounting period will be to obtain 20% more relief in 2023/24, 80% *less* in 2024/25 and 20% more each year from 2025/26 to 2027/28 (where spreading relief is claimed). So, for most business owners in this scenario, 31st March 2024 will be a time to implement reverse year-end planning in order to obtain significantly better tax relief in 2024/25.

Chapter 39

Cost of Sales

The biggest deduction in many business accounts is cost of sales. Unfortunately, that deduction is itself also subject to a deduction: closing stock and work-in-progress.

A deduction from a deduction means an increase in taxable profits and we can save tax by reducing it as much as possible.

Closing stock is a measure of the value of goods still on hand or services not yet completed at the accounting date.

The treatment of goods and services differs a little. In this chapter, we are going to look at goods: tangible products which the business sells.

Closing stock needs to be valued at the lower of cost or 'net realisable value'. Let's look at cost first.

Direct Costs Only
The stock figure in your accounts only needs to include the direct costs of acquiring or producing your product, so the first thing to do is to look at your costing system and make sure that you're not including any indirect costs.

You do, however, need to include production overheads, such as factory or workshop electricity costs and business rates. The electricity or business rates for an office would, however, usually be an indirect cost and should generally be excluded.

Net Realisable Value
Let's say it has cost you £100 to make a product and you would normally sell it for £120. However, to sell the product, you will need to incur advertising and other costs of £10. This still leaves you a profit so you would continue to value the stock of this product at £100.

Let's suppose, however, that a competitor launches a better product, so you can only sell yours for £105 and your advertising and other selling costs increase to £25. The product now has a net realisable value of £80 (£105 - £25).

In effect, you know that you are now going to make a loss on this product. You are allowed to anticipate this loss by reducing your stock value in your accounts to just £80. This will give you tax relief of £20 per item now, even before you sell the product.

It is very often worth having a good look at your stock to see which items can be valued at less than cost in order to provide tax relief for your effective loss now. Things to look out for include:

- Old or damaged goods which are no longer usable
- Obsolete stock superseded by changes in fashion or technology
- Surplus stock for which there is no demand
- Missing items (perhaps lost or stolen)

It's Only a Matter of Time
Before you get your whole workforce out checking stock, it is worth reflecting that stock valuations generally only create a timing difference.

When you sell the items in stock, their accounts value will form a deduction from your sale proceeds. If you reduce your stock value in this year's accounts, you will generally have a bigger taxable profit next year as a result.

Hence, although the savings yielded by reducing stock value can be worthwhile, they are often only temporary.

The position is different, however, if you anticipate having a lower tax rate next year than this year, such as when your profits are expected to fall below the higher-rate tax threshold (£50,270, £43,662 in Scotland). In these cases, getting relief for the fall in the value of your stock this year will actually yield a permanent saving.

On the other hand, if you're expecting an *increase* in profits next year, with a higher tax rate as a result, any reduction in the value of your stock in this year's accounts could give rise to an overall tax cost. You still need to apply the same principles to valuing your stock but you might want to take a more optimistic (but reasonable) view of its net realisable value.

Chapter 40

Bad Debts

There's only one good thing about a bad debt: tax relief. But when is a debt 'bad' and how do you get the most out of the available relief?

Bad debt relief generally follows accounting treatment. Where a debt is written off, or a specific accounting provision is made against it, tax relief should usually follow. (Special rules apply to debts between connected parties, e.g. a husband and wife.)

A debt is 'written off' if it is simply removed from the books of the business altogether: i.e. you've given up all hope of recovering it.

A 'bad debt provision' is slightly different. This is an accounting adjustment you make to reflect the possibility of not getting paid, but the debt itself stays on the books while you continue to pursue it.

"That sounds great", you may be saying, "I'll make a provision against all my debts and get tax relief for the lot!"

Sadly, this would not work. Accounting principles only permit you to make a bad debt provision where there is genuine doubt over the recovery of the debt. If your accounts don't follow generally accepted principles, tax relief would be denied.

However, you can still accelerate relief for bad debts when your accounts are being prepared.

Example
At 31st March 2023, Toshiko was owed £10,000 by Victim Limited, a good customer for many years. By the end of August 2023, Victim Limited had paid all but £2,500 of this sum. At this point, however, Greedybank plc refuses to renew Victim Limited's overdraft facility and the company is forced into liquidation.

In September 2023, Toshiko is preparing her accounts for the year ended 31st March 2023. It is unclear whether any further sums will be received from Victim Limited, so Toshiko can quite rightly make a bad debt provision of £2,500 and will obtain tax relief for this in her March 2023 accounts.

VAT-registered businesses should only make provisions for the net, VAT-exclusive, part of the debt, as the VAT element is not part of your sales and can always be recovered or, in many cases, never paid.

Specific versus General

Some businesses make a 'general provision' to reflect the fact there is always some doubt over the recovery of debts (e.g. 1% of all outstanding debts). This is usually a bad idea, as a general provision is ineligible for tax relief, whereas a properly calculated specific provision does provide relief.

Example

Toshiko's other debtors at 31st March 2023 totalled £80,000. After her bad experience with Victim Limited, she decides to make a further provision of 5% against these other debts, i.e. £4,000.

In October 2023, Toshiko passes her draft accounts to her accountant, Martha, who explains that, while Toshiko will get tax relief for the provision against Victim Limited's debt, she can't claim relief for her £4,000 general provision.

What Martha also does, however, is review which of Toshiko's other debts at 31st March 2023 are still outstanding. These sums are now long overdue and total £8,000. Martha asks Toshiko if these amounts are likely to be recovered. "Possibly," replies Toshiko, "I'd say there's a fifty-fifty chance."

Martha therefore lists the outstanding debts, calculates a provision equal to 50% of the sums outstanding, and includes this in Toshiko's accounts at 31st March 2023 instead of the 5% general provision.

While Martha's provision is the same amount as Toshiko's general provision, it has been properly calculated on a specific basis and is therefore an allowable deduction for tax purposes.

A little extra effort in accounts preparation pays off in tax relief!

Timing of Relief

Where a debt, or part of it, has almost certainly become irrecoverable, accounting principles require it to be written off, or a specific provision made in the accounts. In some cases, however, where the recovery is merely doubtful, there may be some flexibility over the timing of tax relief.

Example

Toshiko's profits for the year ended 31st March 2023 were £40,000 before she made any bad debt provisions, but she anticipates a profit of £110,000 in the year ending 31st March 2024. This gives her an effective marginal rate of combined Income Tax and National Insurance of just 29.73% on her 2023 profit but a colossal 62% for 2024.

Making bad debt provisions in her 2023 accounts therefore saves tax at just 29.73%. Toshiko would be better off if she just waits to see whether she recovers these debts. Any that do go bad during the year to 31st March 2024 will then provide tax relief at 62%.

Does It Really Matter?

Some people take the view that a bad debt is really just the same as a sale that never took place. This is not the case: there are several important differences.

Accounting principles require the sale to be recognised and total turnover, including these sales, is an important measure for many purposes, including the VAT registration threshold.

And, as we have seen, bad debts may sometimes yield tax relief at a higher rate than the tax on the original sale!

Bad Debts: VAT Relief

Many businesses with turnover of less than £1.6m operate the cash accounting scheme and don't account for VAT on their sales until they get paid. Relief for bad debts is therefore automatic.

For those not in the cash accounting scheme, a debt is 'bad' for VAT purposes when it is six months overdue. This means the debt must be unpaid six months after the normal due date. Hence, if you normally give your customers a month to pay, the debt won't be 'bad' until seven months after an invoice is issued.

At this point, relief can be claimed for the VAT included in the bad debt by adding it to the total in 'Box 4' on the VAT Return as if it were VAT on a purchase.

If some or all of the debt is later recovered, the VAT element of the amount received must then be included in the business's output VAT in 'Box 1' of the VAT Return for the relevant period. The same rate of VAT as was charged on the original sale must be used to calculate the VAT element of any sums recovered.

If you're not in the cash accounting scheme, VAT creates an additional cashflow disadvantage on any bad debts. This may give you cause to hold off invoicing a customer if there appears to be little or no hope of getting paid. If you're on cash accounting though, there is nothing to lose.

Chapter 41

Accountants Make Mistakes

One of our readers contacted us a while ago with a shocking story. His accountant, when putting together his business tax return, disallowed £15,000 worth of perfectly legitimate business expenses without consultation.

Fortunately, the reader carefully checked a draft set of accounts before they were submitted and spotted the errors. Most were very standard expenses but were disallowed simply because the accountant's assistant could not find the payments in the company's bank account and assumed they were not genuine expenses.

The two most important lessons from this story are:

- Nobody cares about your tax bill as much as you do.
- No matter how much careful tax planning you do, it's worthless if your accountant doesn't do their job correctly.

The problem experienced by our reader can be avoided by taking these steps:

- When you submit your annual income and expenses to your accountant, ask them to discuss any issues with you before disallowing any expenses (to save on fees, you may wish to set a minimum level for this – e.g. expenses over £100).

- When they send you a draft tax return, ask again whether any expenses have been disallowed.

- When you receive a draft tax return, check that the figures tally with the information you provided. This is relatively easy to do because most sole trader/partnership tax returns should contain a breakdown of your business costs.

- Provide additional information relating to expenses that are more likely to be disallowed. For example, if you spend money on repairs to your premises, you may want to explain more about the exact nature of the work undertaken so that your accountant can make a fully informed decision and discuss it with you.

- Hand over your accounts information early. If your accountant has to rush to meet the deadline, there is a greater chance that mistakes will be made or that there will be no time to consult with you.

- Do not use your accountant as your bookkeeper. It is usually not cost effective to pay your accountant to type up expenses, etc. You will save on fees, and possibly tax too, if you provide your accounting information in an organised format, such as on spreadsheets. Best of all, ask your accountant what information they would like, and in what format – working together produces the best results!

- Question your accountant about who will be doing the work.

- Ultimately, if you cannot get a satisfactory service, consider taking your business elsewhere.

If your business has significantly fewer transactions this year than last year, don't be shy to ask for a reduction in fees.

Finally, if checking over your tax return and accounts fills you with dread, remember the flipside of this tale is equally worrying: If your accountant underestimates your tax bill, it is you who will be accountable. In the end, the final responsibility lies with you!

Part 12

VAT

Chapter 42

VAT Basics

Businesses are usually forced to register for VAT when their 'taxable' turnover in any 12 month period exceeds the VAT registration threshold.

Most business sales will represent 'taxable' turnover for VAT purposes, although there are some exceptions.

Registering for VAT means you will have to start adding VAT to your invoices: usually at the 'standard rate' of 20% (although rates of 5% or 0% sometimes apply). The good news, however, is you can then recover the VAT paid on many of your business expenses.

In the November 2022 Autumn Statement, it was announced that the VAT registration threshold, which is supposed to increase each year with inflation, will be kept at £85,000 until 1st April 2026. It's been held at that level since 2017 and, thanks to the high rate of inflation, this means more and more businesses are being dragged into the VAT net.

The Government has also looked at making more significant changes to the VAT rules, including reducing the registration threshold. Their main bugbear appears to be businesses that deliberately keep their turnover just below the £85,000 threshold to avoid the massive tax blow that awaits them if they have to register.

In October 2018 the Government published a response to its call for evidence on all the various issues. It couldn't decide what to do and therefore decided to simply freeze the registration threshold and allow inflation to drag more businesses into the VAT net. More significant changes could be made at some point in the future though.

Voluntary Registration

It is possible to voluntarily register for VAT. This may be desirable if your customers are VAT registered businesses themselves and don't mind VAT being added to the invoices you send them because they can simply reclaim the tax.

Registering for VAT will then allow you to reclaim the tax paid on your own business expenses.

For businesses that sell to private individuals, voluntary registration is often a bad idea because your customers cannot reclaim the VAT you charge them. You can either raise your prices and potentially lose customers or keep your prices fixed and earn less profit (because some of your revenue will be paid to HMRC).

The position is different for businesses making 'zero-rated' supplies, such as new housing, books, magazines and fresh food. The VAT rate applying is 0%, meaning that you can recover the VAT on your own purchases without increasing the charges to your customers. For these businesses, voluntary registration is generally a good idea.

VAT and Your Tax Deductible Expenses

If your business is not VAT registered, you can claim Income Tax and National Insurance relief on your total business expenses, including the VAT which you haven't been able to recover.

If your business is VAT registered, you can claim Income Tax and National Insurance relief on your net business expenses, after subtracting the VAT that has been reclaimed.

Example 1

Guy is a VAT registered sole trader and pays £100 + £20 VAT for some advice from a VAT registered accountant. He can reclaim the £20 VAT and claim the remaining £100 as a business tax deduction.

Example 2

James is a sole trader but not VAT registered. He also pays £100 + £20 VAT for some professional advice from a VAT registered accountant. He cannot reclaim the £20 VAT but can claim the entire £120 as a business tax deduction.

Calculating VAT Quickly

If you are quoted any price inclusive of 20% VAT and want to calculate the VAT component quickly, simply divide by six.

Example

Simon is quoted a price of £100, which includes 20% VAT. The VAT component is £16.67 (£100/6).

VAT Planning

We showed you how to reduce your VAT in various chapters:

- Chapter 24 – claiming VAT back on certain motoring costs
- Chapter 25 – claiming VAT on fuel
- Chapter 27 – claiming VAT relief on lease payments

In the next two chapters we will look at some of the special VAT schemes available to small business owners.

Chapter 43

The VAT Flat Rate Scheme: Benefits & Drawbacks

Many businesses could benefit by taking a look at the flat rate scheme. For some, the scheme can save time and money but watch out – for some, it can cost money!

The scheme allows you to account for VAT at a single flat rate on your sales. This flat rate is lower than the normal standard rate of 20% to allow for the fact that you generally cannot claim the VAT on your purchases.

Not being able to recover VAT on your expenses is the price you pay for joining the scheme. You can, however, claim the VAT on certain capital purchases (furniture, machinery, equipment, etc) where the amount of the purchase, including VAT, is £2,000 or more.

The scheme is available to most businesses with annual sales (before VAT) of less than £150,000. You can leave the scheme at the end of any VAT quarter but cannot re-join within a year of leaving.

The flat rate you use is based on the type of business you have and can be found by following the link from: *www.gov.uk/vat-flat-rate-scheme*

If you are in your first year of VAT registration you get a special discount – a one per cent reduction in your VAT rate. So the scheme is often beneficial when you first register as long as your purchases are not unusually high at this time.

The rates applying are not as generous as they look, however, as they are applied to your total, VAT-inclusive, sales prices.

Example
Dave sells a table for £100 plus VAT – a total of £120. He operates the flat rate scheme with a rate of 7.5% applying. He must therefore account for VAT of £9 (£120 x 7.5%).

Rates are set on an industry-wide basis and hence, in very general terms, it follows that you may benefit from the scheme if the VAT you pay on your purchases is less than your industry average.

This could arise for a number of reasons but the main things to watch out for are:

- Rent: if you don't pay rent for your business premises or don't pay VAT on it
- Labour: if you employ more people than average rather than paying VAT on sub-contractors' charges
- Goods: if you purchase more zero-rated or VAT-exempt items than is usual in your industry

The scheme has a few pitfalls to watch out for and you cannot use the scheme if you have any 'associated' businesses.

Worst of all, the 'VAT-registered entity' must account for VAT at the same rate on almost all business income of any kind, including:

- Sales that would normally be zero-rated (certain exports for example)
- Rental income (see further below)

Rental Income and the Flat Rate Scheme
Income from residential lettings is normally exempt from VAT but is taxed at the flat-rate scheme percentage if it is received by the same entity that has registered for the flat-rate scheme for their main business.

For example, if a sole trader is under the flat-rate scheme and also owns a couple of flats, VAT will be payable on the rental income. However, there is no VAT payable on the rental income if the property is in a different entity. For example, if the property is owned by a partnership of the sole trader and their spouse, this is a different entity so no VAT would be payable.

Limited Cost Traders

HMRC was concerned that some businesses with very limited spending on goods (service businesses especially) were able to save significant amounts of VAT under the flat-rate scheme.

Therefore a 16.5% rate has been introduced for 'limited cost traders'. A limited cost trader is defined as a business whose VAT inclusive expenditure on goods during a VAT return period is either:

- Less than 2% of their VAT inclusive turnover, or
- More than 2% but less than £1,000 per year (£250 for a quarterly VAT return)

The limited cost trader category is considered each time a VAT return is completed.

Only spending on goods is counted, not spending on services. Goods must be used exclusively for business purposes and exclude, among other things:

- Capital expenditure
- Food and drink
- Vehicles, parts and fuel (except transport businesses)
- Any services
- Goods you intend to sell or hire out, unless this is your main business activity

This is to prevent businesses buying low value everyday items or making one-off purchases to inflate their costs.

Chapter 44

The Correct Retail Scheme Could Save You Thousands

Many retailers work largely with cash sales and do not generally produce invoices, so there is a need for a special system to calculate the amount of VAT due. Thus we have a number of 'retail schemes'.

Some retailers are large, some are small; some have more than one rate of VAT to account for, depending on their product list or the 'lines' they offer. Some retailers have complex computer systems and some operate very simply.

HMRC has therefore developed, over the years, a selection of schemes designed to suit most retailers. Large retailers are able to devise their own variations with the necessary approval of HMRC.

Smaller retailers must choose one of five basic schemes. There may be more than one scheme available and, just because one scheme works well for one particular shop, another retailer might be much better off choosing a different scheme.

The schemes are subject to a number of conditions and some are not suitable for some types of business. Others are subject to turnover thresholds. You will therefore need to check the conditions which apply before choosing an appropriate scheme.

Note that the retail schemes are only used to determine the VAT due on sales. The deductible VAT incurred on purchases is calculated in the normal way and is unaffected by the choice of scheme.

As a further alternative, however, small retailers with annual turnover of no more than £150,000 (excluding VAT) may use the flat rate scheme (see Chapter 43).

The only retail scheme that, in theory, produces a truly accurate VAT result is the 'point of sale' scheme, which basically records every sale with a proper VAT code. This is normally carried out via an electronic till and is then referred to as the EPOS (electronic point of sale) method.

Where such facilities are not available, the other schemes offer calculation methods as follows:

Apportionment Schemes

Scheme 1: Under this method, you simply split the gross takings for the period in the same ratio as your VAT-inclusive purchases under the different liability rates (standard, reduced, or zero). The VAT included in your sales can then be worked out as appropriate.

This sounds fairly reasonable but the important point to note is that if, on average, you have a higher profit margin on zero-rated goods than on standard-rated goods, then you will end up paying more VAT using this scheme because it does not take profit margins into consideration. This aspect of the scheme is often overlooked.

Scheme 2: This scheme is based on the 'expected sales price' (ESP) of goods purchased and again applies the ratio, established from the total purchases under each category, to the retailer's gross takings.

Thus, for example, if the ratio of total ESPs for goods purchased was 50/50 between standard-rated and zero-rated goods, then you would take 50% of your gross sales as being standard-rated and the VAT due would be one sixth of that value (based on the current standard rate of VAT: 20%).

This scheme effectively does take your profit margins into account and will therefore produce a better result than Scheme 1 above where the margin on your zero-rated sales is generally higher than on standard-rated sales.

Direct Calculation Schemes

Scheme 1: First, you establish the total ESP of goods purchased subject to the VAT rate which applies to the fewest sales. You then subtract this total from your gross takings to leave the VAT-inclusive total for your remaining sales. For example:

Gross takings in VAT period	£30,000
Zero-rated purchases marked up to sales value	£12,000
Balance of sales deemed to be standard-rated	£18,000
VAT due: £18,000/6	£3,000

If you have sales at all three VAT rates, you will need to calculate totals for the two rates producing the fewer sales and deduct both of these from your gross takings to provide a VAT-inclusive total for the sales made at your most common VAT rate.

Scheme 2: This operates in much the same way as Scheme 1 above, but is subject to an annual stock adjustment.

Choosing a Scheme

Having checked the relevant conditions for each scheme, you may find that you have more than one choice. Before selecting a scheme, it may be wise to take a look at how it would work out based on the purchases and sales made in a typical VAT period.

For example, let's suppose you have gross takings of £135,000, standard-rated purchases of £50,000 (including VAT) and zero-rated purchases of £50,000. The mark-up on your standard-rated goods is 20% and the mark-up on your zero-rated goods is 50%.

Using Apportionment Scheme 1, you would split your gross takings 50/50, giving you VAT-inclusive standard-rated sales of £67,500. The VAT due would thus be £67,500/6 = £11,250.

If, however, Direct Calculation Scheme 1 was used instead, you would calculate your total standard-rated sales as £50,000 + 20% = £60,000. The VAT due would then be £60,000/6 = £10,000.

Simply choosing the right scheme could therefore save you over £1,000 every quarter.

Part 13

Capital Gains Tax

Chapter 45

Business Asset Disposal Relief

One of the most tax-efficient ways to grow your wealth is to build up a successful business and then sell it. This allows you to convert heavily taxed income into a less heavily taxed capital gain.

Business owners who earn over £100,000 typically face marginal personal tax rates of up to 62% on their income. The many higher-rate taxpayers out there typically face a marginal tax rate of 42%. The rates are higher in Scotland.

But when you sell a business and receive a big cash lump sum, which replaces all this heavily taxed income, you could end up paying less than 10% tax if you qualify for Business Asset Disposal Relief.

Note, Business Asset Disposal Relief used to be called Entrepreneurs' Relief, a much better name in our opinion!

The lifetime limit used to be £10 million of capital gains per person. But in the March 2020 Budget the Government slashed this to £1 million with immediate effect (from 11th March 2020).

The announcement could have been a lot worse. There were fears in some quarters that the relief would be abolished altogether. And because the relief applies on a per person basis, couples can still enjoy £2 million of capital gains taxed at 10%.

Business Asset Disposal Relief is, however, no longer very attractive to serial entrepreneurs, who build up and sell many businesses during their careers. Many will have already exhausted their new £1 million allowance.

Nevertheless, every business owner will benefit from a basic understanding of the special Capital Gains Tax rules that apply to people in business, especially Business Asset Disposal Relief.

Why? Because if you do eventually cash in your chips, there are certain things you need to check and do before you sell.

How Business Asset Disposal Relief Works

Up to £1 million of capital gains per person can qualify for Business Asset Disposal Relief. This is a lifetime limit but can be used for more than one business sale.

To qualify the business has to be what the taxman refers to as a "trade". Generally speaking this means that investment businesses (e.g. property investment businesses) do not qualify.

For disposals taking place on or after 6th April 2019 the business must have been owned for at least two years (previously one year).

Sole traders are generally only entitled to Business Asset Disposal Relief when they sell the whole business (or shut it down and sell off the assets). If you continue trading but sell some business assets, for example your trading premises, you will not be entitled to any Business Asset Disposal Relief.

The only way a sole trader can sell part of a business and still potentially qualify for Business Asset Disposal Relief is if that part is capable of operating as a going concern in its own right (for example, an office or shop in another town). However, HMRC is taking a very strict line on this issue, so it is not something to be relied upon without taking professional advice.

Selling Property

Many business owners purchase business premises personally and rent them back to their company or partnership (this doesn't apply to sole traders because they can't rent their own properties).

The good news is that Business Asset Disposal Relief is available when "associated" assets like these are sold as part of a sale of the business. The bad news is that many business owners will not qualify for the maximum tax relief. To qualify for Business Asset Disposal Relief, the property disposal must generally be accompanied by a sale of at least a 5% interest in the business, or of your entire remaining stake out of an earlier holding of at least 5%.

To qualify for Business Asset Disposal Relief, the 'associated' asset must have been in use in the business for at least two years and must also have been owned for at least three years at the date of disposal.

If the company or partnership pays you rent in respect of any period after 5th April 2008, your Business Asset Disposal Relief will be restricted. The reasoning is that if the property is only available if rent is paid, it is an investment asset and not a business asset.

There are two pieces of good news here though. Firstly, any rent receivable before April 2008 is disregarded and, secondly, rent paid at less than the market rate only leads to a partial reduction in the available Business Asset Disposal Relief. For example, the gain on a property owned since 5th April 2005 and rented to the owner's partnership business for 50% of market rent until its sale (as part of a larger business sale) 18 years later, on 5th April 2023, would have its Business Asset Disposal Relief restricted by a factor of 15/18 x 50% = 42%. (For example, if the gain were £100,000, relief could be claimed on roughly £58,000 of that gain.)

Tax Planning Pointers

Incorporating

Under the previous one-year rule, business owners had to be wary of incorporating a business within one year before selling it. To qualify for Business Asset Disposal Relief you had to own the shares of the newly formed company for at least a year.

Under the new two-year rule, the period you own the unincorporated business is added to the period you own the company shares. Hence, it is not necessary to own the shares of the newly formed company for any particular period, provided your combined period of ownership of the unincorporated business and the company shares is at least two years.

Be Wary of Business Transfers to Family Members

Transfers to spouses are exempt from CGT and can save significant amounts of Income Tax. If the business is sold less than two years after the transfer, Business Asset Disposal Relief will generally not be available on the transferred share unless the spouse already held a share of the business before that.

Chapter 46

How to Pay 10% Tax on Investment Property

Business Asset Disposal Relief lets you pay 10% tax on up to £1 million of capital gains during your lifetime (previously £10 million).

With the top Capital Gains Tax rate now 20% for assets other than residential property, the potential saving is £100,000 per person.

The relief is designed mainly for people selling businesses, in particular 'trading businesses'. A trading business is, for want of a better word, a 'regular' business, as opposed to an investment business which owns assets like rental properties.

Business Asset Disposal Relief is not generally available when you sell investment properties but it may be available when you sell properties used in a trading business, for example your premises.

Fortunately, you may be able to convert an investment property into a trading property in certain circumstances and benefit from the 10% tax rate.

Business Asset Disposal Relief is generally available if you are using the property in a trading business at the time you sell or close it down (known as cessation). You must have carried on the business for at least two years before that time. In cases of cessation, the property must be sold within three years of cessation.

So the basic principle is this: set up a business for two years, use your property in the business, sell the business or close it down, claim Business Asset Disposal Relief on the property sale.

The Structure of the Business

This strategy will not work so well if the business you set up is a company or partnership. When you sell a property that was used by your company or partnership, this is known as an associated disposal. The Business Asset Disposal Relief available on an associated disposal is restricted to reflect any period when the asset was not being used in a qualifying business carried on by the company or partnership.

In other words, if you've owned the property for 20 years and your company uses it for two years, at best you will receive Business Asset Disposal Relief on just 10% of your gain.

However, no such restrictions apply where the property is used by a sole trader in their own trading business or as qualifying furnished holiday accommodation. In these cases, full Business Asset Disposal Relief is available: provided the property is being used in the business when the business is sold, or when it ceases.

Example
In 1982, Abdul bought a shop as an investment property for £30,000. It is now worth £330,000 and he would like to sell it.

Before selling the property, however, Abdul adopts it as his own trading premises for just over two years. He then ceases trading and sells the property, making a gain of £300,000.

Because Abdul used the property in his own trade, he will be entitled to Business Asset Disposal Relief, reducing the Capital Gains Tax due on his sale from £60,000 to £30,000 (ignoring the annual CGT exemption and assuming Abdul is a higher-rate taxpayer).

The important point to note is that Abdul still gets the relief despite the fact the entire gain arose before he adopted the property as his own trading premises!

Note that Abdul would need to use the property in his own qualifying trade – e.g. as a shop with him as sole proprietor.

Using it as the office for his investment business will not suffice. He can, however, employ a manager to run the shop if he wishes.

To determine whether this tax saving strategy will be worthwhile, you will need to weigh up the potential tax savings against the costs (lost rental income, business rates and any other costs associated with setting up, running and then shutting down the business).

In the right circumstances, however, you could save thousands in Capital Gains Tax.

Part 14

Inheritance Tax

Chapter 47

Business Property Relief: Avoiding the Grave Robbers

A very important relief called 'business property relief' often shelters the value of business assets from the scourge of Inheritance Tax.

This relief is one of the most important tax reliefs for business owners in the UK, which is why, in the next two chapters, we are looking at how to benefit from it, how to maximise the savings arising and, perhaps most importantly of all, how to make sure you do not accidentally lose it!

Digging Deep

Let's start by looking at the size of the problem. When most UK taxpayers die, subject to certain exemptions (including business property relief), the entire value of their estate in excess of the £325,000 'nil rate band', and any applicable 'residence nil rate band' (see below), is taxed at 40%.

In other words, even though you will have paid tax all your life, the Government will still want to deprive your rightful heirs of up to 40% of their inheritance!

In the November 2022 Autumn Statement the Government extended the existing freeze in the £325,000 nil rate band by a further two years. The end result is that the nil rate band has remained at just £325,000 since April 2009 and will remain frozen at this level until 5th April 2028: a total freeze of 19 years!

Allowing for inflation, its real value has been considerably eroded, thus exposing a great many more people to Inheritance Tax and adding to the burden falling on those who are caught. If the nil rate band had kept up with inflation we would expect it to be around £550,000 today and significantly higher by April 2028.

'Coffin Up'

Perhaps the best way to illustrate the importance of business property relief is to look at what would happen without it.

Example

Leslie is divorced and, having no children of his own, intends to leave his estate to Yvonne, the daughter of his recently deceased unmarried partner (legally, there is no connection between them, but he helped to bring her up as if she were his own child).

Leslie owns a house worth £250,000 and a share in a small business manufacturing parts for vintage aeroplanes, currently worth £300,000. We will assume Leslie's business share will not qualify for business property relief on his death.

Leslie's current Inheritance Tax exposure amounts to £90,000. This is derived by deducting the nil rate band of £325,000 from the total value of his estate, £550,000, and multiplying the resultant figure (£225,000) by 40%.

Let us now suppose Leslie's assets enjoy a modest increase in value and, by March 2027, his house and business share are worth £320,000 and £400,000 respectively. As we know, the nil rate band will still be £325,000 at this time.

Leslie dies on 1st April 2027. If he had been entitled to business property relief on his business share, its value would have been exempt from Inheritance Tax. His house alone would have been covered by the nil rate band, leaving his executors with no Inheritance Tax to pay.

As things stand, however, Leslie's entire estate, worth £720,000, is exposed to Inheritance Tax. After deducting the nil rate band, he is left with £395,000 to be taxed at 40%, yielding an Inheritance Tax bill of £158,000.

As we can see from the example, without business property relief, even a fairly small business could give rise to a significant Inheritance Tax bill. Poor Leslie is worth just £550,000 today, but his executors will face a tax bill of £158,000 in 2027.

Home Sweet Home

To keep our example simple, I picked a scenario where the only relief available was the nil rate band. In many cases, the 'residence nil rate band', will provide an additional exemption on the deceased's death. For deaths between 6th April 2020 and 5th April 2028, the maximum residence nil rate band is £175,000.

However, the residence nil rate band is only available under certain limited circumstances. In particular, it can only apply where the deceased leaves their home, former home, or, in some cases, funds derived from a former home, to one or more direct descendents. Although legally recognised step children, adopted children and foster children are all accorded the same status as natural children for this purpose, it still excludes many other potential beneficiaries, such as:

- An 'informal' step-child (where the deceased had never married the child's parent, like Yvonne in our example)
- Nephews and nieces
- Siblings
- Unmarried partners

Furthermore, the relief is tapered away once the deceased's estate exceeds £2m in value, including any assets qualifying for business property relief. Any estate worth in excess of £2.7m, including qualifying business property, will be unable to benefit from the residence nil rate band at all.

Hence, while the residence nil rate band will be a valuable relief in some cases, many business owners will not qualify for it. For full details of the residence nil rate band, see the Taxcafe guide *How to Save Inheritance Tax*.

Till Death Do Us Part
At this stage I should point out that things may not be quite so bad if you are married. Assets you leave to your spouse or civil partner are generally exempt from Inheritance Tax.

Furthermore, if you do not use your nil rate band or your residence nil rate band, you will effectively leave these to them too (any part of the nil rate band or residence nil rate band that is not used on a married person's death transfers to their spouse or civil partner).

Even so, without business property relief this generally only delays the problem. Any couple with more than £1m of assets would still be exposed to Inheritance Tax on the second spouse's death. Where they are not leaving assets to a direct descendent, they would be exposed to Inheritance Tax on any assets worth in excess of £650,000.

For those who are single, divorced, or in an unmarried couple, their Inheritance Tax exposure, like Leslie's, starts at a much lower level. Anyone married to a foreign national may face increased exposure too: the exemption for transfers to your spouse will sometimes then be limited to just £325,000 (no coincidence: this exemption is set at the same level as the nil rate band).

On top of this there is the fact that you may prefer to pass your business directly to your children, or other heirs, instead of your spouse.

In short, while the spouse exemption is extremely useful, in the end it is no substitute for business property relief!

What Assets Qualify for Business Property Relief?
In effect, there are three requirements you need to meet in order to qualify for business property relief:

- You need to have a qualifying business
- You need to hold relevant business property
- You need to meet the minimum holding period requirement

A qualifying business for this purpose generally means a business that is wholly or mainly a 'trading business'. Most regular businesses that sell goods or services are trading businesses, as opposed to, for example, businesses that derive most of their income from holding investments.

Professions, such as lawyers, accountants, doctors, dentists, etc, also generally qualify for business property relief.

The minimum holding period is generally two years. So if you have owned a trading business, or a share in it, for more than two years, this will generally qualify. The business itself must generally also have been a qualifying business for at least two years.

The term 'relevant business property' refers to the way in which you own the business, or your share in it. The amount of business property relief you are entitled to is dependent on the type of relevant business property you have.

Several of the most common business structures yield 100% relief:

i)   A sole trader business
ii)   A share in a partnership (including an LLP)
iii) Unquoted company shares
iv)   Unquoted securities (e.g. loan stock) in a company which, either alone, or together with other unquoted shares or securities, give you control of that company

In the following cases, however, the relief is restricted to 50%:

v)   Quoted shares or securities in a company which, either alone or together with other quoted shares or securities, give you control of that company
vi)   Assets held on your behalf by certain types of trust, which are used in your sole trader business
vii) Assets you hold personally (or held on your behalf by certain types of trust), which are used by a company under your control, or a partnership in which you are a partner

In broad terms, therefore, most sole traders, business partners and owners of unquoted companies will be entitled to 100% business property relief. Remember, however, that, whatever business structure is used, there must also be a qualifying business.

In the Pit

There are numerous pitfalls that can lead to the loss of business property relief, and expose your family to an Inheritance Tax bill equal to up to 40% of the value of your business.

For example, in a partnership, a partner's capital account may qualify for business property relief but a loan account (e.g. if money has been lent to the partnership) generally will not. This is a particular problem with many Limited Liability Partnerships.

It is also worth noting that partners who hold business assets personally outside the partnership only get 50% relief on those assets. This situation most often arises in the case of business premises which, for other reasons, are sometimes held personally. Those 'other reasons' are often very good ones but the impact on the business owner's business property relief should be taken into account.

Borrowings: Another Pitfall

Business liabilities, such as business overdrafts and trade creditors, have always reduced the value of a business eligible for business property relief.

Prior to 2013, this did not extend to personal liabilities incurred by a business owner to finance their business: such as personal loans or a mortgage over their own home.

Sadly, however, **any** liabilities incurred to finance the acquisition, enhancement or maintenance of a qualifying business, must now be taken to reduce the value of that business (subject to the comments below regarding liabilities incurred before 6th April 2013).

A liability will be deemed to have financed a business where it is used directly or indirectly for that purpose. Guidance issued by HMRC indicates they are taking a very broad view of what can be taken to have been used to indirectly finance a business.

Liabilities Incurred Before 6th April 2013

Non-business liabilities incurred before 6th April 2013 are exempt from the rules outlined above and may generally continue to be deducted in full from the general assets of the deceased business owner's estate.

However, where a liability incurred before 6th April 2013 is refinanced or varied on or after that date it will be treated as a new liability and will lose its exempt status.

Replacing or varying any mortgages, personal loans, or other non-business liabilities incurred before 6th April 2013 that have been used, directly or indirectly, to finance your business could therefore lead to significant increases in your Inheritance Tax liability.

Coming in to Land

To close this chapter, let's go back to our example to see how business property relief is calculated.

Example Revisited

Let us now suppose Leslie managed to change things before he died, so that his business qualified for business property relief. Let us also suppose his business share was made up of a partnership share worth

£240,000 and the partnership's trading premises, worth £160,000, which Leslie owned personally. His Inheritance Tax calculation will now be as follows:

Chargeable assets:

House	*£320,000*
Partnership share	*£240,000*
Business property relief (100%)	*(£240,000)*
Trading premises	*£160,000*
Business property relief (50%)	*(£80,000)*
Total:	*£400,000*

Deducting the nil rate band (£325,000) leaves £75,000 chargeable at 40%, giving Leslie's estate an Inheritance Tax bill of £30,000.

Chapter 48

How to Safeguard Your Business Property Relief

Do you want to give the Government 40% of your business?

No? Well, in that case, you need to make sure you don't make one of the common errors that could lead to the loss of your business property relief.

In the previous chapter we saw that, without business property relief, your heirs could effectively lose 40% of your entire estate in excess of a nil rate band of just £325,000 on your death. Where your business qualifies for business property relief, however, its entire value will often be exempt from Inheritance Tax.

Losing Out

The difference it can make to your heirs if your business qualifies for business property relief is enormous. Let's say you have other assets that use up your nil rate band and a business worth £2.5 million. Without business property relief, your estate will have to pay an Inheritance Tax bill of £1 million: enough to cripple your business. With the relief, you can effectively pass the business on tax free.

So, it's vital to keep the relief available whenever possible. Generally speaking, this means you will need to have owned qualifying business assets for at least two years.

Under the 'replacement property' provisions, however, you would retain full business property relief as long as you owned qualifying business assets for a total period of at least two years during the five year period prior to your death. In effect, this gives you up to three years to reinvest the sale proceeds of a qualifying business into a new qualifying business without any loss of business property relief. Provided you actually do own qualifying business assets at the time of your death, that is!

The problem, of course, is that it is generally pretty unpredictable when this will be. Furthermore, it may be some time after you cease to be interested in running a business. Most people will want to retire at some point and, unfortunately, this will often result in the loss of the relief.

Selling Up

As soon as you have a binding contract for sale, you are, for Inheritance Tax purposes, no longer regarded as owning the asset being sold. Instead, you are regarded as owning a right to the sale proceeds.

That right is generally not a qualifying asset for business property relief purposes. Hence, at one stroke of a pen, you can lose your business property relief and substantially increase your family's Inheritance Tax bill in the event of your death.

Example
Eddie owns a trading business. The business is Eddie's only asset so, as things stand, he has no need to worry about Inheritance Tax.

Eddie gets an offer from a French company to buy his business for £5,325,000. He decides to accept the offer, so he flies to Paris, takes the Metro to the French company's offices and signs a binding contract to sell his business.

Leaving the office, Eddie looks the wrong way crossing the street and steps in front of a bus. Inheritance Tax bill: £2m!

This is based on a true story and readily demonstrates the ease with which business property relief can be lost and the dire consequences that may result.

An entrepreneur like Eddie might have been intending to reinvest his sale proceeds in a new business venture and hence might have regained the protection of business property relief within a few weeks by virtue of the replacement property provisions.

Perhaps Eddie should have considered taking out some insurance to cover the Inheritance Tax risk during this short interval!

Retirement

Business property relief is lost as soon as a partner retires from a qualifying partnership business. Any capital the retired partner leaves in the business is simply regarded as a loan.

One way to avoid this problem is for the partner to continue in partnership, but with a very small profit share. (Remaining in partnership has commercial implications, which should also be considered.)

When a sole trader retires there is no business so there can be no business property relief. The answer here may be to take on a partner and then, at a later date, to 'semi-retire': i.e. reduce to a very small profit share in the manner described above.

An individual owning qualifying shares in an unquoted trading company can happily retire without any loss of business property relief, as their position depends on their shareholding and not on whether they actually participate in the company's business. Incorporating the business prior to retirement may therefore sometimes be another good way to preserve business property relief.

Buy-Out Clauses: A BIG NO-NO!

It is common business practice for business partners to enter into an agreement whereby their executors will sell their partnership share to the surviving partners in the event of their death.

Similar agreements are also often used by shareholder/directors of unquoted companies whereby their executors sell their shares back to the company, or to their fellow directors, in the event of their death.

While these agreements make a good deal of commercial sense, from a business property relief perspective, they represent a disaster waiting to happen. This is because, at the moment of death, a binding sale contract will come into force and the estate will not hold qualifying business property but, as we saw for Eddie above, will instead hold a non-qualifying right to sale proceeds.

It is therefore essential to avoid any form of agreement that may form a binding contract on the death of a partner or director.

Cross Options

A far better alternative is to use non-coterminous cross options. In other words, the business partners should enter into an agreement whereby, in the event of a partner's death, their executors will have an option to sell the deceased's partnership share and the surviving partners will have an option to buy it.

Similarly, private company directors would enter into an agreement whereby, in the event of a director's death, their executors will have an option to sell the deceased's shares in the company and either the company itself or the surviving directors will have an option to buy them.

To be on the safe side, it is wise to ensure the options are 'non-coterminous'. Broadly, this means the option to purchase and the option to sell may only be exercised at different times. (E.g. the deceased's executors must exercise the option to sell within six weeks of the deceased's death and the surviving business partners, or directors, must exercise the option to purchase more than six, but less than twelve, weeks after the deceased's death.)

HMRC has confirmed this approach is acceptable in the case of a business partnership and there is no reason to suppose the same principles would not be equally valid in the case of company shares.

Using cross options will therefore preserve full business property relief entitlement while also satisfying the commercial objective of allowing the deceased's share of a business to be 'bought out'.

Part 15

Benefits and Drawbacks of Cash Accounting

Chapter 49

What is Cash Accounting?

Individuals and partnerships with small trading businesses can elect to use the 'cash basis' (also known as 'cash accounting'). This cash accounting is not to be confused with the VAT scheme discussed in Chapter 40, which is also called cash accounting!

In this part of the guide, we will be looking at the cash basis for trading businesses. *This* cash basis is not available to property letting businesses, although a different cash basis *is* available to some individuals and partnerships with property letting businesses. (See the Taxcafe guide *How to Save Property Tax*.)

The cash basis for trading businesses is generally only available where the annual turnover (i.e. sales) of the business does not exceed £150,000. Those already using the cash basis may continue to do so, provided their turnover does not exceed £300,000.

The Government claims the cash basis makes accounting simpler for small businesses and reduces a great deal of the administrative burden on them. Personally, I have my doubts. In my view, it still leaves many small businesses facing most of the complexities they faced before, and adds a few of its own!

Nonetheless, it has its benefits too. We will look at those later but first let's look at how the cash basis works.

The basic idea behind cash accounting is simple enough. Subject to a number of restrictions and adjustments (as we will see below) businesses electing to use the cash basis are taxed on the difference between business income received during the year and qualifying business expenses paid during the year; instead of under normal accounting principles (often referred to as traditional 'accruals basis' accounting).

In other words, under cash accounting, income is taxable when it is received and expenditure is deductible when paid.

So, in effect, the theory is there is no need to worry about debtors, creditors, accruals, prepayments, or stock valuations.

The additional benefit (in theory) is that expenditure on equipment, machinery, and most other items will be allowed when it is paid, with no need to distinguish between 'revenue' and 'capital' expenditure (subject to the restrictions examined below).

All these things are just a matter of timing, so the idea is the business will be no better or worse off in the end, even though the amount of profit taxed in any given year may change.

But timing is SO important! Most business owners are much more concerned about how much tax they will have to pay this year than whether they are going to pay the same amount of tax between now and when they sell up!

For Better or Worse?
To assess whether cash accounting might be beneficial for your business, the first step is to consider what the impact on the timing of your business profits is likely to be. In other words, will profits generally be accelerated and taxed earlier, or will they generally be deferred and taxed later?

Under cash accounting, you will not be taxed on your debtors (sales you have made but not yet been paid for). You will also be able to claim a full deduction for expenses you have paid, without any adjustments for closing stock or prepayments.

You will not be able to claim a deduction for business creditors (purchases made but not paid for yet) or accruals (expenses that relate to the period of trading but which will arise later).

Example
Rose opens a new shop on 6th April 2022. In the year to 5th April 2023, she takes £60,000 in sales and makes the following expense payments:

Rent	£13,000
Electricity	£2,000
Equipment	£4,000
Insurance	£2,000
Stock purchases	£20,000

If Rose uses the cash accounting method, she will have a 'profit' for tax purposes of £19,000.

Under normal accounting rules, however, Rose would have a few adjustments to make. Firstly, she would not claim her equipment purchases as an expense but would instead claim capital allowances of the same amount (making this supposed benefit of cash accounting a bit of a 'red herring' as, in most cases, there is no overall effect on taxable profits).

Next, Rose would need to reduce her expense claims to take account of:

Prepaid rent for 6th to 30th April 2023 - £833
Prepaid insurance relating to period post-5th April 2023 - £500
Stock on hand at 5th April 2023 - £4,000

However, she would also increase her expense claims for:

Unpaid electricity bill - £500
Trade creditors (goods purchased not yet paid for) - £6,000
Accountancy fee accrual - £1,500

Finally, she would also reduce her sales to take account of goods returned after 5th April 2023, £333.

These adjustments would reduce her overall taxable profit to £16,000, saving her almost £900 in Income Tax and National Insurance.

As we can see, Rose would be worse off under the cash accounting method in her first year of trading since she would be taxed on a higher business profit. I am not for a second suggesting this would always be the case. It happened in Rose's case mainly because her:

- Business creditors and expense accruals

Were greater than her:

- Business debtors, closing stock value and expense prepayments

And this is the comparison every business owner needs to make in order to initially determine whether cash accounting **might** be beneficial for them.

In short, it will generally come down to a question of whether debtors and stock (current assets) tend to be greater than creditors and accruals (current liabilities).

At this stage, it is worth pointing out this is often where a good accountant proves their worth, by making the adjustments that correctly reflect the true costs of the trading period, thus reducing the value of current assets and making sure all the relevant liabilities are taken into account. This, in turn, brings the trading profits down to the correct level: but the scope to do this is lost under the cash accounting method!

Nonetheless, even after these adjustments, there will be some businesses where the comparison made above will go the opposite way to Rose's, and these businesses might benefit from cash accounting. But only 'might': because there are a few additional problems to be considered!

Cash Borrowing

Any trading business adopting cash accounting is limited to a maximum annual claim of £500 for interest on cash borrowings (business loans and overdrafts) and other associated costs such as loan arrangement fees. Other interest costs, such as hire purchase interest, mortgage interest on business premises, and credit card interest on purchases of business assets will generally be allowable.

Well that's simple isn't it? Buy a piece of equipment on HP and you get the interest allowed; take out a bank loan to buy it and you may be denied any relief for the interest. Really simple, yeah!

Example Part 2

Rose took out a five-year loan of £20,000 to start her business. She paid a £500 loan arrangement fee. She also has a £5,000 business overdraft facility for which she paid a £90 fee. During the year to 5th April 2023, she incurred £300 in interest on her overdraft and £1,200 on her loan. Under normal accounting rules, Rose may claim the following deductions for these items:

Loan arrangement fee (1/5th)   *£100*
Overdraft fee   *£90*
Interest (£300 + £1,200)   *£1,500*
Total: *£1,690*

These reduce her taxable profit for the year to 5th April 2023 to just £14,310 (£16,000 - £1,690).

Under the cash accounting method, she is restricted to a claim of just £500 to cover all these items. This leaves her with a taxable profit of £18,500 (£19,000 - £500), £4,190 more than under normal accounting principles.

This would cost her around £1,250 in additional Income Tax and National Insurance. Furthermore, the differences relating to interest and finance costs are not just a matter of timing: these are permanent restrictions in Rose's deductible expenditure.

On the plus side, it is worth noting that a deduction of up to £500 may still be claimed where the business owner incurs interest costs that are only partly for business purposes.

For example, if interest of £1,000 were incurred on a bank loan taken out to finance the purchase of equipment used only 25% for business purposes, normal principles would restrict the deductible expense to just £250, but a business using cash accounting could claim £500.

Nonetheless, the **total** deduction for all interest and finance costs on cash borrowings is still restricted to just £500 per year.

Capital Expenditure

Apart from cars and unrelieved balances brought forward (as explained below) a business using the cash basis cannot claim capital allowances.

Instead, qualifying capital expenditure can simply be claimed as it is paid. However, while many of the items that are typically purchased by a small business will qualify, there are some detailed rules that prohibit a great deal of other expenditure from qualifying. Items of capital expenditure that cannot be claimed include:

i) Cars. Motor expenses must continue to be claimed under one of the two alternative methods described in Chapter 22, including capital allowances where appropriate (i.e. where fixed mileage rates are not being claimed).

ii) Land and buildings. This includes the cost of 'integral features' (see Chapter 32), and other fixtures that might normally qualify for capital allowances, where these are purchased as part of the purchase of business premises. Additional fixtures that are added to a building later may, however, qualify, and replacements will, of course, usually be correctly classed as repairs and not as capital expenditure.

For example, where a light fitting is purchased as part of the cost of the building, the cost cannot be claimed but, where an additional light fitting is added later, this can be claimed.

iii) Non-depreciating assets. Assets that have an expected useful life of 20 years or more, and which will retain at least 10% of their initial value after 20 years, do not qualify.

iv) Intangible assets. The cost of intangible assets cannot be claimed unless they have a fixed life of less than 20 years. This includes any form of intellectual property, such as patents, trademarks or copyright. Note, however, that most expenditure on software is actually just a licence to use the software, so this would not be prevented from qualifying by this rule.

There are a few other exclusions: but these relate to items that could not be claimed under normal accounting either.

Costs incurred in connection with the purchase or sale of any excluded items (e.g. legal fees, brokers fees, Stamp Duty Land Tax, etc) are also prohibited. This exclusion is extended to the costs of any abortive, or unsuccessful, attempts to buy or sell any of these items. HMRC has long maintained that such 'abortive' costs are also disallowable under normal accounting principles. While this view may be appropriate in some circumstances, they tend to take something of a 'blanket' view on this issue and this approach is not always correct. What the cash basis legislation does therefore, is to ensure their blanket view always applies under the cash basis.

The cost of vans or motor cycles may be claimed under the cash basis, but if the purchase cost is claimed in this way, the mileage allowances explained in Chapter 26 will not be available.

Premiums paid to take out a lease on business premises would be excluded under heading (ii). Under normal accounting rules, part of the premium could usually be claimed for Income Tax purposes (for example, 92% of the premium paid for a five year lease could be claimed over the life of that lease). Those using the cash basis might therefore be better off negotiating a higher level of rent instead of paying a premium.

Finally, remember the above restrictions only apply to capital expenditure. They do not apply to other valid business expenditure, such as the cost of trading stock, repairs and maintenance, or licence fees.

Previous Capital Expenditure

Where a business entering the cash basis has unrelieved expenditure brought forward from the previous accounting period in any of its capital allowances pools (see Chapter 16), that balance becomes fully deductible in its first year on the cash basis.

This deduction is subject to a few restrictions, however:

*   Any applicable reduction to reflect an element of private use must be applied in the same was as for capital allowances
*   Any element of expenditure remaining within the pool balance, that would not have qualified under the detailed restrictions set out under headings (i) to (iv) above, cannot be claimed
*   Any element of the pool balance that has not yet actually been paid cannot be claimed. This will restrict claims on assets purchased under HP or other credit terms

Naturally, it follows from the second restriction that any element of expenditure relating to a car cannot be claimed in this way and only writing down allowances may be claimed as usual. Other items may also be affected but, in these cases, no writing down allowances will be available unless, and until, the business reverts to normal accounting.

Where the third restriction applies, future payments will generally qualify for relief under the cash basis as and when paid.

The main pitfall to watch out for, however, is that, where the unpaid balance on any previous capital expenditure is actually greater than the balance of unrelieved expenditure in the capital allowances pool, the excess will be treated as additional taxable income in the first tax year that the business uses the cash basis, thus leading to an additional tax charge.

At first glance, the ability to claim the entire balance of unrelieved expenditure on the business's capital allowances pools looks like a good reason to go into the cash basis. However, due to the fact the annual investment allowance has been available for many years, most small businesses now have little or no balance of unrelieved expenditure in their capital allowances pools. Hence, there will be little benefit to be gained by entering the cash basis and, worse still, many may be caught out by the charge arising in respect of any unpaid balances on HP contracts, etc.

The First Red Herring
Cash accounting is available to sole traders and partnerships with annual sales not exceeding £150,000. It is not available to companies, Limited Liability Partnerships, or other partnerships that are not composed entirely of individuals.

So, the first red herring to highlight is the so-called benefit of not needing to distinguish between 'revenue' and 'capital' expenditure. Businesses can normally claim an immediate 100% deduction on up to £1 million of qualifying capital expenditure each year. This is more than enough to cover most expenditure by any business with annual sales of no more than £150,000.

Furthermore, the idea that capital expenditure is simpler under cash accounting has been 'blown out of the water' by the restrictions we examined above!

Hence, as far as capital expenditure is concerned, very few small businesses would see any advantage if they used cash accounting and many will suffer from the additional disallowances and charges discussed earlier.

More Red Herrings
Let's dispel a few more 'simplification' myths, shall we?

Under cash accounting, a business proprietor will still need to keep a mileage log if they wish to claim any allowances for use of a car, van or motorcycle.

They will still need to record all business income and expenditure, albeit on a cash basis, and despite not having to worry about capital allowances calculations, they will still only be able to claim expenditure on items of equipment, machinery, furniture, etc, that qualify under the detailed rules above. Private use adjustments will also still be required, where relevant.

In my experience, the hardest part of preparing accounts for most small business owners is not deciding **when** something can be claimed, but **whether** it can be claimed. It takes the average business owner moments to understand the idea of when income is earned and when expenses are incurred, but it has taken me most of my adult life to understand all the nuances of which expenses are allowable for tax purposes!

Cash accounting takes away only the trivial complexities of timing and leaves most of the other problems in place, while also denying many perfectly legitimate deductions such as bank interest in excess of £500.

And, worst of all, when the business owner needs a set of accounts for anything else: a bank loan, student grant application for their children, potential business sale, or just to understand whether their business is really making a profit, they will still need to produce proper accounts anyway!

Cash Accounting Losses
'Negative' results (i.e. losses) arising under the cash accounting method are only available to carry forward for relief against future profits from the same trade. This means business owners cannot claim relief for trading losses against other income arising in the same year or the previous one, or even against the previous year's profits from the same trade. New business owners will also be denied the opportunity to carry losses back for relief against other income in the previous three tax years.

Summing Up So Far
So far, you may have sensed I am not generally in favour of the cash basis, and you would be right. The potential drawbacks and restrictions examined in this chapter mean many small business

owners would be worse off under the cash basis. Restricting interest relief for business borrowings is particularly galling, and represents a major disincentive to any small business seeking to grow.

Nonetheless, despite the potential pitfalls, there will be some small businesses that will benefit from cash accounting, and it is worth considering whether your business may be one of them.

And, at the end of the day, there is still that simplification issue. As someone once pointed out to me, the simplicity of dealing with income and expenditure when it is received or paid, rather than when it arises or is incurred, doesn't particularly appeal to me because I'm an accountant and I've been used to doing traditional accruals basis accounting all my adult life. But, for the average small business owner, it represents a major simplification.

Only you can decide whether the benefit of this simplification outweighs the potential problems highlighted above in your case.

Finally, while cash accounting itself has a number of drawbacks, for an existing business, the process of entering or leaving the cash basis may provide some significant tax saving opportunities. We will look at some of these in Chapters 50 and 51.

Chapter 50

Entering or Leaving the Cash Basis

It is worth pointing out the cash basis is not just available to new businesses like Rose (see Chapter 49). Existing businesses that qualify under the criteria set out in Chapter 49 can enter the cash basis at any time (i.e. in any tax year). This provides some significant tax planning opportunities. But how does it all work?

Entering the Cash Basis

Transitional rules apply in the year an existing business moves from traditional accruals basis accounting and enters the cash basis. In effect, these rules ensure:

- No income escapes tax
- No income is taxed twice
- Expenses cannot be claimed twice

Generally, the transitional rules should also ensure allowable expenses are not omitted, but this is subject to the points examined in Chapter 49.

When an existing trading business enters the cash basis, it must make adjustments for the following items:

i)   Income arising before the end of its previous accounting period but not yet received at that date (i.e. trade debtors)
ii)   Income received before the end of its previous accounting period but relating to sales made, or services provided, after that date (i.e. receipts in advance)
iii)   Expenses incurred before the end of its previous accounting period but not yet paid for at that date (i.e. trade creditors and accruals)
iv)   Expenses paid before the end of its previous accounting period but which relate wholly or partly to a later period (i.e. prepayments)
v)   Stock on hand at the end of its previous accounting period (i.e. opening trading stock)

Items (i), (iv) and (v) are deducted from the business's profits for its first year under the cash basis. Items (ii) and (iii) must be added to the business profits calculated under the cash basis.

Example 1, Part 1

Melody has an existing trading business and draws up accounts to 31st March each year. Up until now, she has used traditional accruals basis accounting but, in 2022/23, she decides to move to the cash basis. This means that, in 2022/23, she needs to make adjustments for the following items that were included in her accounts at 31st March 2022:

Items added to profits:	
Trade creditors	*£18,000*
Accruals	*£2,500*
Less items deducted from profits:	
Trade debtors	*(£12,000)*
Prepayments	*(£1,000)*
Trading stock	*(£20,000)*
Net total	*(£12,500)*

This overall negative net total of £12,500 is referred to as an 'adjustment expense' and is deducted from Melody's profits under the cash basis for the year ending 31st March 2023.

If the net total of the adjustments required is a positive figure, this is referred to as 'adjustment income' and is added to the business owner's taxable income for their first year on the cash basis. However, while it is treated as additional trading income and is subject to Income Tax, it is exempt from Class 4 National Insurance. This generally provides savings at 9% for basic rate taxpayers and 2% for higher rate taxpayers (9.73% and 2.73% in 2022/23) and represents a good incentive for joining the cash basis.

Example 2

River has an existing trading business. Up to 2021/22, she used traditional accruals basis accounting but, for 2022/23, she joins the cash basis.

Her profits for 2022/23 calculated under the cash basis are £12,000, but she has adjustment income of £20,000. This will give her an Income Tax bill of £3,886 (£12,000 + £20,000 LESS her personal allowance of £12,570 = £19,430 taxed at 20%). However, she will only have to pay £9 in Class 4 National Insurance (£12,000 – £11,908 = £92 x 9.73%).

River has effectively saved £1,946 in National Insurance (£20,000 x 9.73%) by joining the cash basis.

As we can see, the greater a trader's adjustment income is, the greater their National Insurance saving will be; especially if they are a basic rate taxpayer in their first year under the cash basis. It may therefore be worth considering taking whatever steps you can to increase your adjustment income. This might, for example, include some of the following:

- Delay payments to suppliers until after the end of your last accounting period before joining the cash basis
- Try to collect as many outstanding debts as you can before the end of your last accounting period
- If possible, try to obtain receipts in advance
- Sell as much stock as possible before the end of your last accounting period before joining the cash basis (but this will only help if you receive payment for those sales before the end of the accounting period)
- Write down trading stock at the end of your last accounting period by considering the points covered in Chapter 39
- Maximise accruals at the end of your last accounting period
- Minimise prepayments at the end of your last accounting period

Note: it will not affect your adjustment income if you buy more trading stock before the end of your last accounting period, provided you do not pay for it until after the end of that accounting period.

While accruals and prepayments are required under traditional accruals basis accounting and must be calculated on a reasonable basis to give a 'true and fair' view of the business's results for the period, there is often some leeway in the exact amounts you need to use.

You will, of course, need to consider the commercial impact of the above measures before taking this kind of action. For example, delaying payments to suppliers may damage your business relationship with them and could do more harm than good.

Amending the figures for accruals, prepayments, and stock valuation as discussed above will also reduce your taxable profits for your last accounting period before joining the cash basis. Generally this will provide an additional benefit, unless you are swapping profits taxed at a lower rate for adjustment income taxed at a higher rate. The most common example of this would be reducing profits taxed at the basic rate of 20% and increasing adjustment income taxed at 40%. Even after taking account of the National Insurance saving on your adjustment income, this would currently leave you 10.27% worse off (40% less 29.73%).

One Way Street
It is worth pointing out that, due to a rather nice quirk in the legislation for changes of accounting basis, an adjustment expense remains fully allowable for both Income Tax and National Insurance purposes, despite the fact that adjustment income escapes Class 4 National Insurance.

Long-Term Differences
The vast majority of any differences between traditional accruals basis accounting and the cash basis will be dealt with via adjustment income or an adjustment expense in the first year after the trader changes their accounting basis, as illustrated above.

However, whenever a taxpayer changes their accounting basis, there is an exception for expenses already claimed on the old basis that would otherwise need to be claimed over more than one tax year after the change to the new basis. In this case, the expenses must simply be disregarded (or disallowed) in all the taxpayer's accounting periods after the change.

Example 1, Part 2
Melody's trade creditors at 31st March 2022 include a £10,000 bill for some repairs to her business premises. She has entered an agreement to pay this bill in instalments of £500 per month, commencing at the end of April 2022.

This means, under the basic principles of the cash basis, she would be able to claim payments totalling £6,000 in 2022/23 and £4,000 in 2023/24. However, she has already claimed the whole £10,000 under the accruals basis in 2021/22.

Hence, the payments she makes in 2022/23 and 2023/24 are simply disallowed for tax purposes. The £10,000 claimed in 2021/22 is not included in her adjustment expense calculation under these circumstances (thus increasing her adjustment expense to £22,500).

This treatment is fairly neutral in Melody's case, as it increases her adjustment expense and effectively defers £4,000 of taxable profit from 2022/23 to 2023/24.

If the same thing had happened in River's case, however (see Example 2 above), it would have been disadvantageous, as it would have reduced her adjustment income by £10,000 and increased her Class 4 National Insurance by £584 in 2022/23 (£6,000 x 9.73%) and £360 in 2023/24 (£4,000 x 9%), assuming she was still a basic-rate taxpayer.

Leaving the Cash Basis

A trading business **must** leave the cash basis if it no longer qualifies. The main reason this will occur is if annual turnover (i.e. sales) exceeds the £300,000 threshold.

A trading business may also leave the cash basis if there is a change of circumstances, which makes it more appropriate for its profits to be calculated under traditional accruals basis accounting.

This part of the legislation is open to interpretation but HMRC has stated this will include cases where the taxpayer wishes to claim more than £500 in interest and finance costs on cash borrowings, or to make a claim to set trading losses off against other income. In other words, the trader may leave the cash basis if it is putting them at a disadvantage.

Hence, applying the same logic, it would also seem appropriate for the business to leave the cash basis if it pays a lease premium for new business premises; or would be eligible to claim the structures and buildings allowance on business property, or plant and machinery allowances on fixtures and fittings, if it were using traditional accruals basis accounting (see Chapter 16).

Other changes of circumstances, such as registering for VAT, or taking on a new business partner, might also be accepted.

However, it appears the business cannot simply leave the cash basis because its owner wishes to, or because there are tax planning opportunities if it does. Indeed, it was stated during the Parliamentary debates on the relevant legislation that the cash basis is meant to be 'an opt in and stay in regime that allows a person to opt out, but only when business circumstances change.'

Beyond the points discussed above the question of exactly what other changes in business circumstances might allow the business to leave the cash basis is, as I say, open to interpretation.

(It is worth noting the cash basis for landlords examined in the Taxcafe guide *How to Save Property Tax* allows landlords to leave at any time: there is no need for their business circumstances to have changed.)

Where a trading business leaves the cash basis and adopts traditional accruals basis accounting (whether this is for the first time or represents a return to accruals basis accounting), similar principles apply to determine whether there is an adjustment expense or adjustment income, although the process is effectively reversed.

The business needs to make adjustments for the same items we examined before (listed as (i) to (v) just before our first example in this chapter).

However, in this case, it is items (ii) and (iii) that may be deducted from the business's profits for its first year under (or back under) traditional accruals basis accounting; and it is items (i), (iv) and (v) that must be added to the business profits calculated under the accruals basis.

Example 3, Part 1
Alex prepares accounts to 31ˢᵗ March each year, and has been using the cash basis for several years. However, in 2022/23, her total sales exceed £300,000, so she must leave the cash basis and adopt traditional accruals basis accounting.

This means she must make adjustments for the following items that would have appeared in her accounts to 31ˢᵗ March 2022 if she had been using traditional accruals basis accounting for that year:

Items added to profits:
Trade debtors	*£15,000*
Prepaid insurance premium	*£2,500*
Trading stock	*£12,500*
Less items deducted from profits:	
Trade creditors	*(£3,600)*
Accruals	*(£2,400)*
Net total	*£24,000*

Hence, Alex has net adjustment income of £24,000 to account for.

Where an adjustment expense arises on leaving the cash basis, the treatment is effectively the same as on entering the cash basis. The adjustment expense is allowed as a deduction from the business's trading profits for its first year under (or back under) traditional accruals basis accounting for both Income Tax and National Insurance purposes.

Where adjustment income arises, however, not only does it enjoy the same exemption from Class 4 National Insurance as we saw for businesses entering the cash basis, but there is also a further benefit, which we will now examine.

Spreading of Adjustment Income
Where adjustment income arises when a taxpayer leaves the cash basis (but not when they enter it), this is spread over the next six tax years. This provides incredible scope for business owners to defer tax on their income.

A proper interpretation of the legislation tells us one way adjustment income may be created on leaving the cash basis is expense prepayments (such as the insurance premium Alex paid in the example above).

However, HMRC's view is that a prepayment already claimed under the cash basis should simply mean the relevant expense is disallowed in future accounting periods (and the prepayment is excluded from adjustment income). Whether you follow the legislation or HMRC's view is up to you; but I know what I would do when the opportunity to both avoid National Insurance on this adjustment income, and spread it over six years, is available.

Do remember, however, that if the prepayment represents an expense that would normally have to be claimed over more than one accounting period after you leave the cash basis (under traditional accruals basis accounting) then HMRC's view is correct. Hence, for example, if a business owner had prepaid three years worth of rent on their business premises, this could not be included in adjustment income.

Subject to this, there are again a few steps you might want to consider taking to increase your adjustment income when you leave the cash basis. This may require a little foresight, as action needs to be taken before the end of your previous accounting period, so you will need to know in advance that your business circumstances are about to change or your total sales will exceed the £300,000 threshold next year. If you have that foresight, the steps you might want to consider include:

- Make as many payments to suppliers before the end of your last accounting period before leaving the cash basis as you can
- Relax your debt collection procedures, perhaps allow your customers more time to pay, so more payments will be received after the end of your accounting period
- In some cases, you may be able to delay billing until after the end of your accounting period
- Build up your trading stock by making additional purchases of non-perishable or long-lasting items, where appropriate (but this will only help if you also pay for these purchases before the end of your accounting period)
- For a service business, build up your work-in-progress by doing as much work as you can, but do not bill for it until after the end of your accounting period

Many of these steps will also reduce your taxable profit for your last accounting period before leaving the cash basis. Generally this will be an additional benefit, but it could backfire if you are reducing profits taxed at a lower rate in the earlier year and creating more adjustment income to be taxed at higher rates in later years.

As before, it is also important to consider the commercial impact of the above measures before taking this kind of action.

For example, allowing your customers more time to pay might get them into the habit of delaying their payments and could eventually lead to increased bad debts. The measures described above may also put quite a strain on your finances.

When calculating your adjustment income, you will also be able to increase it by maximising the opening figures for stock valuations and prepayments (subject to the point discussed above); and by minimising the opening figures for accruals. Opening figures for these items at the beginning of your first year under (or back under) traditional accruals basis accounting should be prepared on a reasonable basis to give a 'true and fair view' of your profit for the year. However, as before, there is usually a little leeway in the exact amounts to be used.

Accelerating Adjustment Income

The tax planning opportunities provided by the ability to spread adjustment income over six tax years are further enhanced by the fact a taxpayer may choose to accelerate their adjustment income: perhaps so that more of it might fall into a year in which they have a lower tax rate.

Example 3, Part 2

As we saw in Part 1 of this example, Alex had adjustment income of £24,000 when she left the cash basis and adopted traditional accruals basis accounting in 2022/23.

In the first instance, Alex's adjustment income will be taxed over six years. This is done by adding an additional £4,000 (£24,000/6) to her taxable income each year from 2022/23 to 2027/28. However, while this additional notional income is subject to Income Tax, it is exempt from National Insurance.

In 2024/25, Alex purchases some new vans for her business. As she gets 100% relief for the cost of the vans under the annual investment allowance (see Chapter 16), her taxable income (before adding adjustment income) is reduced to £37,270 (she is normally a higher rate taxpayer). She therefore elects to accelerate an additional £9,000 of adjustment income into 2024/25, bringing her total taxable income up to £50,270 (£37,270 + £4,000 + £9,000) the higher-rate tax threshold. (The higher rate tax threshold will remain at £50,270 until April 2028.)

This leaves her with £3,000 of adjustment income remaining (£24,000 less £4,000 taxed in both 2022/23 and 2023/24, and a total of

£13,000 taxed in 2024/25). This is now spread over the remaining three years of her original spreading period. Hence £1,000 (£3,000/3) will now be added to her taxable income each year from 2025/26 to 2027/28 (although she could elect to accelerate some of it again if a suitable occasion arises once more).

Assuming Alex is a higher rate taxpayer in every other tax year, accelerating an additional £9,000 of adjustment income into 2024/25 will have saved her an extra £1,800 in Income Tax on top of the National Insurance savings she is already making.

A few people may have both adjustment income spread over six years after leaving the cash basis and transition profits spread over the five years from 2023/24 to 2027/28 (see Chapter 38). That's one for professional advice!

Chapter 51

Turning the Cash Basis to Advantage

As we have seen in Chapter 50, there are a number of advantages to be gained from entering or leaving the cash basis (where it is possible to do so), including the ability to save up to 9% in Class 4 National Insurance on substantial amounts of income (9.73% in 2022/23), the chance to defer Income Tax for up to six years, and the ability to make additional Income Tax savings by accelerating adjustment income into a tax year in which you have a lower rate of tax: typically if you become a basic rate taxpayer.

Entering or leaving the cash basis is also a useful way to undertake marginal rate tax planning (see Chapter 2 for an explanation of this concept). This may be particularly useful in tax years when your business experiences a fall in profits.

Example

Rory owns a small hotel, which he operates as a sole trader. He is normally a higher rate taxpayer but, for the year ending 31st March 2023, his profits (calculated under traditional accruals basis accounting) have been drastically reduced to just £14,000.

At 31st March 2023, he has received £36,000 of payments in advance for bookings over the summer of 2023. His receipts in advance at 31st March 2022 were £16,000.

If Rory joins the cash basis for 2022/23, his taxable profits for the year will increase to £34,000 (£14,000 + £36,000 – £16,000) and he will have adjustment income of £16,000. His tax liability will increase by:

£20,000 x 20%	*£4,000 (Income Tax on additional profits)*
£20,000 x 9.73%	*£1,946 (Nat. Ins. on additional profits)*
£16,000 x 20%	*£3,200 (Income Tax on adjustment income)*
Total	*£9,146*

In effect, this also means £36,000 of income has been accelerated into 2022/23, giving Rory a tax saving of £15,120 (£36,000 x 42%) in 2023/24 (assuming he is a higher rate taxpayer once again). His overall net saving on this income is thus £5,974 (£15,120 – £9,146).

(For the sake of illustration, I have assumed Rory had no other adjustments to make when he entered the cash basis. In practice, all the factors listed in Chapter 50 will need to be taken into account, as well as any of the restrictions discussed in Chapter 49 that might apply)

This saving is all very well but, unless Rory is able to leave the cash basis the following year, there is a risk this acceleration of income could become permanent or at least last for many years.

For example, if Rory's receipts in advance remain at £36,000 each 31st March and he is unable to leave the cash basis, he will not be able to recoup the additional £9,146 cost he incurred in 2022/23 and enjoy his £5,974 net saving until he ceases trading.

On the other hand, if his receipts in advance were exceptionally high at 31st March 2023 and he expects them to reduce to, say, £6,000 at 31st March 2024 (and each year thereafter), his taxable profits for 2023/24 (under the cash basis) will have been reduced by a net total of £30,000. This will save him £12,600 (£30,000 x 42%) in Income Tax and National Insurance as a higher rate taxpayer.

Rory would then have a net saving at this stage of £3,454 (£12,600 – £9,146) with a further £2,520 (£6,000 x 42%) to come when he either leaves the cash basis or ceases trading.

In summary, this form of tax planning, which accelerates additional income into an earlier year when you have a lower marginal tax rate is only worth contemplating if:

a)   The additional income accelerated into the low income year is exceptionally high when compared with the likely level in future years,

b)   You expect your total sales to exceed £300,000 in the following year, or shortly after,

c)   You anticipate a change of circumstances in the following year, or shortly after, which will mean you are able to leave the cash basis (see Chapter 50), or

d)   You plan to cease trading in the near future

And remember, when looking at how much additional income is being accelerated, you need to consider the net total of:

Receipts in advance,
Trade creditors, and
Accruals
LESS
Trading stock,
Trade debtors, and
Prepayments

It is this net total (let's call it 'X') that needs to be exceptionally high for the planning to work where you have no grounds to leave the cash basis in the near future.

Early Relief for Late Payments

Leaving aside the complex nuances of marginal rate tax planning, many business owners just want to save tax ***now!*** Here the cash basis can help again. If the net total 'X' discussed above is negative, moving to the cash basis will defer taxable profits rather than accelerating them. One of the main reasons this could happen is if the business has a high level of trade debtors.

As we saw in Chapter 40, businesses can claim bad debt relief under traditional accruals basis accounting. But this is limited to debts that have gone bad or where the ultimate recovery of the debt is doubtful. Under the cash basis, sales income is not taxed until received. Thus relief for bad debts is automatic. The business also effectively obtains relief for debts that are simply paid late.

Example
Karen owns a small trading business and draws up accounts to 31st March each year. Up to the year ended 31st March 2022, she used traditional accruals basis accounting and, at that date, she had trade debtors of just £3,000, all of which were recoverable.

During 2022/23, several of Karen's customers run into financial difficulties. At 31st March 2023, she has trade debtors totalling £30,000. In other words, the sales income she actually received during the year to 31st March 2023 was £27,000 less than the amount arising (£30,000 – £3,000 = £27,000).

By the time Karen is preparing her March 2023 accounts and 2022/23 tax return (in December 2023), the position with the debts outstanding at 31st March 2023 is as follows:

Received	*£15,000*
Arrangements in hand for payment to be	
made over an agreed period	*£11,000*
Customers made bankrupt and unable to pay	*£4,000*

If Karen uses traditional accruals basis accounting, she will have to include the £15,000 of debts that have now been received in her income for 2022/23. However, she may claim a bad debt expense for the £4,000 she is unlikely to receive.

The £11,000 being paid over an agreed period is the most difficult part to assess under traditional accruals basis accounting. Karen will need to make a reasonable judgement regarding how much of this sum is likely to be recovered and include those recoverable elements within her income for 2022/23. Depending on the circumstances, she is likely to have to include somewhere between 50% and 90% of this income.

In summary, under traditional accruals basis accounting, Karen will need to include somewhere between £20,500 (£15,000 + £11,000 x 50%) and £24,900 (£15,000 + £11,000 x 90%) of the debts outstanding at 31ˢᵗ March 2023 in her income for 2022/23.

If, however, she switches to the cash basis for 2022/23, she will not need to include any of the debts outstanding at 31ˢᵗ March 2023 in her income. (The £3,000 received in respect of debts outstanding at the end of the previous accounting period will be included, but will be matched by an adjustment expense of the same amount, leaving no net effect overall: see Chapter 50.)

In other words, using the cash basis will reduce Karen's taxable profits for 2022/23 by between £20,500 and £24,900.

(As with Rory, I have assumed Karen had no other adjustments to make when she entered the cash basis. In practice, all the factors making up the net total 'X' discussed above need to be taken into account, as well as any of the restrictions discussed in Chapter 49 that might apply.)

Assuming Karen is a typical higher rate taxpayer, using the cash basis for 2022/23 will give her a tax saving (at 42.73%) of between £8,760 and £10,640. In cashflow terms, this is obviously extremely beneficial. The only question is: will she have a higher marginal tax rate when this timing difference reverses in later years? If so, she may end up paying more tax overall in the end, and that is something she will need to weigh up.

Part 16

Other Important Tax Issues

Chapter 52

Avoiding the Child Benefit Charge

As explained in Chapter 2, many parents suffer a draconian tax charge, the Child Benefit Charge, on income between £50,000 and £60,000. This creates the truly horrendous tax rates set out in the table in Chapter 2.

Many of the tax planning strategies outlined in this guide can be used to reduce a business owner's taxable income. When that business owner has income between £50,000 and £60,000 and is subject to the Child Benefit Charge, the savings will be far greater than for most other taxpayers.

For example, in 2022/23, a business owner with income of £60,000 and three children of school age, who simply carries out £10,000 worth of roof repairs at their business premises before their accounting date, would save £6,874!

How much of this is a permanent saving depends on the business owner's income in the following year:

Up to £50,000:   Permanent saving of £3,974
£50,000 to £60,000:   Permanent saving of £3,974 less Child
                      Benefit Charge suffered the following year
£60,000 to £70,000:   Permanent saving of £2,674 less Child
                      Benefit Charge suffered the following year
£70,000 or more: Permanent saving of £2,674

Most of the people affected by the Child Benefit Charge will be couples. This provides additional scope for savings: particularly focusing on some of the techniques we looked at in Chapter 5, where a business owner is effectively able to divert some of their income to their spouse or partner.

Example
Kevin is a sole trader and expects to make a profit of £65,000 in 2023/24. His partner Paula has a part-time job as a secretary, earning £12,570, but also helps Kevin in the business. They also have four children of school age and receive £3,729 in child benefit next year.

Kevin pays Paula a salary of £14,285. She pays Income Tax at 20% on this plus National Insurance at 12% on the amount over £12,570: a total of £3,063. Kevin also has to pay National Insurance at 13.8% on the amount over £9,100. This amounts to £715, bringing the total tax cost of Paula's salary to £3,778.

Paula's salary and the employer's National Insurance paid by Kevin amount to a total of £15,000. The salary and employer's National Insurance are deductible from Kevin's business profits, saving him tax of £6,265 (mostly at 42%).

Furthermore, with his taxable income falling from £65,000 to £50,000, Kevin will no longer have to pay the Child Benefit Charge, saving the couple an additional £3,729. Overall, Paula's salary saves the couple a net sum of £6,216.

Naturally, it also follows that any business owner who is suffering the Child Benefit Charge must have some children: so the strategies for employing children discussed in Chapter 6 may also be useful in reducing the charge.

Example
Sarah's business makes a profit of £60,000. She has five children qualifying for child benefit so, as things stand, she will suffer a Child Benefit Charge of £4,556 in 2023/24.

Sarah's three eldest children help her out in her business from time to time. She decides to put this on a more formal footing and pays them salaries totalling £10,000.

The salary payments to her children enable Sarah to avoid the Child Benefit Charge. Her total tax saving amounts to £8,721, meaning the net cost of paying her children is a mere £1,279!

Chapter 53

The Tax Relief Cap

There is an annual limit on the total combined amount of Income Tax relief available under a number of different reliefs. The total any individual may claim under all these reliefs taken together in any one tax year is limited to the greater of £50,000, or 25% of 'adjusted total income'. Hence, for anyone with total income of no more £200,000, the limit is £50,000.

Broadly speaking, adjusted total income means an individual's total taxable income for the tax year in which relief is being claimed; after deducting gross pension contributions (including tax relief given at source); but before deducting other reliefs.

Ten different reliefs are affected. The most important ones for business owners to be aware of are considered below.

Trading loss relief: Individuals with trading losses can generally set them off against their other income in the same tax year or the previous one. Additional relief applies in the early years of a trade. Losses set against profits from the same trade are not subject to the tax relief cap. Relief for overlap profits is also exempt from the cap, including relief under the transitional rules for 2023/24 (Chapter 37). The current loss relief rules are covered in Chapter 2.

As explained in Chapter 4, trading loss relief is further restricted for some part-time sole traders or partners. Claims by members of Limited Liability Partnerships must also be limited to the amount of capital they have contributed to the business.

Qualifying loan interest: This is the relief given for interest on personal borrowings used to invest funds in a qualifying company or partnership. See Chapter 28 for details.

Share loss relief: In limited circumstances, owners of private companies may claim Income Tax relief for losses on their shares.

Property loss relief: An individual may set capital allowances within rental losses against other income for the same tax year or the next one.

Appendix

UK Tax Rates and Allowances: 2021/22 to 2023/24

	Rates	2021/22 £	2022/23 £	2023/24 £
Income Tax (1)				
Personal allowance		12,570	12,570	12,570
Basic rate band	20%	37,700	37,700	37,700
Higher rate/Threshold	40%	50,270	50,270	50,270
Personal allowance withdrawal				
Effective rate/From	60%	100,000	100,000	100,000
To		125,140	125,140	125,140
Additional rate	45%	150,000	150,000	125,140
Starting rate band (2)	0%	5,000	5,000	5,000
Personal savings allowance (3)		1,000	1,000	1,000
Dividend allowance (4)		2,000	2,000	1,000
Marriage allowance (5)		1,260	1,260	1,260
National Insurance				
Primary Threshold		9,568	11,908 (6)	12,570
Rate: Directors (Class 1)		12%	12.73%	12%
Self-Employed (Class 4)		9%	9.73%	9%
Upper earnings limit (UEL)		50,270	50,270	50,270
Additional rate above UEL		2%	2.73%	2%
Secondary Threshold		8,840	9,100	9,100
Rate: Employers		13.8%	13.8% (7)	13.8%
Class 2 per week		3.05	3.15	3.45
Class 2 threshold (8)		6,515	11,908	12,570

Notes
1. Different rates and thresholds apply to Scottish taxpayers (except on interest, savings income, and dividends)
2. Applies to interest and savings income only
3. £500 for higher rate taxpayers; not available to additional rate taxpayers
4. Reducing to £500 from 2024/25
5. Available where neither spouse/civil partner pays higher rate tax
6. Threshold applying to self-employed taxpayers and company directors
7. From 6th November 2022
8. From 2022/23, Class 2 only payable where profits exceed primary threshold